Management in India: Grow from an Accidental to a Successful Manager in the IT & Knowledge Industry

A real-world, practical book for a professional in his journey to becoming a successful manager in India

Rahul Goyal

BIRMINGHAM - MUMBAI

Management in India: Grow from an Accidental to a Successful Manager in the IT & Knowledge Industry

First published: May 2012

Production Reference: 1180512

Published by Packt Publishing Ltd.
Livery Place
35 Livery Street
Birmingham B3 2PB, UK.

ISBN 978-1-84968-262-6

www.packtpub.com

Cover Image by Sandeep Babu (sandyjb@gmail.com)

Credits

Author
Rahul Goyal

Reviewers
Rajiv Mishra

Kishore Shenoi

Pankaj Ghanshani

Acquisition Editors
Amey Kanse

Kartikey Pandey

Lead Technical Editor
Kartikey Pandey

Technical Editor
Ankita Shashi

Copy Editor
Leonard D'Silva

Project Coordinator
Vishal Bodwani

Proofreader
Aaron Nash

Indexer
Tejal Daruwale

Graphics
Manu Joseph

Production Coordinator
Arvindkumar Gupta

Cover Work
Arvindkumar Gupta

Foreword

Reading this wonderful book by Rahul brought back early memories of my career. It was nearly 15 years ago that I became a manager, almost by accident. Back then I had always prided myself in my creativeness and technical ability. I had this wonderful opportunity working for an exciting startup in the Silicon Valley with three other code wizards. I discovered that while I may never be as good a programmer as they were, I had this innate ability to see the big picture and mobilize everyone to achieve results. After a large company acquired our startup and my leaders quit, my team expected me to lead the integration with the large company. I was elated and petrified at the same time about the important responsibility that I had in my hands early in my career. This became a turning point in my career. I was not only able to integrate the team but many of us were able to build successful careers over the next few years in the large company.

Whether you have always had a career plan to be a manager or if you have become an accidental one, I believe you can excel in being one. Understanding the key principles to being a successful manager and learning to apply them early in your career will make the difference between success and failure. Looking back, I have often wondered what a difference it would have made if I had known what I know now. This is where this book comes in.

In this book, Rahul Goyal has delved deep into his rich experiences as a manager in India and the US to write a guidebook with practical insights on the gamut of competencies that you need to be a highly successful front line manager. In an easy-to-read style he helps you handle the transition from individual contributor to a manager and guides you on all the competencies required for a manager including hiring and building great teams, planning and executing your work, motivating people, making great decisions, handling the inevitable attrition and building an inclusive place to work where diversity is celebrated.

He takes a contemporary approach emphasizing the challenges today's managers need to handle in a globalized and flat world where you need to excel at working across time zones, generations, cultures, and markets. I believe this book is unique in how it applies sound management theory to the practical situations you will run into as a manager and develops it into a set of simple how-to guidelines that we all can follow. I particularly love the way Rahul has applied candor to address the tough situations we all have faced everyday. He has masterfully interweaved examples and stories for each of the principles in order to bring them home to us. We often forget that managers are employees as well and they need to be successful in achieving their career goals. Rahul thoughtfully includes advice on how can a manager think about their own career and the steps they need to be successful

I feel this book will not only be indispensable for a newbie manager that wants to get it right early but also a great reference for seasoned managers who are constantly looking to up their game. In short, this book needs to be the one you keep next to you throughout your journey as a manager.

I have had the opportunity to work together with Rahul for many years and consider him a role model manager. In this book, he speaks from his own direct experiences progressing from a talented engineer to a successful manager and now to a leader-teacher that is grooming others. I wonder how much better a manager I could have been in my earlier years if I had this book to guide me.

In the end, Rahul's message is simple – It's all about the People. Being a successful manager requires many traits and competencies, but it begins with how you put people first while solving for all three stakeholders – People, Customers, and Business. Here in India, we are blessed with a wealth of talent. As we look forward, it is our responsibility as managers to teach how to leverage this wealth to build a great future for us all.

I am inspired by Rahul's contribution and I hope you all do as well.

Vijay Anand
Vice President
Intuit India

About the Author

Rahul Goyal is an accomplished manager with a rich experience of nearly two decades in the software industry. He began his career at UBICS, Bangalore as a programmer working on e-mail systems in India. He started managing people very early in his career and honed his skills in Bangalore, India, and then in Silicon Valley, USA working for Oracle Corporation. He now works as Director of Engineering at Intuit India.

Rahul finds management in everything, such as a game of soccer or a line of ants carrying food or his two sons, sometimes in a tussel for the TV remote or suprisingly co-operating to clean their room. While working at Oracle, he went to IIM, Bangalore to get executive management education in general management.

He is an avid reader and also writes a blog on management which can be found at `http://rxgoyal.blogspot.com`. He enjoys spending his spare time with family and friends or at the course playing golf.

Acknowledgement

I would like to thank my dear friends, Rajiv Mishra, Kishore Shenoi, and Pankaj Ghanshani for their encouragement, input, and critical feedback through the process of writing this book. They kept me going though the entire effort and got me un-stuck many a times.

My sincere thanks to Vijay Anand, who provided me the courage to go ahead and take this journey. Vijay is truly inspirational and one can learn a ton of management just by being around him. Vijay is a role model to many a managers including myself.

To my wife Seema and my sons Kunal and Karan for being so understanding all the time and giving me lessons on management every day. To my parents who taught me to follow my heart and never doubt my instincts. They are my pillars of strength.

Thanks to my first manager, Abhijeet Bhalla, who showed me the ropes and put his faith in me when very few would have. Thanks to my teams, past and present; to my managers in the past and present; to the organizations I worked for, and to my teachers in academics and in sports for teaching me all that I know today.

Finally, thanks to James Lumsden, my publisher at Packt for starting this effort on his visit to our campus and pushing me to get on with it. Thanks to the editors Amey Kanse, Kartikey Pandey, Ankita Shashi, and the project co-ordinators, Zainab Bagasrawala and Vishal Bodhwani for working with me on this book.

About the Reviewers

Rajiv Mishra is currently working with Yahoo! India as a director of product development. He did his B.E in Computer Science from NIT, Nagpur and has close to 18 years of total experience and around 11 years of management experience both in India and in US. In the past, he has worked with Oracle, Citibank and found a startup. Rajiv's interest lies in building complex distributed software systems and high performance teams from scratch. You can reach Rajiv on Linkedin at `http://www.linkedin.com/pub/rajiv-mishra/0/6b0/bab`.

Kishore Shenoi started his IT career as a C-programmer after completing his masters in Physics. He has worked in various capacities in technology and business development, within leading consulting and retail companies in India and the USA. In his current management role, he is using his project management and retail expertise to make a positive influence on the organization.

In the past two decades he has also added two more masters (MBA Business Analytics and MS Operation Management) and certifications including Software Engineering (Harvard University DCE), Data Warehousing (Microstrategy), Project Management PMP (PMI), and Supply Chain CSCP (APICS).

Pankaj Ghanshani has been into software product development for about six years, out of which he has spent the last 1.5 years in a managerial role. He did his B.Tech in Computer Science from Indian Institute of Technology, Roorkee in 2006. He has worked with Oracle, Amazon and is currently employed with Innovation Labs, 247 Inc (formerly 247 Customer), which gives him the experience of working with a very large corporate, a medium-sized corporate, as well as a startup.

He maintains a blog at `http://pankajghanshani.com`, and you can follow him on Twitter at `@PankajGhanshani` and find him on Linkedin at `http://www.linkedin.com/in/pankajghanshani`.

www.PacktPub.com

Support files, eBooks, discount offers and more

You might want to visit www.PacktPub.com for support files and downloads related to your book.

Did you know that Packt offers eBook versions of every book published, with PDF and ePub files available? You can upgrade to the eBook version at www.PacktPub.com and as a print book customer, you are entitled to a discount on the eBook copy. Get in touch with us at service@packtpub.com for more details.

At www.PacktPub.com, you can also read a collection of free technical articles, sign up for a range of free newsletters and receive exclusive discounts and offers on Packt books and eBooks.

http://PacktLib.PacktPub.com

Do you need instant solutions to your IT questions? PacktLib is Packt's online digital book library. Here, you can access, read and search across Packt's entire library of books.

Why Subscribe?

- Fully searchable across every book published by Packt
- Copy and paste, print and bookmark content
- On demand and accessible via web browser

Free Access for Packt account holders

If you have an account with Packt at www.PacktPub.com, you can use this to access PacktLib today and view nine entirely free books. Simply use your login credentials for immediate access.

Instant Updates on New Packt Books

Get notified! Find out when new books are published by following @PacktEnterprise on Twitter, or the *Packt Enterprise* Facebook page.

Table of Contents

Preface   **1**

Chapter 1: Whose Side Are You On?   **7**

What is a manager supposed to manage?   **8**

  How hard can a manager's job be?   10

  Mintzberg—10 roles of a manager   13

    Interpersonal roles   13

    Information processing roles   15

    Decision-making roles   17

    Summarizing the role-play   21

The mai-baap manager   **21**

Visualizing the managerial model   **22**

  The conduit   23

  The hierarchy or leader of the pack   25

  The orchestra conductor visual   27

Some questions answered   **28**

Summary   **30**

References   **30**

Chapter 2: Transition: From Individual Contributor to a Manager   **31**

Watch out for   **32**

Time   **32**

    Your work plus more   32

    Less definition   32

    Multiple roles   32

    Indirect tax   33

    Scope of work   33

  Commitments   33

  Information sharing   33

  Not giving up control   34

  Enforcing your will   35

  Defensive approach—being afraid to goof up   35

Overcoaching	36
Frustrations of being a new manager	**36**
Teaching a man how to fish	36
A slow world around you	38
I don't get enough information	39
I can't get no satisfaction	39
I'm running all the time	40
Making it easier	**40**
Relax a little	41
Understanding the information needs of your organization	41
Know your success measures	42
Learn to say NO	43
Get organized	44
Distinguish between urgent and important	44
Plan your day every morning	44
Find someone to talk to	45
Sign up for formal training and education	45
Summary	**46**
References	**46**
Chapter 3: Basic Skills, Traits, and Competencies of a Manager	**47**
Skills, traits, talents, and competencies	**47**
Skills	48
Traits	48
Talents	48
Competencies	49
Top skills, traits, and competencies expected of a manager	**50**
Love of working with people	50
Easy to approach	51
Myth: I'm easy to approach, I have an open door policy	52
Farmer mentality: sow, nurture, grow, reap	52
Myth: fast moving managers—in a tearing hurry	52
Core values: honesty, integrity, truthfulness, trustworthiness, consideration for others, and more	53
Not a myth: corporate greed	54
Tolerance for ambiguity and patience	54
Good communication skills—especially listening	54
Myth: quiet people can't be managers	55
Team building—hiring, retaining, developing good people, and nurturing team spirit	56
Performance management	57
Myth: maximum output	57
Problem solving	57

Myth: every problem is my problem to solve	58
Always an eye on the ball—results orientation	58
Decision-making	59
Myth: well-informed decisions	60
Project management and execution—delivery	60
Myth about flawless execution	61
Grip on technical knowledge/domain	61
Think customer—customer orientation	62
Emotional intelligence	**63**
Personal competence	64
Social competence—how we handle relationships	65
Summary	**65**
References	**66**
Chapter 4: Teamwork and Team Building	**67**
Why do we need teams?	**68**
Different types of teams	**70**
How to build a team	**73**
Explain the big picture, purpose, and fitment of the team in the larger universe	73
The tough part	74
Defining the composition of the team	74
The tough part	75
Define playing positions	76
The tough part	76
Clear and defined hiring process	78
The tough part	79
Creating visible alignment between team goals and individual goals	80
The tough part	81
Make it easy to collaborate and synergize	81
The tough part	82
Reward collaboration and unreward non-collaboration	83
The tough part	83
Success dose	83
Team spirit	84
Team spirit is created by the team and not by the manager	84
Managers can damage team spirit	85
An environment of trust and respect	86
Group traditions: work, play, and celebrate as a team	86
Don't forget the individual	87
Rotate the champions	87
Why teams fail	**88**
Expectations, alignment, and team direction not clear	88
Leadership deficit	89

Confusion in structure	89
Not enough time for team dynamics to set in	90
Groupthink	90
Summary	**91**
Chapter 5: Communicating	**93**
Elements of good communication	**94**
Clarity	95
Context	95
Two-way	97
Concise	97
Rules of courtesy	98
Watch out	98
Timely	99
Similar vocabulary—apple means apple	100
What managers must know about communication	**100**
Interpersonal communication is a process, not an event	101
Understanding the communication needs of your organization	102
Understanding the communication needs of your role and work	102
You set the communication model for your team	103
Controlling unwanted communication, for example, salary discussions	104
Cutting down the layers, shortening the channels	105
The grapevine—don't worry too much about it	106
Allowing people to vent	107
Scenarios	**107**
Everyday communication	107
Do the Hi exchange	108
Enagage in casual chat	108
Be available to talk	108
Don't always keep looking for a status update	108
Don't keep telling them what to do	109
When someone just walks in with a problem	109
When people share personal problems	110
Communicating bad news to an individual, for example, being denied a bonus	111
Communicating unwelcome news to a group, for example, undesired management changes	112
Difficult discussions—separate the person from the issue	113
Communication in a distributed team	115
Extra communication required	115
Check alignment frequently	115
It's ok to have an accent	115
Acknowledgement response	116
More back and forth required, more questions to be asked	116

Different energy levels	116
Use a mix of methods to communicate	116
Create opportunities for in-person interactions	116
Finally, when to keep mum	117
Summary	**117**
Chapter 6: Motivation	**119**
Understanding motivation	**120**
Desire is given but action is not	120
Everything takes some motivation	121
Everyone's motivation is somewhat different	121
Basic factors are common	121
It's not just your responsibility	122
There's such a thing as self-motivation	122
Demotivators are different from motivators	122
Everyone is motivated to work	122
Motivation theories	**122**
Maslow's hierarchy of needs theory	123
Physiological needs	123
Safety needs	124
Love and belonging needs	124
Esteem needs	125
Self-actualization	125
Putting Maslow's pyramid together in today's context	126
Herzberg's motivation—hygiene and two-factor theory	127
McClelland's motivational needs theory	129
Need for power	129
Need for achievement	129
Need for affiliation	130
All three factors	130
What's motivating in today's workplace?	**130**
Success is motivating	131
Team bonding is motivating	131
Power is motivating: power to choose, power to shape the future	132
A challenge is motivating	132
A manager's confidence and belief in the individual is motivating	133
Hope of achieving greatness is motivating	133
Hope of a better future is motivating	134
What is demotivating?	**134**
Uncertainty is demotivating	134
No social status is demotivating	135
Fear, threats, and disrespect are huge demotivators	135
Lack of adequate and timely compensation is a demotivator	136
Poor working conditions are demotivators	136
Lack of opportunities to show their potential is demotivating	137

Lack of learning is demotivating	138
Signs of low motivation	**138**
Lack of attention to detail	138
Absenteeism	139
Dragging feet	139
Dropped catches…too many misses at work	140
No contest—passivity—low engagement	140
Less social interaction	140
Is money a motivator?	**141**
Summary	**142**
References	**143**
Chapter 7: Hiring	**145**
Understanding hiring	**146**
Understanding your optimal requirements	146
Hiring for potential not just current skills	146
Hiring is a risk	147
Hiring is not an end to itself	147
Be open—talking about challenges upfront	148
Pre-interview: knowing what you are looking for	148
Advertising and sourcing	149
Pre-interview: resume screening	150
Pre-interview: phone screening	151
Sample phone screen	152
How to conduct an effective interview	**154**
Interview plan	154
Reading and analyzing the resume beforehand	155
Interview tips	155
Listen to the candidate	155
Don't ask the same questions to people at different levels	156
Warm-up questions	156
Basics plus deep drill on key areas	156
Look for application and not just theory	157
Look beyond technical skills	157
Past work is important	158
Using behavioral interviews	159
Feedback recording	160
Hiring decision	162
Compensation	**164**
Option 1: compensation on par with a team member with similar profile	165
Option 2: new compensation = previous compensation + 20%	165
Option 3: compensation based on market data	166
Option 4: compensation by negotiation	166
Truth about compensation	166
What is the answer?	167
Closing the hiring process	**168**

Campus hiring	**168**
There is a shortage	169
Campus day 1	169
Only one offer	170
Compensation rules	170
Elimination process followed by selection process	170
Interviewing on campus	171
Campus hiring – allocations	171
Pre-join attrition	172
Campus hires boot camp	172
Summary	**173**
Chapter 8: Performance Evaluation	**175**
Understanding performance	**176**
Purpose of performance evaluation	**178**
Reviewing and reflecting	178
Feedback	178
Alignment	178
Looking ahead	178
Personal development and career planning	179
Tracking progress over the years	179
Positive side effects	179
Used in reward calculations	179
Used in layoffs	179
Organizational improvements	180
Performance evaluation process	**180**
Appraisal form	180
Competencies	180
Goals from last year	181
Open-ended questions	181
Key dimensions	181
Development plan	182
Goal setting for the coming year	182
Final/overall rating	182
Usual appraisal models	182
Employee – manager review	183
Additional external reviewers	183
Additional peer reviews	183
360 degree reviews	183
The usual once-a-year appraisal process steps	184
Using the bell curve in performance evaluation	**184**
Problems with the performance appraisal process	**186**
It has become an event	187
Always done in a hurry	187
Hard to remember the details – especially for a manager	188

Disconnected managers	188
Proximity effect	189
Halo effect	189
Managers shy away from disagreements and having a hard discussion	190
Subjective ratings – depends on interpretation	191
Rating some competencies makes no sense	192
Inconsistency in ratings by different managers	192
High self-appraisal	193
Remote manager	193
Performance management and appraisal as a two-stage system	**193**
Ongoing performance management	194
Short cycle and long cycle performance evaluation	195
Short cycle	196
Long cycle	197
Summary	**197**
Chapter 9: Attrition	**199**
Understanding attrition	**200**
It's going to happen	200
Multiple reasons, but one driver	200
Attrition can be healthy	201
Don't take it personally	201
Top 3 reasons why people quit: 'money', 'career growth', 'manager'	201
Rarely does the decision change	202
Categories of 'quitters'	**202**
The growth-oriented	203
The dissatisfied	203
The mismatched	204
The whimsical	206
The still searching	206
The purposeful	207
The fearful	208
Cost of attrition	**209**
Direct costs	209
Administrative costs of an exit	209
Hiring costs	209
Training costs	210
Indirect costs	210
Loss of productivity	211
Opportunity cost	212
Copy cat attrition	213
Benefits of attrition	**213**
Attrition may get rid of deadwood and misfits	213

Attrition creates space for new perspectives and new energy	213
Attrition may help achieve a balance in the team	214
Internal attrition is very healthy	214
Attrition may lower total costs	214
Attrition may create space for growth	215
Attrition helps a manager expand the network	215
Attrition—watch out	**215**
Managing attrition	**217**
Expect it: anybody can leave	217
Know your people	218
Manage expectations proactively	218
Enhance team capabilities	219
Encourage cross-area awareness	219
Promote openness and be accessible	220
Create documentation and trainings	220
Create a fun work environment	220
Summary	**221**
Chapter 10: Managing – Remoteness, Work-Life, Gen Y, and Diversity	**223**
Managing remoteness	**224**
Remote employee means	224
You can't see him/her – visual observation is lost	225
You only see results, not efforts	225
Distrust creeps in – wonder what he is up to	225
Relationship becomes very 'black box'	226
Out of sight, out of mind	226
Everything becomes harder, requiring extra effort	226
A remote leader becomes very important, just for being remote	227
Making remoteness work	227
Indulge in chitchat	227
Embrace new technology to get closer	227
Set expectations with the remote employee to communicate more	228
Formalize some of the communication	228
Make it two-way	228
Drive by setting clear goals and success criteria	229
More frequent checkpoints	229
Open sessions	229
Get into detail rather than just 'everything is fine'	229
Evaluate if it's working	230
Don't become the only face of the remote team; let them have their identity	230
Don't overdo it – excessive reporting	230
Leverage the 'local' for the remote employee	230
Provision for travel – make it economical	231
Make travel meaningful	231

Work-life balance   **232**

  Understanding work, life, and the balance   233

    What is work?   233

    What is life?   233

    What is work-life balance (WLB)?   233

    WLB is NOT an equal number of hours   233

    Achievement and fulfillment are key   234

    Enjoyment test   234

    Work is NOT life, but work IS life too   234

    Balance now is better than balance later   234

    Why managers should encourage WLB   235

    An individual's WLB is an employee's responsibility; managers only support it   235

  Common reasons of losing WLB   236

Managing Indian Gen Y   **236**

  Some characteristics of Gen Y   236

  Gen Y employee behavior   237

    Smart working   237

    Nothing is impossible   237

    Open and transparent   238

    Secure – there's always another job   238

    Don't Alt-Tab   238

    Very social – diverse   238

    Respect for the individual rather than the position   238

    Ownership, decision-making, and choices are important   239

Managing diversity   **239**

    Diversity is natural   240

    Shun stereotypes   240

    Early training   240

    Diversity doesn't mean the 'same' treatment   241

    Celebrate the diversity   241

    As an individual, learn about different cultures   241

    Be aware of various diversity programs run by the organization   242

    Enjoy the food   242

    No jokes about a particular community   242

    Be quick to stop a conversation that is bordering on discrimination, even in humor   242

  Summary   **243**

Chapter 11: Effective Planning   **245**

Why plan?   **246**

  Making something happen   246

  Stopping something from happening   246

  Educating and making people aware   247

  Helping to prioritize   247

  Increasing commitment   247

  Showing the path – adds confidence, lowers anxiety   247

Planning cycle   **248**

A good project manager   **249**

What to consider when creating a plan   **251**

  The big picture   251

    Identifying the deliverable and greater purpose   251

    Know the larger 'program management' plan   252

    External environment and dependencies   252

    Governing rules and requirements   252

    Know the stakeholders and their requirements   253

    Understand the level of tolerance for problems   253

  Work assignment and execution   254

    Start with a conservative and flexible plan   254

    Players and their strengths   254

    Choosing appropriate methods of execution   255

  What is a buffer?   255

  Execution plan   256

    Checkpoints   258

    Reviewing the plan   258

  Monitoring   258

    Completion criteria and success criteria   258

    Progress and visibility   259

    Checkpoints and re-planning   259

    Advertising your plan and focus areas   260

    Encouraging and expecting planning from your team   260

    Weekly team meeting – last week, next week   260

    Daily stand up meetings – 15 minutes   261

    Personal planning – 15 minutes a day model   262

  Managing changes and risks   263

    Preparing for risk   264

    Being connected   265

  Planning gotcha: don't follow your plan too closely   265

Nuances of planning in India   **266**

  Not saying NO   266

  Too much focus on work – desire to grow   266

  'All is well' syndrome   267

  Too many young players – lack of experience   267

  Regional and cultural issues   267

  Remote teams – out of the loop   268

Summary   **268**

Chapter 12: How to Grow As a Manager   **269**

What does 'growth' mean to you?   **270**

  Another way: find your way one step at a time   272

  Pre-growth checks   272

    Are you having fun?   272

    Are you able to leverage your unique talents?   272

    Do you fit culturally?   273

  Bare essentials for any growth   273

Capability	273
Credibility	273
Opportunity	274
Some dos to grow as a manager	**274**
Grow your people	274
Delegate	274
Almost redundant	275
Trust your team	275
Make decisions	275
Take risks	276
Nerves	276
Deliver consistently	277
Get diverse experience – projects, people, location	277
Make linkages and network	277
Spend the time – the eight-hour workday is history	278
Grow in stature	278
Some don'ts to grow as a manager	**278**
Don't compete with your own people	278
Don't get sucked into the 'busy' paradigm	279
Don't get blind in defending your team	279
Don't be self-righteous, be open to a compromise	280
Don't forget the real job skills	281
Summary	**281**
Chapter 13: Summing it Up	**283**
Know what you manage	**283**
Transition requires a mindset change	**284**
Help yourself, get help	**284**
Know your success measures	**285**
Managers wear multiple hats	**285**
Manager as a conduit	**286**
Team building – define playing positions	**287**
Team building – winning as a team	**287**
Communicate in a timely manner – reduce layers, add clarity	**288**
Motivation – Maslow's hierarchy of needs	**288**
Hiring	**289**
Attrition – expect it, manage it	**289**
Planning and execution	**290**
Decision-making	**290**
Manage – all aspects	**290**
Summary	**290**
Index	**291**

Preface

The software, and knowledge industry in general, has been on a blazing growth path in the last few decades and especially so in India. As the size of organizations grew rapidly, so did the need for managers to manage a growing business and growing teams. As a result, most managers in the software industry today started out as techies, including me. I was lucky to have learned from some of the best managers, but also some not so great ones. Regardless, there is a lot of catching up that new managers need to do.

This book attempts to capture some of those elements, which can help a new manager or soon-to-be manager build a framework of understanding around what managing is in the knowledge industry, how to deal with the transition from an individual contributor to a manager, and how to understand the behaviors that make a successful and respected manager.

Managing people in the knowledge industry has its own unique challenges since it's highly people-dependant. This book discusses various aspects of managing that a manager deals with on a daily basis, such as team building, hiring, motivating your team, planning, and many more. It also attempts to build some thoughts around aspects, such as work-life balance, diversity, Gen Y, and how one can grow as a manager.

The book is primarily based on learning, insights, and experiences and in a few sections, it also brings in some theoretical frameworks applied to the knowledge industry.

Finally, this book is by no means a 'right way' of doing things and neither does it attempt to be complete in anyway. At best, it's a beginning.

What this book covers

Chapter 1, Whose Side Are You On? – Learn about the various roles and responsibilities of being a manager. Acknowledge the dilemmas and build a perspective on what it means to be a manager. These perspectives help a manager make better decisions and manage through the daily pushes and pulls of being a manager.

Chapter 2, Transition: From Individual Contributor to a Manager – One of the most testing times is the transition from being an individual contributor to a manager. Learn about common problems during the transition and possible ways to deal with them. Also, understand the sources of frustration for a new manager as he figures way around in the new role.

Chapter 3, Basic Skills, Traits, and Competencies of a Manager – In this chapter, we try to answer the question: what are the key ingredients that make a good manager? Understand the meaning of skills versus talents versus competencies. Walk through the top skills and competencies that are expected of a manager in the knowledge industry. Also, look at some of the myths around managerial work.

Chapter 4, Teamwork and Team Building – Team building is the holy grail of the management function. Understand the purpose and nature of a team. Look at the various aspects of 'how to build a team', such as defining team composition and alignment of goals. Also, peek into the difficulties of doing the same. Finally, understand some of the reasons why teams fail.

Chapter 5, Communicating – Communication is a top skill for a manager in the knowledge industry. In this chapter, we look at the elements of good communication. Then we go on to build an understanding of the communication process in an organization. Then we walk through common communication scenarios, such as how to deliver tough news to your team or how to respond when someone just walks in with a problem. We also look at communication in a remote team and finally closing with pointers on when to keep quiet.

Chapter 6, Motivation – Keeping the team motivated is an ongoing responsibility of a manager and key to delivering results for the organization. In this chapter, we build an understanding of what is motivation? We will have a brief look at some of the famous theories, such as Maslow and Mcclelland's theories of motivation. We look at what is motivating in today's workplace and also what is de-motivating. Finally, we peek into signs of low motivation that managers can potentially spot and how to adopt measures proactively.

Chapter 7, Hiring – Hiring is a key function for a manager. In this chapter, we understand the various aspects of hiring, such as defining your hiring needs, sourcing potential employees, pre-screening candidates, and arriving at a short list. We take a detailed look at the pre-interview and conducting a good interview process. We analyze the compensation process and strategies that can be applied when deciding the compensation. Finally, we peek into the campus hiring process in India since campus hiring is a significant contributor to the workforce.

Chapter 8, Performance Evaluation – This chapter focuses on the performance evaluation process, which is a key part of a manager's responsibility. We look at the purpose and usage of performance ratings and typical review methods. Understand the usage of the Bell curve in performance ratings and build understanding of the common issues in the annual review cycle, such as the proximity effect, disconnectedness, and halo effect.

Chapter 9, Attrition – Attrition is a fact of life in a professional work environment and every manager needs to deal with it. In this chapter, we build a framework of understanding on why people leave a job. Enumerate the direct and indirect costs of attrition and wonder if attrition can be 'beneficial'. Importantly, we will look at common signs of impending attrition and how perhaps a manager can proactively avoid some of it from happening. Finally, we will go over how to manage attrition so business can be conducted, almost as usual.

Chapter 10, Managing – Remoteness, Work-Life, Gen Y, and Diversity – In this chapter, we build some understanding of some common but critical management scenarios. Look at challenges of working in a remote team and how it impacts the working model, followed by how to make it easier by creating lines of communication and setting expectations. We'll discuss the ever elusive work-life balance and build an understanding of work and life and the difference between the two. Another key component of the workplace is the new generation, Gen Y. What makes them unique? What makes them tick? And understand the common behaviors of Gen Y. Finally, we approach the sensitive and crucial diversity dimension of management and discuss why diversity is important and how we can support a diverse workplace.

Chapter 11, Effective Planning – In this chapter, we take a detailed look at the planning function of a manager. Review the traits and behaviors of a good project manager. Understand the planning cycle and various considerations of it, such as the external ecosystem in which the team operates. We also get into creating an execution plan and other key aspects, such as regular monitoring and review. Finally, we look at some planning issues and specifically the issues of project planning in the Indian environment.

Chapter 12, How to Grow As a Manager – A short chapter on understanding your own growth aspirations and listing the key ingredients for growth. Are you ready to grow in your current role or organization? We walk through the behaviors that will propel growth, such as trust, consistent results, diverse experience, and many more. Finally, we look at what behaviors hold managers back from growth.

Chapter 13, Summing it Up – This is a summary chapter where we take a visual journey to recall some of the key things that we discussed in the earlier chapters.

Who this book is for

- This book is most contextual for new managers in the knowledge industry
- Aspiring managers and soon-to-be managers
- MNCs who want to effectively manage employees at their Indian offices
- All managers who wish to be more effective by better understanding the management frameworks and how they apply to the Indian IT and ITes sectors – IT Product Development, Services, Backend processing, and BPO
- Management principles remain the same across all sectors and so people from other sectors will also benefit from this book

Conventions

In this book, you will find a number of styles of text that distinguish between different kinds of information. Here are some examples of these styles, and an explanation of their meaning:

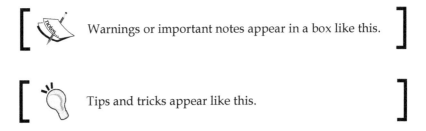

[Warnings or important notes appear in a box like this.]

[Tips and tricks appear like this.]

This book uses 'him' and does not always use him/her at many places. This is done only for ease of reading and the content applies equally to all genders.

Reader feedback

Feedback from our readers is always welcome. Let us know what you think about this book—what you liked or may have disliked. Reader feedback is important for us to develop titles that you really get the most out of.

To send us general feedback, simply send an e-mail to `feedback@packtpub.com`, and mention the book title via the subject of your message.

If there is a book that you need and would like to see us publish, please send us a note in the **SUGGEST A TITLE** form on `www.packtpub.com` or e-mail `suggest@packtpub.com`.

If there is a topic that you have expertise in and you are interested in either writing or contributing to a book, see our author guide on `www.packtpub.com/authors`.

Customer support

Now that you are the proud owner of a Packt book, we have a number of things to help you to get the most from your purchase.

Errata

Although we have taken every care to ensure the accuracy of our content, mistakes do happen. If you find a mistake in one of our books—maybe a mistake in the text or the code—we would be grateful if you would report this to us. By doing so, you can save other readers from frustration and help us improve subsequent versions of this book. If you find any errata, please report them by visiting `http://www.packtpub.com/support`, selecting your book, clicking on the **errata submission form** link, and entering the details of your errata. Once your errata are verified, your submission will be accepted and the errata will be uploaded on our website, or added to any list of existing errata, under the Errata section of that title. Any existing errata can be viewed by selecting your title from `http://www.packtpub.com/support`.

Piracy

Piracy of copyright material on the Internet is an ongoing problem across all media. At Packt, we take the protection of our copyright and licenses very seriously. If you come across any illegal copies of our works, in any form, on the Internet, please provide us with the location address or website name immediately so that we can pursue a remedy.

Please contact us at copyright@packtpub.com with a link to the suspected pirated material.

We appreciate your help in protecting our authors, and our ability to bring you valuable content.

Questions

You can contact us at questions@packtpub.com if you are having a problem with any aspect of the book, and we will do our best to address it.

1
Whose Side Are You On?

Am I supposed to listen to people's personal problems?

He was out for a month due to injury; should he get the same bonus percentage as another guy?

How much time should I spend with my team?

I'm up to my ears with work, and Sameer, the key developer on the project, walks in with a problem of his own. What am I supposed to do?

My boss wants me to change the design we have already invested in, but I really don't agree with him. Should I fight against the change?

The guy looks good in technical interviews, but seems to have an attitude problem; should I still hire him?

I can stop this guy from leaving the company if I can promise him a promotion soon but I really don't think he deserves it right now, but again, I have a key accounts project that can use his skills.

How do I explain why somebody didn't get a raise?

Is it my job to explain why a layoff happened? After all, I didn't make that decision.

How do I motivate the team when they already know there is not going to be any pay hike this year?

We have just completed a long, tough project delivery. Everybody is looking for a break, but we have more work coming. How do I avoid a burnout?

These questions, and many more such questions, are what trouble managers today. Each and every question can be real and every individual manager will make a choice and go with it. How many such choices result in good business and improve the overall well-being of the team and the organization, will decide how successful a manager will turn out to be.

Being a manager brings with it lots of questions. Let's start with the most basic one.

What is a manager supposed to manage?

Let's look at what organizations ask for in a manager. A typical job description from one of the popular job portals includes the following:

- Hands on
- Expertise (in some technical or functional area)
- Good communicator
- Build and refine processes
- Work in global teams
- Plan and drive on-time delivery, following global processes
- Analyze and monitor the business impact
- Manage a team of 10-25 people
- …and on and on

So what is this company really looking for in a manager? Somebody who is hands-on technically, has expertise in some areas, is a good communicator, can build and manage people, work and co-ordinate across borders, build and refine processes, deliver on time, and monitor the business impact! In other words, they want a superman!

There isn't a more confusing job description than that of a manager.

What would this manager do on a daily basis? He can't come into work and say, "It's Monday, so I've got to focus on processes today, then Business Impact tomorrow". Can business impact wait until tomorrow?

So, what is a manager really supposed to manage? What do we mean by **management**?

The classical definition of management, as also found on Wikipedia, is as follows:

> *Management in all business areas and organizational activities are the acts of getting people together to accomplish desired goals and objectives efficiently and effectively. Management comprises planning, organizing, staffing, leading or directing, and controlling an organization (a group of one or more people or entities) or effort for the purpose of accomplishing a goal.*
>
> *Resourcing encompasses the deployment and manipulation of human resources, financial resources, technological resources, and natural resources.*

Let's break it down to some key words. Management is to:

- Get people together to accomplish organization goals
- Plan, get people, direct, control, use the resources
- Deploy resources including people, money, machines, material

This definition still applies to any business, but it's a 30,000 feet view of management, and doesn't fully describe the functions of a manager in today's knowledge industry.

Applying this to today's knowledge industry, we see the following characteristics:

- Plan: Work plan, prioritize, schedule, and delivery.
- Staff: Get the right people.
- Direct: People and resources based on a plan and react or pro-act to events.
- Control: Whatever you can or need to control. Mainly, people and resources.
- Resources: People — the most important resource.
- Resources: Money — this is limited, most of which is spent on people.
- Machines: Mostly simple and can't do much without people using them effectively.
- Material: Mostly information, which is to be deciphered and used by your people.

Clearly, in the knowledge industry, you manage people and whatever affects people, because everything is linked to people and their performance. You manage people's work, their expectations, monitor their output, set the culture, get instructions, give instructions, reward people, respect people, punish people, hire people, fire people.

People! People! People!

People are the center of a manager's world.

Why? This is because, in the knowledge industry, people drive everything. They constitute a major part of the cost and the quality of work is reflected most by the quality of people.

Other hardware and machinery is a fraction of cost and are very reliable that they don't need as much management attention.

Now that we understand the definition of being a manager, let's look at the next question.

How hard can a manager's job be?

It's often a great pleasure to make jokes about managers, especially your own. Here are some:

Q: How many managers does it take to change a light bulb?

A: Three! Two to hold the ladder and one to screw it in the faucet.

Q: How many managers does it take to change a light bulb?

A: Don't know. Let me call a meeting to discuss it first.

Q: How many managers does it take to change a light bulb?

A: None, it's not their problem.

Jokes aside, most people don't have an idea of the challenges of being a manager, some managers included.

It's widely believed that one key aspect to being a manager is taking decisions. But how hard can decision making be? You can always take simple analytical decisions, that is, look at the available choices, evaluate the outcomes, and make the best choice. Right?

Unfortunately, it's never been so simple, and despite all the technology, it isn't about to become that simple. Let's look at a scenario.

Consider this: you manage a team of five developers and are working on an important deliverable that is due on the coming Friday. Everything is going as planned and you seem confident that you'll make it. You have kept the pressure on the team to keep working at feverish pace to definitely make it by Friday. Actually, you have a little buffer and you are targeting everything to finish by Thursday evening IST itself, which gives you a clear, one day buffer.

On Wednesday, you have your regular weekly meeting with your senior manager, who incidentally is based out of San Diego. You are all set to report the "All is Well" status and the meeting starts with, "Hey, we got to take care of this new issue".

While your manager explains some more details, your mind starts racing and the faces of your team members flash before you; how hard people worked and how you asked folks to cancel their vacation.

What do you do?

Would you say, "We have all been working really hard at this point in time, and we are really close. It would be a tragedy to divert our attention to something else and miss making the date we really wanted to"?

Are you going to be your management's man, and say, "Certainly, I'll take care of that! But the Project Hilo delivery will slip"?

It's important to understand that how you respond to this situation may depend on how you view yourself. Are you representing the management, and therefore the organization, to your team, or are you representing your team to the management and the rest of the organization?

Whose side are you on?

Various scenarios can be played out and which one is best-suited will depend on many aspects. Let's list some of those down:

- Priority: The priority of the new task is certainly primary to decision-making, but priorities are not absolute and are as perceived. In most cases, your manager guides your priorities, which is where this conversation stands. It is true that your manager may set the priority, based on information from various sources, including you. However, the information your manager has about your team is always less than and not as current as what you will have. It is possible that your manager may set priorities in the absence of enough information around your project.

- Personalities of players: It would also depend on the personalities of the people involved; are you an 'accommodating type' personality? Is your manager bullish and usually does not budge?

- Communication skills of your manager and you: There is a lot that you want to say about the hard work and the heartbreak that looms over your team. Given a remote meeting, a lot of information needs to be conveyed with the right tone. Your manager also needs to have a good ear for listening to details and concerns.

- Nature and history of the relationships that exists between you and your manager: Do you have a history of good decision-making and delivery of projects? Do you share a trust relationship with your manager?

- It would depend on how much time you have to discuss this topic: Contentious issues take time to understand and sort out. Is there enough time to discuss this issue? Your manager perhaps allocated only a small amount of time, expecting this to be a straightforward conversation.

- It would depend on how fruitful you think the conversation would be: Do you believe that your manager will be willing to listen to you and possibly change the decision?

- It would depend on how much you personally put into the work: If you have happened to toil along with your team, you have a personal stake and can experience the pain first hand. This would be good motivation for you to push.

- It would depend on how connected you are with the team and the effort being put into it: Are you well connected with your team? Can you feel the empathy?

In this one hour conversation, decisions may need to be taken and commitments may need to be made. Commitments will have an impact on you and several team members. Your decision-making skills will be tested. How empowered do you feel to be able to make the decisions?

A seemingly simple situation has many influences and dilemmas. As a manager, you are destined to face these dilemmas on a daily basis. Managerial decision-making depends on more than just the immediate facts of the task at hand. It's the entire gamut of influences that exist in your ecosystem. These influences are created by the organization in general and you in particular. There are so many things a manager is supposed to do.

At different points of the day and each day of the week, you'll end up playing different roles. Let's try to put together a framework for understanding the different managerial roles.

Henry Mintzberg, one of the foremost researchers on management, published a research paper describing the roles of a manager. This was widely acclaimed and added new understanding of managerial work at that point in time.

Mintzberg—10 roles of a manager

Reference: *The Nature of Managerial Work*—Henry Mintzberg—1973—HarperCollins—US—ISBN—9780060445560.

Mintzberg defined 10 roles that a manager plays. These roles are categorized into three categories:

Interpersonal	Informational	Decisional
Figurehead	Monitor	Entrepreneur
Leader	Disseminator	Disturbance handler
Liaison	Spokesperson	Resource allocator
		Negotiator

While this research was published in 1973, the roles listed are still very relevant and provide a simple framework to understand managerial responsibilities. Let's explore the Mintzberg roles and apply them in context of today's knowledge industry.

Interpersonal roles

Interpersonal roles are the set of roles that a manager plays while interacting with his team and other people in the organization, as well as outside the organization.

The figurehead

A manager performs certain ceremonial and symbolic duties. In today's knowledge industry, far fewer ceremonial duties exist, as many of the functions have become automated and self-service through technology portals. Some continue to exist, such as the following:

- Default representative of your organization: When people don't know whom to contact in a particular team, they'll find the manager.

- Signing legal documents: For example, work contracts, third-party software usage agreements, service-level agreements.

- Providing signoffs on various activities. For example, provide a sign off on a software module that needs to be delivered. Sign off on requirements documents that may come from another team or customer.

- Verifying and approving timesheets.

- Operational functions like approving leave applications and job offers to be rolled out.

Leader

The manager is the leader of the team. This is a rather large bucket of interpersonal behaviors; multiple behaviors will fall under this category:

- Growing the team
- Creating a good work environment for people to work in
- Inspiring and motivating the team
- Encouraging skill development for people in the team
- Setting the basic culture and norms in the team
- Setting examples for others to follow
- Helping people plan careers
- Keeping a long-term view of the team's well being and work towards that

A leader is one of the key roles that all managers play in the knowledge industry, and many people believe that this is the primary function of being a manager.

A leader, by definition, leads the way, sets the precedents for the organization, shows the light when the team needs direction, connects with people, and earns their respect so they follow willingly.

A leader nurtures the team and creates a healthy environment for it to prosper and grow.

Liaison

A manager creates and manages a network of external relationships. This is an extremely important role in today's interconnected world.

There was a time when systems and processes were smaller, simplistic, and independent in nature. Things have changed in the globalized world, where systems are large, complex, and interconnected. Changes in one place have ripple effects in different parts of the system. When your team is connected to the network of dependencies, you may create a change for others or you may be required to respond to a change created by someone else. A manager's liaison abilities will be exercised on every such occasion.

In a software development world, some examples would be:

- Liaison with other teams, which may have a dependency on your output or where your team depends on their output; for example, software components that integrate with each other.

- Liaison with teams that participate in the lifecycle of work. For example, product managers, account managers, customers, and customer support teams.

- Liaison with customers and customer representative.

- Liaison with press and other entities which showcase the organization or its work.

Interpersonal roles define your interactions with the people who matter to you and your team. As you grow as a manager, the importance of these roles grows even more.

Information processing roles

Let's look at the information processing roles that define how managers are required to deal with information.

Monitor

This one is a generally well-understood role. A manager needs to monitor the internal organization as well as gather relevant information from the rest of the organization:

- Status of the work progress, issues faced

- Deadlines met or missed

- Monitor the external environment and watch out for changes which may impact the work

- Status of dependencies

- Monitor people and other resources

Some managers mistake this to be the primary role and drive through monitoring. They become status managers. Their primary function becomes getting statuses and delivering statuses.

The status meeting becomes the most important meeting of the week. Very soon, most important decisions will be taken during that meeting, as opposed to focused meetings across the week.

Status becomes the driver of work.

Many organizations spend way too much time tracking statuses and building monitoring systems. Current environments of large, complex, and interconnected work makes people worry about statuses too much.

Status, in itself, becomes significant work.

A manager needs to balance the monitoring with the real execution and build the trust that eliminates the need for excessive monitoring.

Disseminator

Much information lands up on the manager's plate for one reason, which is to disseminate, that is, to spread the information. The sources of this information can be internal or external. Some examples of information that a manager disseminates are as follows:

- Overall progress within the team and those of dependencies
- Issues that are of concern
- Organizational changes
- Changes in policies and guidelines
- Message from the higher management
- Organization goals and priorities

Disseminating information is an extremely important function for managers, as lack of correct information leads to people making assumptions. Inter-dependency in work also requires information to be available, so the alignment between different teams is within an adjustable range.

In today's world of e-mail and internal wikis, it has become much easier to disseminate information. There is often the problem of plenty and multiple sources of information.

One very powerful channel of information that every organization has is that of the grapevine. The grapevine has only become stronger over the years, as people have gotten more connected and information can travel faster. Also, teams are more distributed, which can lead to an information gap that is readily filled by the grapevine.

This has created a new kind of challenge for managers — that of finding a reliable source of information and keeping an adequate flow of information, so that teams don't rely on the grapevine and look towards their managers to get the information.

Spokesperson

A manager speaks for the team. This is an important responsibility and a privilege. There are various forums where you speak for your team, delivering the status information, and displaying new achievements or current problems being faced or risks to the deliveries.

The audience includes:

- Groups outside the organization such as customers, partners, and vendors
- In larger direct organizations like administration, your internal customers, HR, and so on
- In peer groups and teams where you have interconnected work dependencies
- Higher management to convey the position of the team on various issues

The information processing roles are increasingly becoming more important as the amount of information and the mode of information have changed and has been changing rapidly since the Internet became part of the corporate world.

In the Indian context, this role is very pronounced as the manager is the primary contact point for the teams in other parts of the globe. In many cases, the person on the other side (in the US, Europe, or elsewhere) never really meets or talks to anyone else but the manager of the team.

Decision-making roles

The decision-making roles are perhaps the most challenging of the roles. These make or break a manager's career and have a huge impact on the effectiveness of the entire team and the organization.

Entrepreneur

Being an entrepreneur (manager) doesn't come naturally to most people. In fact, there are several distinctions people make between entrepreneurs and managers.

So, who is an entrepreneur?

By definition, an **entrepreneur** is someone who believes in a new idea and assumes significant risk to implement that idea.

In business, we would assume that the entrepreneur does that to create new business opportunities by creating a better product or service or provide services with better quality and efficiency.

A manager, being responsible for the business delivery from his organization, has the opportunity to act as an entrepreneur to create new products and improve upon existing products and processes.

For example, you may run a product support organization, where the delivery may be measured by customer issues solved per week. You may already have a set of processes that guide the organization to deliver the service. Improving the processes involved, so that customers get a faster time for resolution and better quality of the solution, would be an entrepreneurial effort.

There's a risk that the manager presumes when new processes or systems will be introduced. The current systems may be negatively impacted. The manager will need to sell the idea and get the buy-in from the top management and his/her own team. The manager will need to develop the idea into one that can be implemented and work with other departments or teams to participate or facilitate.

A manager acts as an entrepreneur to design and create a change in the organization. For example:

- Create innovations in the product. Add new creative features to the product or process improvements to increase overall productivity.
- Future plans for the team in the short term and long term.
- Innovate within the boundaries. For example, use **Scrum** methodology to manage work.
- Manage the associated risks.
- Sell the idea for new innovations within the team and outside it.
- Nurture the new product or processes when these stabilize.
- Advertise success or learn from failure.

Organizations today support and encourage innovation. In our fast moving world, governed by technology, no organization can choose to stay with the old one for too long. It is not the purview of a few to think of improvements. Every manager on the ground can and should be able to improve what they do today by creating new processes and products.

An MNC manager in India has a significant opportunity to be innovative and add new adaptations to the global processes, such that those processes can achieve the objectives and work in the local environment.

Disturbance handler

Any activity or event that disrupts or can potentially disrupt the normal flow of work can be termed as a **disturbance**. These can be big, like a political strike that brings down the city to its knees or smaller ones like key people unexpectedly taking a break due to family or medical issues. Disturbances can be long drawn, like the SARS (a deadly virus that spreads in the air from human-to-human) threat that created a fear of travel among people the world over or can be short-lived like key systems not being available.

Many disturbances can be proactively avoided by looking out for them as a matter of routine, and that is one reason why managers build networks and keep an eye on externally connected and dependent components of the system.

However, many of the disturbances show up as fire drills and will knock at the door at just the wrong time. You are expected to just work through those while making sure that impact on the business is as minimal as possible.

Some examples of disturbances are as follows:

- Key employees leaving on short notice
- Layoffs and the impact on morale of the existing team, besides the fact that others need to pick up extra work
- Deviant employee behavior due to dissatisfied employees or people acting out their grudges
- Larger policy changes
- Larger organizational changes, like re-orgs and mergers
- Managing negative circumstances like backlash from dissatisfied customers

Indian managers also get to play this role and manage many disturbances locally. Disturbances in India have their own nature, like political strikes. While you handle disturbances effectively and save any impact on the organization's business, make sure that you report the issue and the resolution to your management chain. Many managers do the hard work of managing the disturbances, but never create any visibility of the same with higher management. Your overseas managers must know the situation on the ground, the resolution, and the fact that you managed it well.

Resource allocator

This is another well-understood role. A manager is supposed to manage the allocation of resources to get the best productivity from the team.

Resources are mostly people, but also include hardware, software, network, help with expertise, and of course money.

A primary function and a role of the manager is to optimally deploy the available resources to deliver the results:

- Create schedules and work plans. These could vary from a high level to a very detailed level. Plans are typically weekly or monthly or any duration in-between. The nature of planning depends on the nature of a project and a manager's comfort level with detailed planning.
- Prioritize among multiple projects and demands for bandwidth.

- Allocate other non-human resources such as machines, software licenses, and so on.
- Set policies for sharing resources.
- Manage shortfall by creative sharing or borrowing from somewhere else.
- Allocate budgets for resource spending.

Re-plan

Managers need to update and re-plan as the work progresses. Given the flexible nature, highly people-dependent work, and ever-changing requirements, it has become harder to plan with reasonable accuracy. Instead, most managers plan out a reasonable amount of buffer that needs to be added to each task or milestone, such that the intermittent milestone dates aren't too far off from plan. Nobody complains if the work gets done earlier than planned, but a slip in the delivery date isn't taken with as much enthusiasm.

Negotiator

With the work becoming people-centric, the negotiator role is a key role to be played. Unlike machines, people seldom take exactly what is given to them. They either want more or want less. How much more or less given depends on the negotiation skills of the two parties.

Negotiation is an important art, as it impacts more than one person. If one person negotiates to get less work, the others will have to bear it. If one person negotiates to get more rewards, there will be less to go around for all the others.

Hence, although negotiation is a one-on-one activity, it must be viewed in the larger context of the team. A manager usually will:

- Negotiate in larger organizations for work, delivery of work, and resource allocation
- Negotiate the terms applicable for work to be done
- Negotiate internally, within his/her team with different individuals on various subjects, technical and non-technical
- Negotiate with team members on various topics, work allocation, vacation planning, and many other tasks

Negotiation should be distinguished from haggling or having your way. Negotiating with your management is not the same as negotiating with someone outside the organization. Don't keep pressing too hard to get your way. You may succeed a few times, but your manager may figure out your disposition and may block you out later in further situations, expecting a hard negotiation.

Summarizing the role-play

Although the roles listed may not be complete in today's scenario, and certainly have scope for more dimensions to be added, they do capture the large part of the role-play. More importantly, it goes on setting the expectation of multi role-play for a manager. Once a manager becomes aware of the multiple roles to be played, he can work on developing and sharpening the same. (Foot note: Mintzberg published another book, *Managing in 2009* (ISBN978-0-273-70930-5), which goes into greater and finer grain details on managing.)

Every organization and situation will require one or more of the role-plays to be enhanced. For a new team being set up, the **leadership** and **negotiator** roles may be the most prominent ones. In a stable team, where people and processes are working well, the disseminator and resource allocator roles may be more prominent.

As a manager grows in the organization, the responsibilities including team size also grow. Overtime, there will be senior people in the team, even other managers who may be directly or indirectly reporting to you. A different leadership style will be required to manage a mature team. A more relaxed style of functioning and more open information sharing will be required. Senior people in the team are more like partners to you and are capable of running the business by themselves without much direction and monitoring.

An individual may find comfort in one role or another, based on his/her skills and personality. However, it is important that a manager be able to play most of the previously-mentioned roles. If you want to grow as a manager, you should find positions where your strength roles are leveraged the most. For example, there are several cases where people exclusively work as a manager in a start-up company. The moment they get acquired by a larger company, they look for an exit, despite being given top compensation.

The mai-baap manager

The Indian manager has a unique role to play, that of **mai-baap** (mother-father, that is, parents). Many team members also expect the manager to play almost a parental role. I, personally, have had people walk into my office and open up with their family and personal issues, as personal as spouse abuse and divorce. Some of the expectations were to simply open up and lighten their hearts, perhaps to explain the stress they were going through, which may have had a dent on productivity, or perhaps to get advice from someone who has seen more of the world. This will certainly not happen in the western world.

A manager, in the Indian context, may have to bear the expectations of a guide and a philosopher.

Sometimes, managers can also become like mai-baap, and behave like parents. They indulge in probing team members on personal matters and throw in the free advice. They form opinions about people based on what they hear about the employee's personal life and not just based on the quality of work done.

Many a times, there may be conversations which are not that personal, like someone contemplating higher studies, or a change in career, or getting involved in volunteer activity, sometimes even life goals like starting their own company one day, or going on a world tour on a bike.

It's perfectly fine to hear people out but be discreet before you give them your opinion on such matters and whether you can support something like that or not, from an organizational perspective.

Sometimes managers tend to get the idea that they control and impact every aspect of an employee's life and behave like a mai-baap. Good advice to such managers is to not behave like a parent. Remember your boundaries and stay away from personal matters of others in the organization. While you have to hear people out sometimes, never initiate or encourage a very personal conversation. As smart as you may be, you aren't qualified to handle it and from an organizational perspective, you are better off not knowing those details. There isn't anything you are supposed to do about it.

All said and done, there is an expectation of a mai-baap role to be played.

Visualizing the managerial model

"A picture is worth a thousand words", as clichéd as it sounds, also remains true. Visualizing is a great way of putting information in perspective. Decision-making becomes so much quicker once you visualize something. Our minds are perhaps designed to work with visual information.

When we operate in any environment, we have the following perspectives:

- A model of how and where in the scheme of things we stand
- A model of how things work in a given model
- What contributions we have to make and what contributions others in the ecosystem should be making
- The way we interpret the environment guides the way we process information
- The way we process information will guide the actions that we take

Here are some of the models for being a manager.

The conduit

Managing is a bridging role. A great way of visualizing your role is by using a conduit analogy. A **conduit** is a channel, a delivery mechanism, or a means to transmit something. Let's explore:

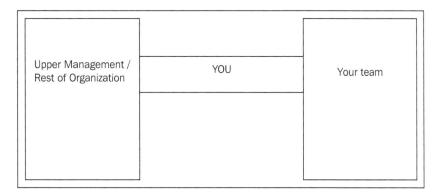

A manager's role can be visualized as a conduit. What your team sees is highly dependent on you, the conduit. You are the primary (not the only) source of information, priority, nature of work, and philosophy for your team. How much of an organization and a management's philosophy is passed on to your team, will heavily depend on you.

On the other side of the conduit are your manager and the rest of management. What your manager sees of your team is highly dependent on you, the conduit. The effectiveness, productivity, and well being of the team depend on the conduit.

The conduit (you) has the ability to color the picture in any shade; how big or small and also control the view of the picture to smaller or bigger. The conduit doesn't need to be uniform and can be a funnel. The conduit can control the flow of content in either direction. Here's how you can visualize the forms of a conduit:

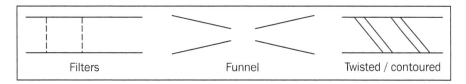

What flows through the conduit:

- Work content and priorities for the team, as defined by higher management.

- Work content and directions may need to be elaborated and broken down into a level of detail that suits the execution.

- Monitoring and status information about the team, as reported by you to the higher management.

- General information about the organization and external information to the organization.

- Cultural influences and positioning on various aspects of managing.

- Rewards to you and the team.

- Visibility of the work being done: In remote teams, this channel is very important. At the same time, today's networked systems help create visibility outside of this channel.

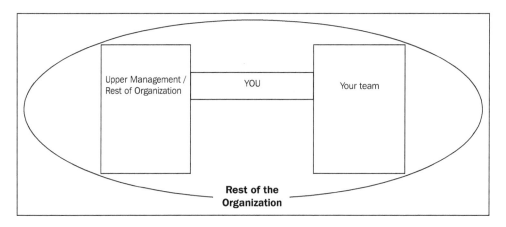

The rest of the organization is all around you and influences everyone in the picture. You, the conduit, may have a change of shape and flow of matters based on pressure/ influence/expectation from the environment around you. Your team may have multiple channels of information and cultural influences due to the organization around them. The upper management may be forced to share more information, rewards, and work based on how the rest of the organization is working.

The conduit model does not mean that the manager has no power, or he/she isn't a thinking being. The manager controls being a conduit and hence holds great power. Controlling the flow, twisting, coloring, translating, and enhancing the work, culture, and rewards is a very empowering position.

The conduit also serves as a reminder of the fact that the power of a manager depends on the power of the two sides. A good team and a good upper management are both necessary for a manager to contribute.

The hierarchy or leader of the pack

Most people tend to think of a manager primarily as a leader and in a hierarchy, perhaps an influence from the most powerful form of organizing, the military. The verbal communication reflects that too, for example, "20 people under me". The growth path and designations also match this expectation; the first designation is Software Engineer, then Senior Engineer, then Project Lead, and then Manager. The visual is that of a reporting herirarchy. Most companies have an organization chart displayed on internal portals that support this vision of a manager:

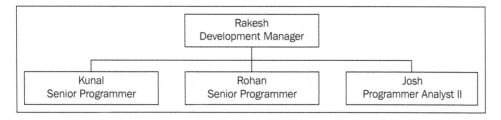

It is indeed true that leadership is the key to being a manager. A mindset of responsibility and fronting the organization helps shape many other behaviors of a manager.

Unfortunately, the hierarchical view promotes a sense of superiority in managers and they find themselves at odds with today's reality.

The hierarchy is the fundamental representation of authority and responsibility and displays the relationships between people.

While looking at the chart, one must remember:

- The manager is not smarter than everybody in the levels below
- The manager doesn't have to control ALL that happens under him/her
- The manager is responsible for the delivery of work being done by people in the hierarchy
- The manager is responsible for facilitating the people in the hierarchy to perform optimally
- The manager's authority is not absolute over the people in the hierarchy

The leader should view his/her immediate organization as part of the larger organization and understand that the leader of the smaller organization is also being led. If we increase the scope of the visual, we'll see the following figure:

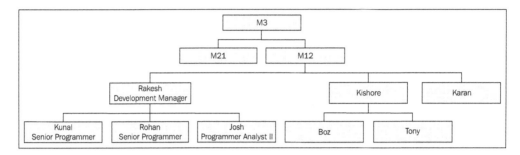

In today's knowledge industry, the leadership isn't limited to the manager, and the team members are capable of providing leadership in various aspects. For example, it is very likely that the technical leadership in the team or liaison leadership may come from different members of the team. The manager becomes more of a focal point of the system, managing different aspects of his/her organization.

The visual can be flipped on its side and this is how it'll look:

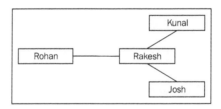

The larger organization will look similar to the following diagram:

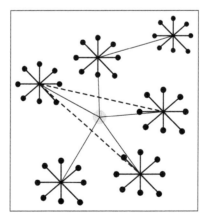

The system now looks like more of a hub and spoke model rather than a hierarchical one and is more applicable in the knowledge industry. The manager is really in the centre of the team he/she is managing while connected to the larger hub. There may be lateral connections between hubs as well, leading to a complex network structure and placing the manager not only at the centre of his/her own hub, but also connected to and hence being influenced, and in turn influencing, other parts of the organization.

The orchestra conductor visual

Some people liken the manager's role to be similar to that of an orchestra conductor, as displayed in the following figure:

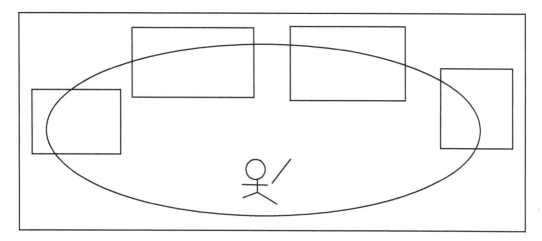

The orchestra conductor isn't the expert at every instrument, but is responsible for setting them in action, at the right time and at the right intensity. The orchestra conductor has a larger picture of the overall score and the overall execution plan. If anything goes wrong, the orchestra conductor has the best chance of course correcting.

The model works in certain cases in today's knowledge industry. The team members are typically highly skilled in their trade, just like the musicians in the orchestra piece. Most require only minimal direction to complete their task and have the maturity to work with other people in the team. There may be multiple small teams with different expertise. They need to be in sync with each other and play their part. Finally, all of them are required to make the score complete.

However, this model works only if the team has all members with high expertise and maturity. High technology and highly experienced team managers can potentially work in this model.

This model doesn't fit in many ways too, for example, today's manager's job is always changing and isn't a very well laid out plan. In fact, there's hardly any plan that doesn't change. The model also ignores the larger organization picture and the networking required to work in today's industry. Hence this model is only partially applicable and only in very specific situations.

Some questions answered

Here are responses to the questions posted at the beginning of the chapter. Let's see if your thoughts match mine:

Q: Am I supposed to listen to people's personal problems?

A: Not exactly. You may listen, but don't necessarily have to opine and certainly don't need to resolve.

Q: He was out for a month due to injury; should he get the same bonus percentage as another guy?

A: Evaluate the overall contributions for the bonus period as the primary guide to deciding the bonus percentage. Use standard organizational policies to decide the bonus amount. Don't worry too much about a month gone due to injury, another person who may be healthy may come to office but produce precious little.

Q: How much time should I spend with my team?

A: As much as you can. You are a model for your team and always take center stage.

Q: I'm up to my ears with work, and Sameer, the key developer on the project, walks in with a problem of his own? What am I supposed to do?

A: Listen to him. If you are in the middle of something and don't want to be interrupted, ask him if his discussion can wait for a little bit. If not, at least listen to him for a few minutes and decide if further discussion can wait. This is assuming that Sameer isn't a habitual walk-in with trivial problems.

Q: My boss wants me to change the design we have already invested in, but I really don't agree with him. Should I fight against the change?

A: First of all, try to understand the reason behind the requested change. Voice your disagreement with your boss's request and set up a discussion. Most managers will not shy away from a good technical discussion. On your side, be open to understand the perspective of the other side. You have to be able to voice your opinions and stand by them. That's part of your job description.

Q: The guy looks good in technical interviews, but seems to have an attitude problem. Should I still hire him?

A: Probe your opinion a little bit more. Do you think the candidate's personality is a detriment to the job function? Will it fit into the organization and team culture? In the end, respect how you feel too.

Q: I can avoid this guy leaving the company if I can promise him a promotion soon, but I really don't think he deserves it right now? But again, I have a key account project that can use his skills.

A: Never buckle under a threat of someone leaving. Attrition is part of life and it's better to deal with it rather than promoting someone you don't believe in. The cost of having a person in a wrong position can be very high.

Q: How do I explain why somebody didn't get a raise?

A: Well, you must have a reason why someone did not get a raise when you took that decision. Explain it. Even if you did not decide the raise, you are still responsible to explain it to your team member.

Q: Is it my job to explain why a layoff happened? After all, I didn't make that decision.

A: Layoffs are sensitive. Spend some time with your manager and HR and figure out what to say and how. Yes, it is your job to explain, even if it's not your decision. You represent higher management to your team members.

Q: How do I motivate the team when they already know there is not going to be any pay hike this year?

A: Money is only one of the factors that impact motivation. Look for other factors that can appeal to the people and get them motivated. For example, working on new technology may be very motivating for some or a new customer facing role for another person.

Q: We have had a long, tough project delivery just completed. Everybody is looking for a break, but we have more work coming. How do I avoid a burnout?

A: Work on a detailed plan to know exactly how much the pressure is. Take it to your management and discuss adding more bandwidth and perhaps reducing the scope of work. On the other side, work with your team members on the plan and make them party to the planning process. Seek ways to optimize.

Summary

If there's one thing that is true about being a manager, it's the multiplicity of everything and the variety of everything. No two managers have the same challenge or the same prescription of the problems.

To be able to perform well as a manager in the organization, you need to understand that there are multiple roles that you are expected to play. The nature of business and organization culture will demand that some roles are primary and more valued than others. You may need to understand the different systems and players within the organization that are essential to align with in order to successfully play these roles. You will need to work on these competencies and develop skills required to succeed in the role.

And finally, you need to watch out for when the priority of a role changes.

That being said, if your organization has trusted you to be a manager, you certainly have many of the required qualities necessary to be a manager. The important factor is to continue to enhance these key qualities and grow as a manager.

Being a manager is a journey like no other; it's like Alice in wonderland, Slumdog Millionaire, and Terminator 3 all rolled into one.

In the following chapters, we'll explore several other key aspects of being a manager and unravel some facts and some myths, so you can form your own opinions and get a larger understanding of the bends in the river ahead.

References

The Nature of Managerial Work — Henry Mintzberg — 1973 — HarperCollins — US — ISBN — 9780060445560.

Managing in 2009 (ISBN978-0-273-70930-5).

2

Transition: From Individual Contributor to a Manager

"I don't know who I am anymore", said Venkat to himself, with a puzzled look on his face.

Venkat had been a star performer for the last three years. This was his second job, and he admits that he struggled initially to adjust to the processes and systems of a large multi national. However, he started with the basics and worked hard at his assignments, spent twice as much time as anybody else around, and read all that was to be read (even stuff that seemed unrelated). After his first deliverable, Venkat felt somewhat confident, and he has never looked back since. He enjoyed the work, and volunteered for all meetings and status report preparation that his manager asked for. He enjoyed the special status he received from his peers, and volunteered to help them out on technical issues. He earned the top rating in performance reviews three years in a row.

Venkat got promoted to a manager recently, and he got a great project to work on as well, which was technically challenging but with tight deadlines. He had a small team of three developers, and he knew at least two of them well, while the third person was new to the job.

After so many years of success, now he was finally in charge. However, Venkat didn't feel the same high. He was a little lost, unsure of what to do and just didn't like the feeling of low confidence.

Even though nothing was critically wrong with the deliverable, Venkat wasn't his usual self.

Venkat's story isn't fiction; it's an often repeated reality in most organizations. A solid individual contributor doesn't seem so solid in a manager responsibility.

In this chapter, let's examine some of the aspects of making that transition.

Watch out for

As you move into a manager's role, there are a few things to watch out for.

Time

If there's any one thing you'll have less of, it'll be time. Unfortunately, most people never do active time management; instead they settle into a set pattern of time spent that works in the given set of work circumstances. Every time there's a significant shift in the work and the environment, there is bound to be some disruption in the pattern, leading to a time crunch. Let's examine some factors that lead to a time crunch in your transition.

Your work plus more

For a manager, the deliverable is a sum total of deliverables of the team members, including your own. Almost always, a new manager also tends to retain a significant part of the work he used to do as an individual contributor. So you not only have to code your own module, but also look at the quality, completeness, and delivery of the work from your team members.

Less definition

As an individual contributor, a lot of what you do is defined well, for example, a specific software module to write or a set of issues to fix. Your primary responsibilities are your own deliverables. As a manager, the work that arrives at your door may require further definition and also need to be broken down into executable units, so it can be understood by your team and executed well.

Multiple roles

As we know from *Chapter 1, Whose Side Are You On?*, a manager plays various roles, and you get to spend time on many of these various activities. For example, as a liaison role, you may be invited to a meeting on a new architecture discussion, or as a resource allocator, you may spend time working with the IT department to get new hardware for your team.

Much of the time spent on these other activities goes unaccounted for.

Indirect tax

As a manager, you are responsible for making sure everybody progresses. You will spend time trying to unblock somebody. This unblock activity may be simply debugging some code, or de-mystifying a customer issue, or working with an external team to get the dependencies delivered.

Most of these unblock activities are unplanned, and will show up on a daily basis. Once again, time spent here goes unaccounted for.

Scope of work

When you become a manager, the scope of work gets wider. As an individual contributor, you could get deep into one area and that would help solve many problems. However, as a manager, you may have too many things in different areas to be able to find the time and dive deep into any of the areas. The skill needed to manage multiple areas is very different from the ability to dive deep, just the way that the skill of a deep-sea diver is very different from that of a lane swimmer.

Commitments

It is common for individual contributors to evaluate and estimate the time taken for a delivery based on their own capability and past experiences with the delivery process. While taking on a new project or deliverable, often new managers tend to evaluate and estimate just the way they used to, that is, based on their own abilities. A manager needs to understand his team and other factors like the experience available in the team, the time to be invested in learning and ramp up, and many more.

New managers are also quick to commit an aggressive date, since they would like to have the satisfaction of a completed deliverable, sooner rather than later.

It is also tough for a new manager to say NO to more work. More work than what can be handled, given the circumstances.

Information sharing

Information is, perhaps, the most valuable asset in today's environment. The conduit visualization applies well, when analyzing information sharing.

As an individual contributor, the information you really need is usually technical or directly deliverable-related such as a time line or expected quality. As a manager you tend to get a lot more.

You may receive information about the deliverables, about other dependent deliverables, about what is happening in the environment, future plans, about people, and about policies. As a conduit, you have the necessary context and a better understanding of the two sides. Basic information at one end may be critical data points on the other side.

As a manager you need to figure out how to manage this information.

Treatment #1: Some of this information needs to be shared as is no change required.

Treatment #2: Some needs to be changed to make it fit the context and reduce complexity of details.

Treatment #3: Some just needs to be kept with you.

Treatment #3 is really the one to watch out for, as it's hard to keep information from your trusted team or peer or a friend. Dishing out details that others don't know also illustrates a sense of power, and being in-the-know, so it's easy to slip into a model where you routinely dish out details that are not to be talked about to that audience.

All of the previous treatments also apply to the movement of information from you to your manager/management chain. As a manager, you are supposed to report the status of deliverables as well as the general status of the team, which includes the problems being faced, achievements, and what's working versus what's not working for the team. Very often a new manager finds it difficult to make the choice between the three treatments.

Not giving up control

This is probably the hardest of things to do, and for most new managers, this conflicts with the idea of being a manager. Everyone expects to have more control as a manager; however, a key part of being a manager is to give up control to your team members. Many decisions that you used to take as an individual contributor may now be left to folks who are more in the thick of things.

In order to increase the scope of your knowledge and influence, you may have to give up on the depth of involvement. The folks who take up the work from you, in those areas, are the right people to take those decisions and should be allowed to do so.

Another key aspect to understand is that, in most cases, there are no right or wrong decisions. For example, a software design can be done in many, many ways, and each design will have its own merits and demerits. Similarly, how a customer's problem can be supported may have many solutions. A manager is better off when he has a reputation and influence in the team so that team members come to him whenever there is a critical-enough decision.

Many new managers tend to keep all the decision making to themselves, creating a level of distrust and slowing down all the processes.

Enforcing your will

One of the subtle aspects of being a manager is to enforce your will. People in the knowledge industry are well educated, perhaps very analytical, and there's a lot of scope for different viewpoints and discussions. This can sometimes lead to too much discussion and not enough execution.

Once again, there are many ways of doing things and everything can be debated. At times, managers are compelled to make decisions by consensus, which isn't always easy to come by.

Managers need the ability to arrive at a decision, while taking many viewpoints, but it'll be rare to get a 100 percent consensus.

Once a decision is made, a manager would need to endorse it and stand by it. Everyone else who may need to follow or support the decision should have no confusion regarding following the decision. A manager must be able to enforce his will when required.

The other end of the spectrum also exists, that is, a manager always enforcing his will regardless of others' opinions. Being a manager doesn't really mean that you are technically best or always right. The team members are equally bright and should be able to influence decisions that impact them.

Always enforcing your will may lead to alienation and distancing between the manager and his team.

This aspect always goes with the feel of things. Too much or too little can create trouble.

Defensive approach—being afraid to goof up

Every new role and responsibility brings about its own challenges. Your response to these challenges makes you unique and contributes to your successes. It is also true that it's usual human behavior to be cautious when in a new situation. Being cautious is different from being defensive. A defensive mindset may lead to inaction, which leads to inefficiency and loss of productivity.

Some of the ways this manifests are as follows:

- Checking for e-mails from your manager all the time, and trying to respond to them immediately (even when they may not be urgent)

- Reviewing your composed e-mails again and again, before sending them out
- Seeking the status of things, many times a week
- Over analyzing every issue before taking a decision
- Trying to report good status all the time
- Trying to close down on discussions too quickly
- Trying to look for hidden meanings, in everything
- Looking for information all the time from various sources

Since managers are leaders, they are also responsible for setting an example for their team. Sometimes new managers take this too far and run a risk of becoming uptight:

- Spending too much time at the office and trying to be the last one to leave
- Afraid to admit you could be wrong
- Trying to look serious all the time, especially in meetings where your manager is also present

A defensive mindset can easily seep down into the organization and is not typical of successful teams.

Overcoaching

New managers can also get into a habit of spelling out everything and 'helping' or 'correcting' every aspect of their team members. The team members get a lecture and detailed instructions to do everything. Managers watch the progress too closely and 'correct' a mistake even before a mistake is actually made. It's a manifestation of part 'defensive mindset', part 'eagerness to help', and part 'demonstration of superior skill'.

Frustrations of being a new manager

The process of transition will bring about many frustrations; let's look at some common ones now.

Teaching a man how to fish

One of the biggest problems to overcome for a new manager is the thought process that says, "I can do this myself, better and faster". Every time there is a task to be done, you have a choice to make regarding whether this work should be delegated to somebody else, or whether I can do this myself. As an individual contributor, it is natural to take on work that comes to you and the mindset is still largely the same when you transition into a manager.

Here's what happens.

A certain work, say, preparing a document on design, needs to be done. Now the choices are:

- If you assign it to another member, Tom, then you have to do the following:
    - Explain what you'd like to be done in there
    - Monitor when it's being done
    - Review what's done
    - Take a deep breath and go back to *step 1* for changes
    - Continue the cycle till you are satisfied

It is very tempting to just take it on and do it yourself, especially if the work is exactly in the same area that you owned as an individual contributor. It is indeed true that it will be faster and easier if you do it yourself. Here are some more reasons why a new manager will not let someone else, say Tom, take on the task:

- Tom has not done this kind of design work before
- Tom has other things to do
- The last time you gave something to Tom, you had to explain it many times
- It's just faster otherwise
- This work is too important to be given to someone else
- Let me just get it over with

But here's why it may be worth letting Tom take it on:

- Tom learns the design process.
- Tom learns your thought process and creates alignment.
- Tom builds on the work he did last time. You get to leverage the groundwork you did last time.
- Tom gets a boost of motivation to be part of an important assignment.
- Tom and you strengthen a trust relationship.
- Next time, Tom can be even more independent.
- You get to do more of something else.
- Though the initial document may be done quickly by you, everything takes many revisions. The next iteration may need new hi-fi diagrams, which may require even more time from you.
- You get the satisfaction of coaching someone.

At times, it may require extreme patience to see things move slowly and mistakes being made, but that's part of the natural learning process.

Teaching a man how to fish makes him into a food provider and possibly capable of feeding not only himself, but also many others. Your work actually decreases when you have many hunters in your team.

A manager needs to be a coach too and would need to spend the time to develop the team and build the skill sets required to deliver. A coach's primary job is to teach his/her teammates how to play. The success of the coach is in how well the students play. Anybody who has taught would know that it requires patience and empathy. These are some of the qualities a manager would need to develop to be able to take on a larger scope of work and rise up in the management chain.

Also, a manager needs to coach the entire team and not just a few core members. Many a times managers tend to get close to the top performers, and work closely with them and lose out on the opportunity to influence and develop the entire team and build a trust relationship with them.

A slow world around you

While you are geared up to produce the results and deliver more, it seems like the world is geared up to slow you down. Everything seems to take more time than it is supposed to take, and for no apparent reason, but some might be as follows:

- People take too long to respond to you
- People take too long to make simple decisions
- People are slow to understand what you are saying
- People take too long to finish simple tasks
- Processes are slow
- The hardware and network is slow!

All of the previous points can be partially true. However, it is likely that you are expecting everything to be faster than it is. It would be great if everybody could be paced the same way, but that is never the case. The organization has its own pace, and some of it can be influenced by you, but most of it would not be. Truly, a faster pace may not be required, or may not be desirable, given the circumstances.

However, as a new manager, you are likely to be working hard and would like to see things move faster to see results faster.

I don't get enough information

You work in a very connected world today with multiple sources of information, but may still feel that you don't get the information you need. You may feel a lack of timeliness and quality in the information you get.

Here are some information gaps:

- Not enough detail being given by your team when reporting their statuses to you:
    ° You hear, "It'll take some more time", instead of, "It'll take two more days"

- Your manager doesn't provide all the required details and background when assigning you new deliverables

- People respond with short sentences:
    ° You asked the architect's opinion on something, and he responded, "It'll work"

- The data is incomplete and comes without enough context

- People just forget to update you

Your information needs are much higher as a manager, as you are supposed to gather information and disseminate information, but you may be fumbling for information all the time, especially for the information that you really need at that point in time.

Information is useful when it's timely and it can be relied upon. You may need to understand and set up the channels of information, such that:

- You can sift through it quickly

- It has enough context

- It is accessible when you need it

I can't get no satisfaction

Imagine a 400 meter steeplechase, which really tests everything you got. It's long enough that you need a lot of stamina and short enough to run hard and it has got the obstacles to jump over. Now imagine you being the guy who is just one meter behind the leader and pushing hard but not getting there, no matter what you do.

Sometimes, a new manager may feel just like that runner in close second place. You are doing everything right, running hard and keeping stamina and jumping over the obstacles, but just not getting there. It's a feeling of helplessness, as you have exhausted your abilities in all departments.

Some of the manifestations are:

- I'm pushing hard, BUT people are not responding equally
- I'm getting the support that I need, BUT some more would really be great
- We made the deadline, BUT it would be better if we finished with some time left to review more
- I'm happy with the work, BUT we can do even better

New managers can be hard on themselves and on the people around them because they have a point to prove and they may be bursting with ideas having watched all their managers as an individual contributor.

I'm running all the time

Your day starts with looking at e-mails and picking out the work items from your manager and some follow-ups from past deliverables. While you are trying to figure out how to do those, one of your team members comes by and wants to have a one-on-one as he is very demotivated. Meanwhile, you look at your calendar and see that you have been invited to two meetings, one from administration on relocation from your current place and another from a dependent team to discuss some design interfaces.

At the end of the day, you end up doing only half of what you wanted to. You feel helpless and appear to be running from one thing to another. You are always trying to complete tasks that others have imposed on you (either your manager, or your team members, or supporting teams, or peer teams). You seem to get little opportunity to implement all the good things that you wanted to.

As a new manager, it is easy to get overwhelmed. You may try hard to finish as many work tasks as you can, but more keep showing up. These untimely work items take precedence over other initiatives that you had in mind for yourself and for your team.

Making it easier

Here are a few things you can do to make it easier on you.

Relax a little

New managers feel an extra pressure to show results and to prove themselves in a new role. In most cases, this pressure is self-generated. In fact, a new manager may have a little bit of a honeymoon period, since the senior managers understand that there's a learning curve involved. The extra attention you may be getting could also be because people want to help you and not just scrutinize you.

Different people respond to pressure in different ways. Some may respond aggressively and try to do too much and others may become too circumspect and try to do too little. Either way may not be the best way forward.

Let's look at some scenarios and responses from different viewpoints:

Scenario	New manager says	New manager's manager's (senior manager) thoughts
Deliverable needs some things to iron out	Let me explain in detail what is left out and why.	No big deal. I just need a list of work pending.
You came in late and missed a meeting	Sorry to have come in late and missed the meeting.	No thoughts. It can happen to anybody.
You need to ask for a vacation	Let me explain the reason for the need for a vacation and how things will be taken care of when I'm out, and by the way, here's my cell number.	Enjoy your vacation. Let me know who is incharge while you are out.
New additions to project	Yes, we can do it. Let me stretch to accommodate this within the given time.	Is it possible to fit? How much more time and resources do we need?

Understanding the information needs of your organization

A large part of any job today is to deal with information. However, every organization has its own way of dealing with the information, and every individual has his/her own way of working with, and requiring, information.

As a new manager, you would deal with a lot more information than you did as an individual contributor. You will also generate information for others to consume, like the status of your team to be sent to your manager or any important project-related decisions to be shared with your team.

While sending out information, consider the following:

- Urgency of the information
- Is this information time critical
- Level of detail required for the information being provided
- Does the context need to be set for the recipients?
- Is there a culture of sharing information voluntarily or sharing only when required
- How formal should the information be?
- How to share confidential information
- Preferred means of information sharing, such as written information, e-mail, wiki, or Word documents

Besides learning how to process information for your organization and for your immediate manager, you will also need to identify the key channels of data. For example:

- Let your team know what to report and the level of detail required, that is, let them know of your information needs
- Which meetings are key to attend
- Communication from key people and important broadcasts, which need to be read and should not get lost in the sea of e-mail
- View only channels, where you just want to be connected and don't have to respond, such as a support mailing list for related products.
- Informal channels to be connected to the grapevine

Finally, learn how to archive information so you can find it later. A lot of stuff goes around only to come back, and having the past references can make a big difference.

Know your success measures

Many problems arise because it's not clear what is considered a success. It is extremely demotivating when you don't see recognition despite doing everything right.

Every organization has a certain set of criteria to be met before something qualifies for success. For example, in a software project, you may complete the functionality in time and with good testing done as such. However, if you did not create automation tests, the management may still see it as incomplete and consider the quality questionable.

Take some extra time when defining the project to list down the key criteria to be met besides the core deliverable. Similarly, work with your manager to define the key aspects of the job, and what is considered as success at the organizational level. Also, some of the success measures for you may be different for your peers, since you work in different areas.

Learn to say NO

This is a difficult one, especially for new managers. It is indeed true that nobody likes to hear a NO, after all, if someone expected a no, why would they ask?

While it is perfectly all right to take on more, and say YES, it's always better if you say that willingly.

Many a request will come to you, and many will add work for you and for your team. Most of this work may be unexpected and may lead to an overstretch of your resources. As a manager, you are supposed to utilize and nurture your resources. An overstretch may not be in the best interests of the team.

It is an art to say no to people and an integral part of business communication. Here are some tips:

- Understand that it's well within your right to say no. Don't be guilty about it.
- Be firm and understanding of the other person's needs and expect the same from them.
- Or, defer the decision till you have all the facts, including looking at the calendar or discussing with other team members before you commit.
- Don't be upset that somebody is asking you to do more. Be polite and express your inability.
- "I don't know if I can take that one", or a more direct one, "I wish I could, but I really can't".
- Offer some alternatives.
- If you are unable to do the above, sign up for some soft skills courses on assertiveness.

The art of saying NO without leaving a bad aftertaste will serve you well, not just in your career, but also in your personal life.

Get organized

Planning and preparation are absolutely necessary to manage a larger scope, especially when most of the things are not in your control. The level of planning that worked at the individual contributor level will not be sufficient for a managerial role, and the nature of preparation needed is very different as well. We'll look at some tips for this now.

Track the time spent

Just like financial management starts with knowing where you spend your money, time management starts with knowing where you spend your time.

Spend 10 minutes at the end of the day to quickly look through how time was spent that day.

Start using a calendar

For some strange reason, individual contributors don't like to use the calendar. It is not a daily routine for ICs to look at the calendar; instead, most ICs rely on a **to-do** list.

A to-do list is a great way to know what needs to be done; however, it's NOT a plan.

Distinguish between urgent and important

Every task and activity is not at the same level of urgency or importance. Urgent is stuff that cannot wait, and will take precedence over many other things to be done. Important are the activities which are crucial and must be done in order to accomplish your goals with quality and consistency.

For example, attending to a hot customer problem is urgent and cannot wait. While a quality review of your deliverable is an important activity, which must be done, it doesn't have to be done right now.

(Reference: *First things First*, by **Dr Stephan Covey**, is a recommended read and explains this concept in great detail.)

Plan your day every morning

Start the day by looking at the calendar and planning out how you are going to spend the day. Knowing what is coming in the day and in the week helps you set your expectations and avoids the panic and uncertainty. It's ok if you can only accomplish part of your plan due to other reasons. Over time, it can only get better.

Find someone to talk to

It's human nature to talk and find solutions through discussion. However, it may not be easy to find the right person to talk to. If you can, find a mentor. Somebody who has seen more than you and can help you charter the waters. A mentor can provide you with an outside perspective and bring about some validation when you need one.

If you can't find a mentor, have a peer support group where you can learn from the experiences of other managers.

One word of caution, a mentor or support group is not your therapist. Don't go there to only get advice or empty out your frustrations; instead, go there to share and learn. Also, this does not shift your responsibility; you still need to make your own decisions whatever else follows. While you share, be discreet.

Having some validation for decisions or more information will help you go into a decision with more confidence and may help you see better as you navigate through your career.

Sign up for formal training and education

The need for managerial training is well recognized by most organizations, and if you are lucky, your organization may have several different short-term courses. Unfortunately, many people do not spend enough time and effort in leveraging this training. Since you are reading this book, it's likely that you do believe there's more to learn. Some suggestions to consider are as follows:

- Time management
- Assertive communication
- Project planning
- Performance appraisal
- Self improvement training such as the *Seven Habits*© Franklin Covey programs

If you find the time and support, talk to your management about a more involved program that may be run by an external agency like IIM or any other institution of repute.

Summary

Becoming a manager is a life goal for many. Being a great individual contributor doesn't necessarily make you a great manager. While the key abilities that made you a great individual contributor are still very relevant and required in your new role, there is a new set of skills and many new perspectives that need to be developed. The good news is that most of this is easily achievable once there is awareness. In the next chapter, we'll explore in more detail the personality and skills required to be a great manager.

References

First things First, by **Dr Stephan Covey**.

3
Basic Skills, Traits, and Competencies of a Manager

In India, being a Manager is highly valued. A majority of people see themselves taking a managerial position some day. However, can anyone become a manager? A really good manager? Are managers born or made? Do all managers, at least all good managers, share something in common?

When we look around and see the journeys being taken by different managers, their working styles and behaviors, we can hypothesize that:

- Managers are born and made. Some folks have a natural flair to be a manager and some acquire essential skills to be a manager in a given situation.

- Not everyone may enjoy being a manager. While you may be 'promoted' to become a manager, you may find that you don't really enjoy the time spent talking to people, driving them to results, and compiling status reports for your management.

- It appears that good managers do have many things in common, even though they may have their own style of execution.

In this chapter, we will explore the skills, traits, talents, and competencies that are usually required and expected for playing a manager role, and also burst some myths surrounding managers.

Skills, traits, talents, and competencies

We all have heard these terms. Let's try to understand what they mean and how they are different or similar to each other.

Skills

Skill is defined as the ability or capacity to do something, acquired through specific training.

Skills are learned abilities. Technically, anybody can take a course in a specific subject and acquire that skill. Of course, the person should have the aptitude to learn those skills.

Developing skills does not need to be in a formally-structured or schooled way. Babies develop motor skills as a natural process of learning. People develop communication skills, which are part formal learning and part informal learning.

How well somebody can translate that acquired ability, that is, skill, goes beyond the definition of skill.

In order to be an engineer, you need to acquire the engineering skills, or in order to become a chef, you need to acquire cooking skills. This alone will not make you a good chef or an engineer.

Traits

Traits are at the other end of the spectrum. Traits are personal. Traits are often linked to a person's character. Being shy is a trait. Some people are introverts and others are extroverts.

Traits determine your response or behavior in a wide variety of situations. Some people are fearless by nature and others are cautious. Traits are often described in pairs of opposing behaviors; for example, extrovert-introvert and honest-dishonest.

Many people consider traits to be innate, and that can definitely be true. However, it is not always true. There are traits that people develop by their upbringing and the environment they live in. As people progress through life they acquire new traits or modify ones they already have; these are called **learned traits**. Also, people display contradictory traits, so an honest person can become dishonest and vice versa.

Talents

Talent is an oft-used word in business today. A pure definition of talent from *Webster's Dictionary* (1913) is as follows:

> *Intellectual ability, natural or acquired; mental endowment or capacity; skill in accomplishing; a special gift, particularly in business, art, or the like; faculty.*

It sounds like a lot of things, but the key phrases are **intellectual**, **natural**, and **skill in accomplishing**. Talents are supposed to be God's gift to you being applied to a specific craft or job. Specific application is the key phrase here.

In a usual conversation, we say, "This person is very talented". Most Indians would concur that "Yuvraj Singh is a talented cricketer". In these statements, we clearly imply the fact we refer to the potential of Yuvraj Singh as a cricketer, his applied skill.

It is very possible that Yuvraj Singh could have become a successful soccer player had he chosen to pursue that. Anyway, we are all glad that he chose cricket.

Michael Jordan, the basketball legend, is an excellent golfer now and he tried his hand at professional baseball as well. Both Yuvraj and Jordan have most certainly a combination of different talents, such as physical stamina, focus, and discipline, which when applied to a particular sport created a great performance.

Competencies

Competencies are behaviors an employee displays in order to translate the knowledge and skills and leverage the traits to deliver a performance on the job.

Competencies are related to a given job function. Hence different jobs will require different competencies. An offshore software engineer needs to have the necessary technical skills to write the code and written and verbal communication skills to effectively communicate across the world, among others. In this case, the communication competency is highly valuable, given the offshore nature of the work.

If the job description changes to that of a software engineer working as a database administrator, a slightly different set of competencies apply. While related technical skills are very important, in this case, expertise will be desired given the fact that databases are critical to the business and scope for errors is less. Communication competencies are always required but basic communication may be enough for this function. However, a meticulous attitude and handling high levels of stress will be important, given the requirement criticality of the infrastructure.

Competencies are the application of all that we know and can do. Almost all employers describe a job function in terms of competencies and results required. Also, almost all employee appraisal forms will attempt to grade people in terms of competencies on some scale. For example, a competency of 'Result Orientation' may be measured on a scale of 1 through 5, and an appraiser may be advised to comment on the reasons behind the rating.

Top skills, traits, and competencies expected of a manager

Let's look at some key skills, traits, and competencies that are expected of a good manager.

Love of working with people

Most managers will spend a majority of their time managing people, and everything that is connected with people, even more so in the knowledge industry.

Do you find yourself talking to people all the time? Do people tend to bring their problems to you? And when they do so, do you see it as adding value to finding a solution, or do you see that as a headache which you shouldn't have to deal with?

If you find satisfaction in just being with people and helping them achieve their results, you have a primary quality to be a manager.

Going to parties and having a good time with people also displays that you love being around people and surely shows your love for food or drink, but not the essential part of helping people achieve their goals.

Although all interactions count, including phone conversations, e-mail, or Instant Messenger, it's the face time that has the most impact. If you'd rather spend your time in your own office by yourself, perhaps a manager role isn't for you.

You can, of course, force yourself to spend time with people as part of the job requirement, but unless you really enjoy that time, it will be hard to sustain and excel as a manager. You may end up limiting your interactions to a select few, where comfort levels are high, at the risk of alienating others.

Global managers today get less and less face time with some of their team members, sometimes as little as 12 hours in the entire working year. Without the love of working with people, the interaction with remote workers can really become difficult, as it'll take an extra effort to be connected at a deeper level than just work.

If you like to work with people, you are likely to be high on empathy. When people approach you with a problem, you may feel the problem to be your own. Even before the person tells you there's a problem, you already know there is a problem by the look on his/her face, the voice, and the body language. Your body language will be inviting and welcoming. While the person describes their problem to you, you listen intently and non-judgmentally, even supporting them so that he/she is encouraged to open up. If you are high on empathy, you may also have a feel of what kind of suggestion will work with this person and how it should be put across. You follow up and when you see the person getting over the problem you feel a sense of satisfaction.

Empathy also helps in understanding and working in a diverse environment, for example, working with people who grew up culturally different from you. Especially in India, there is a high degree of diversity with people from different backgrounds, and also while the working population is highly skewed towards men, women have a growing presence, especially in the knowledge industry.

> Please note that a manager doesn't have to be an extrovert to love working with people. Extroversion is often equated with being outgoing, and that isn't the same as having a love of working with people.

Myth: nice manager

Sometimes managers wish to be seen as popular, someone who everyone wants to work for. A nice manager, who listens to his people and rarely says no to anything, be it taking vacations or a promotion. Being a people person doesn't mean being nice all the time. While being a people person is a great thing, usual business rules still apply. A good manager balances the priorities of the people and business and can be nice and tough at the same time.

Easy to approach

While you may love to work with people, the people around you should also love to work with you, and a measure of that is the number of people who feel comfortable coming up and talking to you.

A non-threatening, if not friendly, demeanor would certainly help. But even more important is the rest of the interaction that will follow. Do people come to you for problem solving and leave with more problems to solve? Do they come to you to share the overload of work and leave with more work to do? Is there a fair give and take in your interactions with people?

Myth: I'm easy to approach, I have an open door policy

Approachability is not to be confused with accessibility. Accessibility is a measure of the number of channels and the time you are accessible to others. Today, channels of accessibility are hardly an issue, given the multiple modes of contact, including Instant Messengers. Time availability will always remain an issue and you'll have to consciously make time for people. Approachability isn't the same as availability or an open door policy. Your approachability is defined by the way you respond to people's attempts to get in touch with you. Do you respond quickly and positively, or do you buzz them off for a few days? Do you have a friendly disposition towards people? Do you let people speak? Do you listen to what they have to say before responding? All of these define the degree of approachability you exhibit.

Farmer mentality: sow, nurture, grow, reap

There are thousands of types of jobs, but none of them is as involved, as complete, and perhaps as spiritual as farming. It requires hard work, investment, belief, knowledge, teamwork, patience, faith, ownership, and a sense of creativity. And of course, the elements of risk, especially in India where farmers still depend on the monsoon.

Farmers go through a cycle of preparation, investment, nurturing, protection, seeing it grow, and then enjoying the benefits of all the effort. They go through this year after year and while they make it better every cycle, they take the losses when decisions go bad. Nevertheless, the basic approach remains the same.

Managers need to develop the traits of a farmer. You need to have a sense of preparation and investment, since it's the most basic, key part of the process and then wait while nurturing and supporting for the benefits to roll in. This needs to be done with every person, process, and project.

Myth: fast moving managers—in a tearing hurry

Some people believe that a hotshot manager is always juggling many tasks and pushes everyone to move faster, but that simply isn't true. Most exceptional managers have a farmer mentality.

Farmers are always required to be patient. You can't push certain processes to be faster than the natural cycle. You can help and catalyze, but improvements are usually marginal and need to be evaluated for the long term. Too much of anything, even the catalyst, can yield bad results. Managers also need to be patient and respect the personal growth cycle for each individual and for different processes. Managers can help catalyze the process but need to allow the cycle to take it's own course. Once a growth or improvement cycle is over, the next growth cycle can start.

Core values: honesty, integrity, truthfulness, trustworthiness, consideration for others, and more

There is no substitute for core values like honesty, integrity, and trustworthiness. These are very important for any employee in general, and are even more important for managers, as managers have a high impact on people and processes.

There will be many challenges that will come a manager's way and many decisions that managers need to make. Core values will be a guide in all of these. Many questions cannot be answered by looking at the rulebook, but very easily answered by using the value system yardstick. There will be lots of opportunities for a manager to make quick gains, by using a shortcut and possibly lowering the value standard. This would usually be impossible to sustain, and will come back to haunt you in the longer term.

Consider this: Vijay comes to his manager's office and expresses the monetary problems he is facing. He is a good contributor and quite important to the current project. Vijay mentions that he has an offer for about 30 percent more than what he makes right now and although he likes the company, he'd like to resign. The manager's options are to relieve him in a month's time or promise him more than 30 percent in a few months' time when the annual salary revision is due. The manager knows that it may not really be possible to give Vijay 30 percent because the expected budget may not allow that; however, Vijay may stay until then and the project will be past the critical stage. At the same time, the manager is not breaking any rules, as he is fine with giving Vijay a 30 percent raise if the budget is available, plus the manager can always say that upper management rejected the change.

Even simpler situations such as taking a day off for being sick while you are really not or using the official network and resources to watch adult material or taking office stationary home are all situations which call for basic values to be applied.

Values are the foundation of good behavior and nothing less is expected from a leader.

Not a myth: corporate greed

The recent financial crisis the world underwent is a grim reminder of corporate greed, which of course is a result of a few individuals propagating a culture of greed through the system. Poor governance and integrity standards have led to many a scandal with dire consequences. Satyam in India or Worldcom in the US have cost thousands of jobs and the loss of credibility for the entire industry.

Tolerance for ambiguity and patience

We all know: the better the map, the easier it is to follow, but unfortunately the working map in an organization is not always clear. Sometimes the destination is not clear and there are multiple ways to get there and also, there are too many detours. You'd be lucky if the map does not change half way through. It would be great if the directions to follow were clear, but who is supposed to make it clear and easy to follow? A manager needs to deal with this ambiguity—find the best way given all the other factors.

Ambiguity is the order of today's knowledge industry. A lot of things are fuzzy and need definition. It takes time to remove some of the fuzziness, and a manager needs to deal with it. It will require tolerance for fuzziness and patience to figure it out.

Some people are pre-disposed to display patience, and others can learn to be patient. Patience defines the quality of your daily interactions, your responses, and some people believe, your respect towards others' opinions. Simple day-to-day necessity, like good communication, requires you to be patient. Patient people wait for others to complete their thoughts so they can take the time to respond well and with complete information.

Good communication skills—especially listening

Communication is the bread and butter for a manager. There is a lot of information which needs to be processed and communicated by a manager in all directions, to his directs and beyond, to his management chain, and also to many other parallel groups.

Communication is NOT smooth talking. Many people confuse good communication with fast talking or smooth talking, where one person dominates a discussion and the other party.

Good communication is not a love of talking. A rather quiet person, who can listen to others and respond with clarity, is a much more powerful communicator than somebody who simply loves to talk.

Communication includes all forms of communication, the usual written communication such as e-mail and formal memos, letters, and so on. New age communication such as SMS, Instant messaging, and so on, and verbal communication, via phone or video conference and with the person face-to-face.

Body language is also part of communication, although it's becoming less of a factor given that a majority of communication is not face-to-face anymore. Even people who sit half a floor away communicate via e-mail or IM. The tone of your voice over phone or tone of your instant message plays an important part in perception of the message.

Good communication skills also include understanding your audience and communication in such a way that the audience can understand and communicate back to you. As such, your communication style will change a little based on the audience it's intended for.

Finally, the single biggest factor in good communication is listening. Unfortunately, the importance of listening gets lost very often and a large population of people suffer from a lack of listening.

Especially in India, people tend to cut into a discussion or start talking before the other person has finished, and perhaps get impatient to answer with the assumption that they know what the other person is talking about. Indian managers do need to work twice as hard to develop good listening skills.

Myth: quiet people can't be managers

Many people believe that managers are people who stand up and speak at every opportunity. It's not uncommon to see meetings where the manager takes all the talking time with very little being said by anyone else.

Remember the term **talkative**. The term instantaneously takes us back to middle school, when kids who would talk too much in the class were called talkative. It's often believed that managers need to be talkative. At every opportunity they get, they talk. It is indeed true that a large number of managers tend to talk too much, and unfortunately the problem grows over the years. Over time, people tend to avoid managers who ramble.

You can be a quiet person as such, and as long as you don't shy away from speaking when it is required, quietness will be a strength. I have been fortunate to meet a lot of highly successful managers, who are quiet by usual standards but have an impeccable record of delivery and team management.

Team building—hiring, retaining, developing good people, and nurturing team spirit

Another key competency for a manager is to be able to build teams. Although, at a literal level, a team is made up of a set of people, in reality a team isn't really a team without the binding glue called **team spirit**. A manager is as good as the team he/she builds. A manager's capacity and ability to deliver is equal to the capacity and ability of the team.

To start with, building teams requires good hiring skills. It requires:

- Position identification.
- Defining skill requirements for the position.
- Defining the process for identification and skills testing. Most organizations will have a pre-defined process and supporting team to do this.
- Look for fitment.
- Deciding appropriate compensation.
- Following required organizational process for completing the hiring process.

Besides having a team, it is important to configure a team. For example, a team of 10 people may need to be balanced in terms of experience, youth and freshness, and a variety of technical skills.

A team needs to have defined positions and each team member should know what role and position he/she is supposed to play.

Finally, a manager needs to create an environment to foster team spirit and bonding, so that a set of people works as a team and not as multiple individuals.

Once a team is in place, a manager needs to constantly nurture the team and also the individuals. Most people love to work in a team, but they are individuals too and have unique needs and aspirations. This will lead to better retention, which is a definite success criterion for a manager in today's knowledge industry.

Performance management

Ensuring good performance and consistent performance from every individual is a core competency of a manager and absolutely essential for success. In a way, performance management is a side effect of many other competencies, such as result orientation, communication, project management, people skills, and so on. A balance and purpose in all these skills will bring about good performance automatically.

Performance management is the long-term management of performance of the individual and the overall team.

Myth: maximum output

Performance management is NOT about getting the maximum output. Often managers confuse delivery of the maximum using as little resources to be a mark of performance. Signing up for more work, and then putting people under pressure to work harder and longer hours is not performance management. Continuous pressure on people may result in burnouts and hard to repeat performance. The keyword in performance management is consistency. What is valued is performance of the team and the manager that is consistently high.

Problem solving

One of the key competencies for a manager is to be a problem solver. A manager is in a unique, perhaps the best, position to solve a problem. Close enough to the ground realities to understand the basics of the problem, and far enough away to understand the big picture and consequences.

He/she has the resources, technical and physical, which may be required for problem solving. He/she needs to rally his/her team and the supporting cast to come together to solve problems.

The nature of the problem could be technical or administrative or personnel-related. Given the job profile, a manager may face more technical problems, hence technical and analytical skills may be most important, or most of the problems may be co-ordination-related, hence communication and organizing skills may be most important. Regardless of the skills required, everybody expects managers to be problem solvers.

Approaches to problem solving may differ and the working style to solve problems will also differ from one manager to another. It is often seen that two managers from the same organization and even performing similar roles have very different styles of problem solving, and both may be successful at it. However, the popularity score of one may be different than the other.

Myth: every problem is my problem to solve

Problem solvers love to solve a problem. However, not every problem that shows up at your door is yours to solve. Every time you see a problem doesn't make it yours to solve; although you may have the capability to solve it, it's better for the right area owners to take care of the problems. This leaves you with more time to focus on other issues in your own area. It's of course ok to help if you can.

Especially in India, managers tend to take on more than their fair share of problems. Part of that is culture, where the leader seems to become responsible for everything.

In general, anything that is handled by any of your team members, as a matter of routine, should be delegated immediately. If it needs to be given priority, indicate that in your communication and follow up as necessary. However, don't try to do it yourself. At times, things may be escalated and may require extra skill or experience. In such cases, even routine tasks may be required to be handled by the manager. For example, a customer requested bug fix can be delegated in general, but if this issue is very complex, has been going on for a while, and is escalated to higher management, it will be prudent for the manager to get involved closely, including making the code fix, if required.

Always an eye on the ball—results orientation

Everybody loves a positive result. And consistent good results are very highly valued in the business world today.

Achieving results is not easy, as most managers end up with a lot of different priorities and little time. Besides, fire fighting has become part of the daily routine for many a manager. It is very easy to get busy in the daily work and lose sight of the end results to be achieved.

Besides, in today's dynamic environment, even simple tasks may not turn out to be simple, and unexpected problems show up all the time. In today's knowledge industry, the biggest problem is loss of people, which creates multiple problems of overload, transition, and commitment.

Successful managers will keep an eye on the ball, where things are and where they are going, and carefully chart the course so the end results are met.

A manager's success will be partly defined by the quality of results and partly by the journey to the result. If the journey to the good results is not great, it'll leave a bad taste for all the people involved, and will make it harder to repeat a good performance, hence impacting the consistency of a manager.

Decision-making

Decision-making is one of the casualties of today's knowledge industry. Since there are many players in the decision-making process, the decisions get put off for another discussion. In general, many people seem to shy away from making a decision, since decisions bring a responsibility with them and perhaps an onus to follow through. Do you tend to avoid decision-making by either waiting it out till somebody else makes it or getting into an analysis paralysis?

Decision-making will typically involve:

- Information analysis of various kinds
- Looking at alternatives
- Involvement of multiple parties
- Risk analysis
- Prioritization
- Impact on people and processes
- Impact on a team or a company's external image
- Consideration for ethics and values
- And of course, multiple outcomes or consequences to be considered

Most of all, decision-making requires someone to be ready to take on the responsibility of the decisions and not be fearful of getting blamed. Some of these abilities are a result of exposure to decision-making as we grow up.

Especially in India, parents tend to bubble wrap the child from the vagaries of the real world. There are many kids who go to college and still have their wardrobe being decided by their mothers. Many have their parents accompany them when they go to a new town, so they can be helped. Thankfully, a large number of people do get the independence to make their own decisions, at least enough of them.

A manager is expected to make decisions and stand by them. Not all decisions require a detailed process and are done as a matter of routine. But even routine decisions are required to be consistent. For example, a simple decision of approving casual leave for a team member requires you to be consistent about when and how often casual leaves should be taken. One team member should not be questioned more than the others unless there's a good reason. Decisions based on core values will tend to be consistent.

There are decisions that have a long-term or high impact and require a detailed analysis. For example, policy decisions and financial decisions usually have long-term impact. Some decisions may not have a long-term impact but may impact a large number of people across multiple teams. For example, a simple decision to have everybody verify and confirm some personal data seems to be a simple one and perhaps takes only about 5 minutes of an individual's time, but when calculated across a 50,000 people organization, strain on network resources, follow-up, and reporting, the cost of such a decision is not trivial.

A manager's decision-making abilities will be tested everyday and are instrumental in the successes of the team and the manager.

Myth: well-informed decisions

Many decisions are delayed for the want of more information. Everybody wants to take well-informed decisions, since a well-informed decision is likely to be accurate. The reality is that most decisions get taken in absence of all the information or because someone has the confidence in making that decision (or perhaps the ability to deal with the consequences if things don't turn out well).

The problem lies in the fact that there is too much information that needs to be analyzed. Even if you can spend the time to do all the analysis, the decision may still not turn out well, since some parameters may change.

Managers need to make a call sooner or later and get just enough confidence to go ahead.

Project management and execution—delivery

Most managers will have some delivery responsibility, either it's product features, projects in IT organizations, or better service efficiency in KPO/BPO industry. Every individual in the team has some measurable deliverable, and the manager will have a sum total or a larger than sum deliverable.

In order to make successful deliveries, effective project planning and execution skills are necessary. While most organizations have set processes and planning tools, these are best utilized in the hands of an effective manager. Also, all good processes and tools leave some flexibility to be exploited by a skilled professional.

Finally, a plan is just a map on paper, and ground realities will almost always force you to re-calibrate and adapt to changes as they happen around you. In today's complex networked world, problems will show up that'll force you to re-plan and re-evaluate the goals, and sometimes reset the expectations of the stakeholders. These are skills that are most likely acquired through experience.

However nice and loved a manager is and however smart and educated he/she may be, the ultimate test is the delivery test. If a manager can't deliver, there isn't much point in having him/her around in that role.

In order to deliver, a manager needs to understand the success criterions or parameters of success that are expected. For example, an important software module, a fairly complex piece of code, may be delivered on time with bulletproof working and great performance, however, it may fail the success criteria of maintainability and being easy to debug, or security, if these were not taken into account.

Some of the skills tested for execution are:

- Planning and tracking
- Allocating resources and budgeting
- Responding to contingencies
- Managing change and course correction
- Calm under pressure
- Defining clear success criterions and communicating the same to the team
- Reporting and keeping the organization informed

Delivery is what the organization is set up for. All other competencies and skills are really for achievement of delivery.

Myth about flawless execution

There's an often-used term called **flawless execution**. It's many a times understood as, **execution without any problems**, which is completely contrary to the real world. Many managers become fearful of making a mistake, or worse, they run into issues and hide them for want of being seen as flawless. While it is always good to foresee a problem and plan for it beforehand, in the real world, unseen problems are part of any execution. Managing unexpected problems also displays strength in execution.

Grip on technical knowledge/domain

A manager is not about just managing people or processes or spreadsheets or outcomes. A manager needs to know the product in great detail, including technical or specific domain-related details.

If you are managing a team of technical people and managing a technical product, there is little chance that you'll command respect from your team and peers if you aren't able to keep up with the technical details. It'll also be extremely difficult to contribute to your team members' work and estimate or evaluate the work being done or make decisions if you aren't at the desired level of technical expertise.

It also applies to managers who manage a work process. Without the domain knowledge and in-depth process understanding a manager will find it hard to manage.

In India, a lot of people become managers very early in their career, and tend to lose touch with the technical aspects. Although they manage since they have a strong foundation in technical aspects and started in the trenches, they would be able to do even better if they had the inclination to be connected technically too.

Think customer—customer orientation

Good managers understand their customers. They understand the impact of the work on a customer's business. They understand how the work being done may benefit or may harm a customer's business. After all, customer benefit is the underlying theme of all work being done.

From a very simple perspective, everything that an organization does is meant to eventually deliver value in shape of products or services to the end customer. The customer pays for it and must get what he/she needs from the products an organization is selling. Customer orientation is a key competency for any organization, and almost all managers get evaluated on this. Unfortunately, many a times, customer orientation tends to get lost in the layers of the organization.

Managers are expected to understand who their customers are. Customers can be internal or external.

In the product development organizations, the end customer may not always be visible, but internal customers should be. Sometimes, organizations choose to use the word **consumers** instead of customers, especially in the case of product development teams that are responsible for building framework or infrastructure that other higher-level products may use. For internal support organizations, like network support, other internal organizations, which are users of the network, are the customers. In services organizations, the end customer is the client people are working for, but there's also the client's customer that needs to be kept in mind. In BPO organizations, like telephonic support for a PC maker, the employees are the closest to the end customer. In outsourced BPO operations, the customer is the client and client's customers.

Typical expectations from managers on customer orientation are as follows:

- Understands who customers or consumers are
- Understands the customer scenarios
- Works to understand the customer needs and maps them into the work being done
- Prioritizes work based on customer impact

It is often not easy to know what will eventually have the most impact on the end customer, since the eventual impact on the customer is a combination of many things that an organization does, it is extremely important that managers understand the impact their work can or must have on the eventual customer.

A very typical example is the way User Interfaces get designed in a software product. A simple "Order Entry" form may have many fields that are laid out in a single form. The layout of the fields is extremely critical to the productivity of a user. If an operator is taking the orders over the phone, the layout will be very different than the order being filled out online, directly by the buyer. A smart manager would think about the usage of the product and not only try to create a form that simply lays out all the details of the form, as listed in the requirements document.

Any discussion on managerial competencies would be incomplete without understanding emotional intelligence. While the concept of emotional intelligence was being researched and talked about for a long time, it became a big topic of interest after the publication of the book *Emotional Intelligence* by **Daniel Goleman** and the subsequent bestseller book, *Working with Emotional Intelligence*.

Emotional intelligence

Emotional intelligence is described as social intelligence that involves the ability to monitor one's own and others feelings and emotions, to discriminate among them, and to use this information to guide one's thinking and action (definition by **Solovey & Meyer**, 1990: Referenced from the paper *Emotional Intelligence: What is it and why it matters* by **Cary Cherniss**).

To understand emotional intelligence, consider this example: a top Indian software company hires two fresh graduates, Jay and Veeru, from a highly-rated engineering college. After four years of education and being in the classroom every day, they are looking forward to the professional world and some real action. They know they are supposed to have one month of technical training. Two days after joining, they are both gathered in a large meeting room and told that they'll have three months of technical training boot camp due to a recent policy change. Everybody, including Jay and Veeru, is frustrated at the thought of hours and hours of lectures and classroom time. Veeru stands up and asks the question, "Why did you hire us, if you think we need to be trained for so long?" There is a stunned silence in the room and then murmurs of agreement followed. Veeru is encouraged and adds, "You should not play with people's careers". The coordinator simply replies something to the effect of, this is a policy decision and they should talk to HR manager if they'd like to. On the other hand, Veeru's friend Jay asks a simple two-part question, "Can we have a choice of different courses, so we don't do exactly the same basic training and can we simultaneously work on a small real project on the side?"

Who do you think is more likely to succeed in future or turn out a better job performance? Frustrations and unexpected turns are part of any job today, especially when we deal with large, complex problems. Both may have similar grades (a measure of technical or academic capability) coming out of college, or Veeru may have much better grades than Jay. Veeru let his emotions get the better of him; he feels cheated and angry and is unable to control or channel the anger. He resorts to accusation and wrongdoing. Jay is not happy to hear either and is perhaps, equally frustrated. However, he tries to understand the problem a little more by trying to get some more background, and possibly find a solution in the given situation, where he has no control whatsoever. However, he does have control over his emotions.

It is argued that the EQ matters more than the IQ in long term job performance. While IQ and technical skills are important for getting into a job, once there everyone around may have a similar level of IQ. The differentiation and professional success is highly likely to come to people who are high on EQ.

Dr Goleman also describes the five dimensions of Emotional Intelligence in the *Emotional Intelligence Competence* framework. Three of these dimensions, self awareness, self regulation, and motivation, fall under **personal competence**, which determines how people manage themselves and two, empathy and social skills, fall under **social competence**, which determines how people handle relationships.

Personal competence

Personal competencies determine our understanding of self and how we control and leverage our emotions:

- **Self awareness**: This is all about knowing yourself, your emotions, and the effects of these emotions on you. When do you feel happy? When do you feel satisfied? When do you feel hurt? Do you understand which emotions make you bonkers? As a person, what are your strengths and weaknesses. Do you consider yourself high on confidence?

- **Self regulation**: This is the management of yourself, your emotions, your responses, controlling your impulses, and leveraging your strengths and managing your weaknesses. Self regulation also applies to managing your indulgences and greed and staying honest and trustworthy.

- **Motivation**: This is about emotional tendencies that guide and facilitate reaching goals. Do you have a drive to achieve? Do you strive to attain your goals? Do you try to improve in order to exceed the set standards of excellence? Do you have a resolve to complete what you started and attain the results, despite problems? Do you align your efforts with the efforts of others in order to get the synergy required and attain larger goals?

Social competence—how we handle relationships

There are two dimensions of social competence, namely, empathy and social skills:

- **Empathy**: This is the awareness of others' feelings, needs, and concerns. Often visualized as being in somebody else's shoes, empathy helps us understand the other side of the equation and helps understand the perspectives of the other people concerned. Empathy is key in service orientation and understanding of customer needs and responding to them in an effective manner. Empathy also helps in today's diverse environment, especially in India, since India is easily the most diverse country in the world.

- **Social skills**: These are your models of interaction with the individuals and the general population around you. It's the adeptness at inducing desirable responses in others. Communication is primary to social skills; it includes listening and the ability to convince others. It also includes the influence that you have on others as a virtue of leveraging your strengths. Social skills help you bring people together for a common purpose and keep them focused. Social skills can help you resolve conflicts and get you out of a jam.

Summary

So, what's the verdict? Is a manager born? Or raised? Or created in a management institute?

Perhaps the answer is the usual option D: all of the above.

There are quite a few listed up there, but you don't need to be a master at all or any of these. There's a learning curve in managerial skills also, just like technical skills and if you work consciously and apply thought, these skills will get enhanced.

Besides the usual skills and competencies, quite clearly emotional intelligence is core to a manager. Some of the EQ seems like inborn and natural tendencies, a lot of it is a result of the social environment we grew up in and learnt as we grow in our professional and personal lives. It appears that self-regulation may improve as people work on it.

A lot of the other skills and competencies, such as project management and communication, can also be learned and improved upon. Many managerial programs aim at enhancing these skills. However, empathy and self-motivation are hard to cultivate. Core values are part of our core and not easily replaced.

It's possible to manage work by sharpening your project management, hiring some good talented people, assigning tasks to them, and measuring people based on empirical success parameters. This will likely get the job done, possibly also get the manager a promotion over the years, and most certainly a salary raise.

However, without the soft skills required, without empathy and love of working with people, without people-centric management, without core values, it would be impossible to be a manager that people admire.

Finally, are great managers created in top management institutes?

Certainly not! People who learn management formally really acquire the knowledge about the various aspects like finance and operations, which will certainly help understand the business aspects much better than most others. They also learn about how to break down problems and manage processes, hence making them skilled at execution. Besides, management students also learn about various human aspects and theories on human behavior, which will hopefully help them understand people a little better. Top management institutes already shortlist academically high ranking students, so IQ is high to begin with. So management graduates should be ready to manage work and if the same management graduate happens to have all the other essential people skills, this person can be the right person to work with.

References

Emotional Intelligence by **Daniel Goleman**.

Working with Emotional Intelligence.

Definition of Emotional intelligence by **Solovey & Meyer, 1990**: Referenced from the paper *Emotional Intelligence: What is it and why it matters* by **Cary Cherniss**.

4
Teamwork and Team Building

The National Geographic channel is a great place to learn about animal behavior and, if you are so inclined, it's also a great place to observe teamwork. The toiling ants look very inspirational and a pack of wolves is as ferocious as it gets. Most animal instincts are often explained as being driven by the simple needs of survival of self and are natural.

It's fair to assume that humans too are predisposed to work in teams. While prehistoric examples of humans living together are too dated for this book, joint families or even the nuclear families of today are a valid example of a team. A family is also a team with common goals (survival included), differentiated skills, and shared values. At school, we worked on various projects and assignments as a team. Almost on a daily basis, we played gully cricket and soccer in teams.

Each of these teams was different. Each had a different level of challenge, different number of people involved, different skill levels, different objectives, and different leaders. Each was created as a matter of fact, or randomly at best (a teacher picking four people for a chemistry lab assignment). While many of these teams worked well, there were several occasions when they didn't (dysfunctional families are known to exist, and we love to hear the debate on the team combination of our beloved cricket team).

By virtue of these, almost everybody has extensively worked in a team environment, even before they start their first job. With so much experience of working in teams, it should be possible to simply hire people and expect them to work well with each other. However, teamwork and team building still remain high priority item in business. Companies routinely invest lakhs of rupees (or thousands of dollars) in team building exercises, the results of which are highly debatable.

For managers at all levels, a solid team is a basic requirement. Your capacity to deliver and to have an impact on the organization is dependent on the capacity and capability of the team. A good team can make or break a manager's career.

In this chapter, we will examine some of the basics of teamwork and look at possible ways to build the right team.

Why do we need teams?

Let's start with the very basic question of the need for creating teams, besides the evolutionary fact of humans being predisposed to work in teams:

- A task is too big to be accomplished by one person:
    - Most work today is designed to be large and requires more than one person to do it. Although it is true that eventually work needs to be done individually, that individual's work may be insufficient to qualify as a meaningful delivery.

- Variety of skill sets required:
    - Work today is fairly complex. Sometimes it's the technical complexity that requires specific technical skills like in software product development, where specific skills in J2EE and database may be required. At times, as in a backend processing, the work may not be technically challenging, but may require domain expertise like insurance and taxation. In almost all cases, there's a need for various levels of experience to validate and de-mystify work.

- Integration requirements:
    - Work today is like pieces of a jigsaw puzzle. Each piece needs to fit into its right place in the puzzle. Working closely in a team makes it easier to build the pieces that fit together well. The communication within a team is much higher than communication across multiple teams; besides formal channels, many informal channels also exist. The water cooler chat is also an important channel where people exchange information. People are more open to share information within a team, which helps correct problems early on and avoids costly rework and delays.

- Continuous nature of work:
    - ○ Most work today builds upon existing work. For example, in product development, new features tend to build upon existing features or add new strengths to existing features, such as adding mobile access for a product that is currently available on the Internet. Developers fix bugs on the code that was written much earlier. Working in a team allows this continuous and leveraging activity to happen. The knowledge is shared and the risk is reduced in a team, for such continuous work to happen.

- Mitigate risk:
    - ○ The IT and BPO industry is notorious for job-hopping. It's not unusual to find a resume where there are four jobs in four years or less. Besides job-hopping, people may fall sick and need to take time off from work. Working in a team enables managers to ensure business continuity, so the end customer does not have to see the impact of any internal problems like attrition, organization changes, and so on.

- Power of compounding:
    - ○ Working in teams enables people to produce more than they would if the same set of people were working independently. People build on each other's ability and can get more work done in terms of volume and also in terms of complexity.
    - ○ Brainstorming is a good example where people bounce ideas off of each other to come up with solutions and new ideas. In my experience, most good solutions require a good brainstorming session. When people work in teams, each individual has much more confidence to take on a challenge and deliver on it, knowing that someone is around to lend a helping hand if need be.

- Enhanced productivity:
    - ○ Being in teams creates a sense of belonging and affinity among team members. Many satisfied team members often define the team as their extended family. This leads to people being interested in higher goals for the team and team members. Good teams also tend to show lower absenteeism and longer working tenures for team members.

Different types of teams

While all teams consist of people, there are several variations due to the objective or nature of the work being performed by the team. Let's examine some types of teams found in the knowledge industry:

- Perpetual teams:
  - This is the most common form of a team in long running product development organizations like Oracle, Microsoft, Yahoo!, and so on. A product like Oracle Database© Oracle, or Oracle Financial© Oracle, or MS Office© Microsoft is supposed to be on the market for a very long time. While the product will evolve over a period of time, it may retain its branding and basic purpose. Teams working on such products are also supposed to be long term, almost till eternity (which could be anywhere between 10-20 years in the IT industry). Of course, team re-organizations may happen and there will certainly be new players; the team, as such, will still need to exist and function with a new structure and new people.
  - Perpetual teams are built like a family and at least some people will tend to work there for a very long time. These teams will have very experienced senior team members, who may or may not be managers.
  - Perpetual teams also tend to have people of various experience levels, including some fresh from college since there is a variety of work (development, maintenance, new features, design, and so on) due to the long life of the product.

- Project delivery teams:
  - Project delivery teams are created for the purpose of a project delivery to a client. These projects may be short to medium term, and can be part of an existing long-term relationship with a client. For example, an Indian services company may already be engaged long-term with a large retail chain from the US, and they may have a new module (say reporting) to be implemented. A new project delivery team will need to be created with the required technical and leadership expertise. The leaders are typically handpicked and may have worked on a similar project or with the same client earlier, and the technical resources including experts may be drawn from the pool of people on the bench or seeking transfers into another project.

° Eventually, a number of people, who may have never met before, come together for execution of a project and delivery to the customer. The life of this team is equal to the life of the project. As a project nears completion and handover, the team size starts to reduce and soon enough the team is gone as another specialized (perhaps production support) team takes over.

- Crack or SWAT teams:

  ° These are short-term teams created, usually, to solve a difficult problem. For example, a team created to rescue miners trapped in a coalmine or a team created to design a complex software system. The team will have required experts from multiple fields (one who is a telecommunications expert and another who is a performance expert). Another example would be of a team created to win over additional business from a customer account. These teams have high energy and an extremely high focus on the goal. Typically, the people may be focused on one and only one mission. The team is bound by fierce focus on achievement of the goal. There's likely to be an urgency and high pressure, and there may be a clear leader, but no hierarchy. Opinions of all will be highly valued and expertise will be respected. There's no real team building required in this form of team, except picking the right people with high expertise, high experience, and temperament for a big job.

- 24x7 teams:

  ° These are teams that ensure 24x7 work, for example, global support teams, which are located in US and India. The US team may work from PST 9 A.M. to PST 5 P.M., which happens to be IST 9:30 P.M. to IST 4:30 A.M. India team 1 may work from IST 4 A.M. to 1 P.M. and India team 2 will work from 12:30 P.M. to 9:30 P.M. A customer issue may be worked upon by someone in the US team, and then passed on to carry forward by India team 1 and if still not resolved, it may pass to India team 2 and if needed again, to the US team.

  ° The team members are connected to each other on a daily basis and are usually experts in their respective areas. So a US team member working on, say, database backup, will tend to hand over issues to another database backup expert in India team 1.

  ° This kind of a team is very common today in services, which require 24x7 uptime such as e-mail, networks, production databases, and so on.

- ° 24x7 team members have a unique problem that they share their work with people who they may never see in person. Minimal personal interaction will happen, given the minimal time overlap between them and given the fact that one of them is at the end of his/her working day. Hence they have a very peculiar position of working purely on the basis of the written word and laid down procedures.

- ° There's a high dependency on each other, since work passes hands daily and builds on work done in each shift. Quantity and quality of the results is tied together, but there's very little control over each other.

- Cross organizational team:

  - ° These are the teams, which work across the entire organization and play either an integration role, or a specialist role, or a policy role. For example, there may be Release Management team or Program Management team, wherein one or more Release/Program managers work with multiple organizations to ensure overall integration of the product. Another example is the HR teams and Standards teams who ascertain policies and monitor the implementation of policies across the organization.

  - ° Teams who manage common infrastructure such as Operations teams, Real Estate teams, and Support teams also fall into this category. These teams manage common resources and ensure fair distribution.

  - ° These teams are engaged in a lot of customer (internal or external) facing activities, and people should be adequately equipped to be able to do so. A high sense of fairness and ability to stand your ground under pressure will be handy.

- Committees:

  - ° These are typically teams that comprise members from other teams who come together for review or implementation of some activity, for example, a design-review committee or a process-review committee. While there is a specific agenda for this committee to come together, the people are not dedicated to this agenda. They have their own deliverables and primary day job to work on.

  - ° These committees typically have suggestive powers and help drive initiatives that are good for the entire organization.

For further discussion, we will focus on Perpetual teams and Project Delivery teams, as the primary challenge lies with these.

How to build a team

Building a team is no easy task, and requires all of the manager roles (as discussed in *Chapter 1, Whose Side Are You On?*) to be applied.

Explain the big picture, purpose, and fitment of the team in the larger universe

Every team should know its purpose and fitment in the immediate organization and the larger corporate as well.

Things that should be clear to every team member are as follows:

- What the team is supposed to contribute
- How this contribution is important to the organization
- The size and complexity of the task for the team
- How work flows to this team and how the output of the team flows to other teams
- Different kinds of work that is expected
- How customers use the product or service
- What is important for the eventual customers or consumers
- How the products and services get delivered to the end customer
- What the important factors are for the team and the organization
- What behaviors are appreciated and valued by the organization
- The life stage of this particular team in the context of other teams

A big picture is essential to connect the dots and make decision-making more effective. People can automatically make better decisions and understand why certain aspects are important. Team members are aware of how team output fits in the larger strategy and can relate their individual work to the team's work and finally the organization's work.

The following are a few of examples:

- Case 1: Software developers working on a module that runs on a television set. If something goes wrong, it may be very easy for the developer to make the fix. However, the cost of up-taking that fix on the consumer's device is very different. Updating a fix on a TV is infinitely higher than a simple download on a handheld. Hence zero-defects is a key criterion for TV software developers' success. The quality team members and development team members need to collaborate closely to be successful.

- Case 2: Software developers working on a browser-based Order Management application. In this case, patching the application for any defect is fairly easy since the deployment will be internal to an enterprise. However, the key aspect of this application is the usability of the application by the end users. Does the application allow users to navigate around easily and find the details they are looking for, without wasting any time? The domain knowledge and the understanding of the usage scenarios are critical to the success of the product. A developer with great coding skills will require the domain expertise of a product manager to build a complete product.

- In a BPO, working on credit card payments, a team may be responsible for reminding consumers about their pending payments. The tone in which the representative talks to the customer makes a big difference to how the message will be taken. Team members hear each other and can help each other fine-tune communication skills and encourage each other to create a better customer experience, as the same customer may end up talking to another team member and the positive, or negative, experience may be carried into the next call.

The tough part

Explaining the larger picture has no real difficulty, except the willingness of managers to spend the time to do so. It's just easy to ask for something to be done, rather than explaining why it needs to be done and how it fits into the larger context.

Explaining the larger picture is not a one-time activity. It is more of a habit, perhaps a cultural thing. Every time there's an opportunity, you can talk about the larger picture. Over a cup of coffee is also an excellent time to discuss the larger picture around the work happening around that time. For me, some of the very free flowing and imaginative discussions about the product's features, users, market, and economics affecting the product, have happened on a coffee or a late evening beer.

Defining the composition of the team

As a manager, you need to figure out what skill sets are required, how many people are in each skill set, and the experience-level required.

A simple example is any sports team like a soccer team or a cricket team. All batsmen or all bowlers will not work. All players of the same age and experience will not work. All batsmen who can play great defense will not work, and at the same time, all batsmen who are aggressive, like Sehwag, will not work either. It's always important to get the team combination right.

For example, in a product development team engaged in a product which runs on the Internet, you may require five people with J2EE skills, of which two should be experts in UI technologies like JSP or ASP and two should be experts in non-UI technologies like SOA or Web Services or EJBs, and one person with expertise in Oracle databases. Of these, based on which area is more complex or which area has more of a challenge, the person should have more experience, say 9-10 years. In UI technologies, you may wish to hire one person with 4-6 years' experience and one with 0-3 years' experience. Perhaps, similar composition for the backend team also.

The team composition plays a big part in team dynamics. By introducing variation in experience level, you allow mentorship to happen. A more experienced person gets a chance to impart knowledge and bring someone up. As people grow in experience and wisdom (if we can use that word), there's a need to play a nurturing role to use their skills to have an impact at a personal level and not just at the product level. Besides the technical challenge, now there's an additional challenge to train someone technically and otherwise. This person gets to play a larger role and build a relationship with someone who he/she will also share successes with. The younger, less experienced folks bring in more energy and enthusiasm that will rub off on the senior folks, while the senior folks will bring the patience into the system.

When there are many people of similar skill sets and similar experience, there are higher chances of conflict. The team is also an ecosystem, where a balance is needed. More species of the same kind will lead to more contention for similar resources as needs are similar too.

The tough part

Most of the time, you never get a chance to build a team from scratch. You actually inherit a team that already exists. The team may not fit the composition that you may think is ideal, but there is likely to be no choice but to work with the team you already have. While a balanced team composition is the ideal situation, you need to make the best utilization of what you have. If certain skills need to be developed, identify the people who may have interest in learning those skills and spend the time and effort in skills enhancement for those people.

The good news is that over time there will be opportunities to start getting the composition right. There will be attrition as well as opportunities for people to move into a different role or take on other assignments.

Define playing positions

Just like any ecosystem, each entity has a place of its own, and that position supports the ecosystem to the maximum.

In a soccer match, each player has a playing position and you get players in the team based on what position they can play best. Each player relies on another player to play their position and almost always be there to take the ball. While others can assist as required, and in some grave emergencies, even the goalkeeper can move up the field, otherwise he/she would be expected to be near the goalpost.

Now imagine a scenario when some players come together for the first time to play as a soccer team. For experimental reasons, we can possibly lower them into a soccer field and ask them to play against a well-organized team. There will be complete chaos and despite good players, team may end up loosing.

Managers need to define the sphere of work of each team member. There are some direct deliverables for which a person is hired; for example, a programmer is supposed to program and a test engineer is supposed to test. Besides these broader categories of work, there will be other responsibilities or tasks; a developer may also be responsible for aligning development and QA activities. This may require additional meetings, status exchanges, and so on. Sometimes, these responsibilities may be high visibility, such as presenting or sending out team status to higher management and hence would seem attractive to more than one person, especially if there are multiple people with a similar career level.

Usually a manager gets to decide who takes on these additional responsibilities; in the absence of clear positions to be played, there's usually redundant work, and people criss-crossing each other, leading to conflict situations. These hurt the team spirit and lead to heartburn, and people try to outdo each other rather than aligning for shared success.

The tough part

Setting playing positions is a very challenging task, especially when you have a talented and ambitious team. Most contention comes around the lead positions.

Rajesh's five member team had two senior programmers, Gaurav and Sanjay. Both of them were hard working as well as smart programmers and both were capable of taking on leadership responsibilities. It was quite common to see both Gaurav and Sanjay get into a discussion, technical or otherwise. Rajesh could observe that and he was thankful that the discussions were still largely constructive. Both Gaurav and Sanjay indicated that they want to play a lead role for the project. Rajesh listened to each one and indicated that the team does need a lead. However, here Rajesh will need to make a decision between the two people.

Very soon, both Gaurav and Sanjay started getting into each other's way. If there's an e-mail from Rajesh or some other stakeholder, both Gaurav and Rajesh will respond separately and in great length. In fact, sometimes, Gaurav will ignore the response already given by Sanjay and respond in another thread instead of adding on. The other team members started to get technical decisions from each of them, sometimes contradictory to each other. Team meetings became longer since the two senior people could not agree on several issues. Essentially, these two were playing for the same position and getting in each other's way and also creating confusion for everyone else.

Rajesh had a choice to make, and he couldn't wait any longer. He decided that Gaurav will lead in the team. For now, Gaurav will be the Tech Lead and will have the responsibilities of triaging issues and responding to the support forums. Sanjay would be responsible for addressing any issues in a number of functional areas as well. These areas were listed. Any other communication will be done by Rajesh, and he intended to re-direct to either Gaurav or Sanjay, and was hoping that in due time, a pattern will set in.

Rajesh knew that Sanjay would not be too happy about this change. He had a long discussion with Sanjay and explained his reasons for making this change. He also listened to Sanjay, as Sanjay went into great detail on his contributions over the last few years. It was important to make sure that Sanjay's contributions were well known to Rajesh, and well appreciated by him. Rajesh also explained that there were newer opportunities coming up in a few months and that Sanjay's expertise and experience would be required there.

Rajesh got closely involved with the activities for the next few weeks, as the new dynamics set in, always making sure that he was not undermining Gaurav's authority while also giving due weight to Sanjay's viewpoints. He also sent Sanjay to attend the company's annual product conference in San Fancisco, USA.

By defining the playing positions, Rajesh improved the productivity in the team, reduced the confusion, and set up clearer authority structures. He also paved the way for Gaurav's career growth, as well as addressed the aspirations of Sanjay, and gave him due respect.

Did Rajesh run the risk of losing Sanjay? Yes, he certainly did, but the situation demanded clear and firm direction setting. Letting the confusion prosper would not have helped in any way and there weren't any signs of things turning around on their own. It is possible that Rajesh could have ended up losing both Gaurav and Sanjay, and some other team members as well, if he had let these issues run unchecked.

Clear and defined hiring process

Once the team composition is decided, the next step is to get people on board. Hire!

Hiring is one of the rather painful activities that comes with no guarantee of a payoff. In the knowledge industry, especially so in India, managers spend a fairly significant amount of time on hiring activities.

While different models of hiring and interviews will work in different scenarios, some golden rules apply. These are as follows:

- Have a clear process of hiring: Written test or not? How many rounds of technical interviews? In which areas? Most organizations set up a series of technical interviews and if a candidate comes out successfully from these, he/she is considered worth hiring. However, the hiring process is more than just technical interviews. Technical skills are critical but so are soft skills and fitment into the team, organization, and culture.

- Establish the core skills required for a given position. Ensure that the core skill requirements are easily met and perhaps surpassed by the candidate.

- Be flexible around non-core skills. Evaluate if other people or mechanisms in the team can meet those gaps.

- Use a different process and questions based on experience. Many organizations get set into a pattern of interviewing, and follow it regardless of the career level, and then adjust the expectation.

- Hiring interviews test mostly for technical skills, but soft skills are equally important. Ask all interviewers to also note down and provide feedback on soft skills. Lack of soft skills is more likely a reason why someone may not fit into a team.

- Ask a candidate what he or she wishes to accomplish, and be candid about what would be a reasonable expectation if the candidate were selected. In a tough hiring market, managers oversell a job and to make it attractive, end up being too far from reality. Once selected, it's only a matter of time until an employee knows what is being offered. A team member who feels cheated will find it hard to be part of the team.

- Don't promise future compensation. Managers often show all possible compensation that can possibly be earned by a candidate, without clarifying the conditions that go with it. For example, managers promise a performance bonus of N percent to a candidate, without mentioning that the performance bonus depends on performance ratings, the company's performance, and budgets.

- Say NO to technically good people, if you see large differences in goals. This is most relevant for perpetual teams, where you want people to stay for a long time. A large percentage of Indian knowledge workers aspire to work in a different country for multiple reasons, including money, status, and international exposure. Many candidates are very clear about this goal, and disclose this candidly during the hiring process. Over the years, most organizations have moved into a model where the work is predominantly done in India, with a very small percentage of people on site. You may be tempted to hire the candidate since the opportunity does exist for that small percentage, but it's better to have a very honest and transparent discussion, and if you sense that candidate is looking predominantly for an onsite opportunity only, you may want to say no.

Hiring is also driven by the pressures of hiring fast and getting people on board and these are key parameters for a manager's success. Hiring will be discussed in detail in one of the later chapters.

The tough part

Do you ever have a feeling that the person you are interviewing does not fit into the team but you can't necessarily put a finger on it?

There are candidates where the technical ability is satisfactory and experience is acceptable, but there's something with the way a candidate responds, something in the body language that makes the interaction somewhat of a bumpy ride.

As a key decision maker for hiring, you must listen to your gut feeling also. Listen to the little clues given out during the interview process. Does the candidate say something and then back track? Does he sound bitter about his last job of five years? Does he take a little too long to get to the point?

It is hard to quantify these observations, but in my opinion, it's ok to listen to them and dig a little deeper. Don't take these as make or break, but rather a sign to dig deeper around these aspects.

Similarly, pay due credit to aspects like a candidate who gets it instantly, who seems to be on the same wavelength as you, or who has the same disposition to people and situations as you do, while his technical ability is just baseline and not stellar. Consider hiring this person if you think he/she can catch up with the technical skills and has the attitude to work hard at it.

Creating visible alignment between team goals and individual goals

Once people are on board and part of the team, they need to all pull together in one direction, and hopefully that is the direction the team needs to go in. People pulling in different directions can never help. Not knowing which direction to pull in is one of the biggest problems team members face. They get assigned tasks, which they duly complete, but have no idea how that task helped the team or them as an individual. If the team works on a particular technology or a domain, the team members must invest time and energy into that technology or domain. People can certainly learn different things, but not at the expense of what is required to achieve the team goals. The need to experiment and to learn is great to fulfill in the knowledge industry, and aligning the learning and experimentation with the team goals makes it easier for people to contribute to the team goals.

Whatever the task, allocated deliverable, or personal growth goal for a team member, it should be aligned with the team deliverables or the larger goals. This alignment needs to be visible to the individual team member and to the rest of the team as well. Contribution is infectious. When people see others contributing, they'll tend to put in more contribution as well. Having the visibility allows people to collaborate and contribute to each other's tasks also, and since it's aligned in the right direction, the team gains.

Let's look at some examples of finding alignment.

Praveen, Senior Programmer, had a long-term goal of working in a customer-facing role like a Product Manager or Account Manager. In the medium term, he wanted to get some vocational management education to get a foundation in commercial aspects of the business. Ranjan, his manager, had an important delivery in six months' time, and lots of work in between. The team already had a team lead, James, who was interacting with the customer, so there wasn't another customer-facing role that was open. The options seemed limited, but Ranjan gave it a shot. Ranjan had a discussion with Praveen and the following happened:

- Accepted the goals that Praveen had, no questions asked.
- Explained the significance of the delivery in six months and expectations from Praveen.
- Explained the corporate policy on higher education.
- Offered to create opportunities for Praveen to work with James to get a customer-facing experience. Praveen can then evaluate if he likes what he sees.

- Praveen may have to work extra to spend time on customer issues while having other deliverables.
- Planned a review with Praveen in six months' time.

Ranjan saved a misalignment and possible employee attrition by being open to the needs of the employee and not making a compromise of team goals. He ended up directing Praveen's energies in the direction where Praveen will put in the most effort, and the team will gain overall along with Praveen. Alignment usually creates a win-win situation.

The tough part

The tough part is that asking people to forego personal goals for team goals is a non-starter. It is indeed very difficult for most people to get over the 'what's in it for me?' perspective. You can attempt to draw a larger picture where aligning with the organization's goals will actually help the individual achieve his goals. If there isn't an alignment found, it's better to lay it out as such, instead of drawing a completely improbable picture. Even if there's no alignment and you establish that, your team members will respect your honesty and openness.

There have been many cases in my career where this has been visible and we simply asked the candidate to continue contributing in the current position till we found a replacement and at times, also help the team member transition into a role where his career goals are met.

Make it easy to collaborate and synergize

Everybody understands that synergy is important and knowing this, most people try to collaborate and work together. Despite the desire to collaborate, it doesn't always happen due to the conditions and systems in place. For example, if it takes too much effort and is generally difficult for two people to talk because of time zone differences, the amount of talking between them will be less and will likely become lesser if the logistics are not addressed or newer ways of collaboration are not devised.

Making it easy is about the logistics of collaboration; simple things help:

- People who need to collaborate should be in close proximity, ideally seated next to each other. Teams are usually put together to begin with, but in today's virtual environment, teams may be spread out physically.
- If two people are in time zones that are hard to sync up, consider a different pair up. Most times you may have to live with the constraint and devise methods to make it easier for both the parties. Share the burden of late nights, equally, as much as possible.

- Create forums where people can demonstrate their work and see others work. It is not uncommon to find that people sitting next to each other may be on different pages.

- There are a lot of mailing lists that one becomes a part of. However, a team mailing list, which is very exclusive to this team, would be very helpful. Mailing lists have become impersonal, and nobody clearly knows the expanse of most lists, hence people tend to be careful about what to send to those lists. A closed forum allows people to announce personal achievements and smaller milestones, even birthdays and congratulations on becoming a parent.

- Create open forums for discussions on topics of interest. These topics may be directly related to work or open topics of general interest. The fact that a forum exists for this purpose will encourage people to think about ways of participation in this forum.

- A common place for sharing of content that is accessible to the entire team. It's good to create public and team private sections on this portal. It becomes easy to share documents, demo scripts, and even personal artifacts like photos from a team picnic or book reviews.

- Encourage summarization and easy read sections in documents. Most documents detailing someone's work like a design document or a process document can become a pain to read and understand. There's too much to read and too much language to sift through. Encourage people to create initial sections that explain the concepts and details at a high level and using diagrams. Use language and flow that is easier to read, perhaps even enjoyable. One of the teams I know of used to encourage creating a small presentation with every important document. Presentation format forces one to think of summarization, short bullet points, and transition from one slide to another, thereby forcing a thought process of simplicity and flow.

Most of the logistics are technically easy to achieve in today's environment, but may still require conscious attempt.

The tough part

Making it easy to collaborate may demand changing existing organization boundaries or even going against the organization culture, which can be a daunting task. For example, an organization may be very calendar-oriented, that is, all meetings between people are generally pre-planned and agreed upon. If you wish to see a shift to Instant Messaging, which is a very disruptive communication model, there is likely to be huge resistance, and it's possible that it may be a counter productive move. Evaluate what will work in your conditions and thoughtfully initiate the changes.

Reward collaboration and unreward non-collaboration

Make it known to the team that collaboration is rewarded. Everybody runs into issues that require help and sometimes, just another person to look at. Encourage people to collaborate to solve problems and leverage each other's skills, rather than trying to do it all by themselves.

Make "attempt to collaborate" a part of the success measures, asking questions such as the following:

- Is the work reviewed by other people in the team?
- Has the design been presented to the team?
- Has there been a knowledge sharing session?
- Are the lessons shared with the team, after problems are solved or projects completed?

If someone presents a solution to a problem to the larger group, expect that to be a joint presentation.

The tough part

While rewarding is easy, unrewarding is always difficult. Most managers, especially in India, have trouble with tough conversations. A simple way to unreward is to simply let an e-mail out to the relevant team members only. The e-mail can state something as simple as, "Ramesh, please ensure that the reviews are completed before we check-in the code". Disapproval from the manager is unrewarding in its own right.

Success dose

It's a chicken and egg situation: do good teams create success or does success create good teams? However, there's one clear answer: a team that doesn't taste success is not going to last for too long. It is important for teams to create successes and celebrate them to feel the high of a success and the desire to replicate it. That is why there's a need to create smaller milestones that can provide the success boost along the way to larger success.

Sometimes, especially in product development, the timelines are such that market release of the product takes over a year. Team members may not get a sense of accomplishment for a long time, and start to lose motivation, thereby hurting the team. In another extreme case, the work may be perpetual like backend order processing or a BPO call center, where the work doesn't have a logical end as such. Managers will need to create some milestones that can bring closure to the work being done and bring a sense of completion and success to the team members.

Team spirit

There's no team without team spirit. Team spirit is the glue that makes a team out of a few people put together. Universally, great teams have great team spirit. When team spirit exists team members exhibit behaviors where they place team interests ahead of the individual interest, value a harmonious team environment, and demonstrate these behaviors over and over again.

On various dictionaries on the World Wide Web, team spirit is defined as the spirit of a group that makes the members want the group to succeed.

Team spirit is one of those fuzzy things, an undercurrent that is hard to quantify, and hence hard to nail down a process by which team spirit can be created.

Team spirit is created by the team and not by the manager

Team spirit is really owned by the team and the manager acts as the facilitator. Why would a team member wish the team to succeed and act in the best interest of the team, even ahead of individual interest?

The answer is unclear. It's the same question as why would you help someone? (Such as holding the door for somebody, giving money to charity, or being nice to other people).

We choose to do lots of things that aren't technically in our best interest, as such. Giving away money to charity is only taking away money from what we can spend on ourselves. How is it supposed to do any good for us? Perhaps the universe will reward us for helping others with our money, or more likely, it just feels good to do so.

Team spirit is such a thing too, and it has a better justification. If the team does well, it's likely that team members will gain in the long run. When team spirit prevails, team members feel good to contribute to the team in as many ways as possible. People give away their personal time to work harder on a delivery, with no direct monetary gain in the short run or possibly even in the long run. People fill in for others who are not available. People take up extra responsibility such as interviewing, late night meetings, training for new joiners, and more.

The same things when asked by a manager will have some resistance if the team spirit does not exist.

When team spirit prevails, the team drives itself. In summary, in an environment where everyone in the team feels they own a stake, have a strong say, and know and trust each other, there will be strong team spirit. Here, the manager is almost always the caretaker, coach, and facilitator — and not a director.

When it comes to hiring, teams should be empowered to conduct the interviews, and very likely they'll select someone who would not only be technically qualified for the job, but also fit in well with the team. Hiring by the team indicates inclusion in the group. It's likely to be more effective than the hiring being done by managers alone or some other set of people.

When the team has to decide on deliverables, it's best for the manager to let the team drive those. The team decides, the team delivers. The team is the largest stakeholder in the deliverables commitment. Individual team members need to come together in order for the team to succeed. It lifts the team spirit, when teams have the power to decide their commitments. Manager will need to guide and nudge the process, so it gets completed in time, with the buy-in of the team.

Managers can damage team spirit

Managers have a high impact on team spirit. They may not be able to create team spirit, as much as they can damage it. A manager controls many different aspects in a team including hiring, rewards, flow of work, visibility, and more. A weak manager, defensive and insecure about himself, can really break team spirit. Decisions may become centralized, with the team playing a minimal part and not being part of the decision-making. Communications can become guarded when managers don't show strength and are not confident about their own abilities and the team's abilities.

Managers need to be confident about themselves, their abilities, and the team's abilities to give up control, and let the team spirit flourish.

An environment of trust and respect

Fairness and equality in the team are essential for team spirit. Everyone in the team has a place, whether that person is new to the team or has been around for a while; whether the person is a man or a woman; whether the person has high credentials or just average. Every team member is part of the team and has a contribution to make to the best of their abilities. They should be allowed a chance to do so.

Treating everybody equally does not mean that hierarchies are not to be set up. The best teams have the leaders emerge from the team due to their contributions and peer recognition. Managers should recognize these leaders and they are the best candidates to be placed in the formal leadership positions.

When people have an assurance of being treated fairly, they can focus on the task at hand and not worry about being left behind or not getting their due. People become forthcoming because they know they will not be judged prematurely.

An environment of trust develops. Before being a programmer, a process executive or a business analyst, each one is a human being and wants to be treated fairly and trusted, and they will reciprocate in the same manner.

Group traditions: work, play, and celebrate as a team

Working like a team becomes so much easier when everybody can come together and celebrate. There's a saying, "Families that eat together, stay together", and a version of this applies to a team. "Teams that celebrate together, stay together". There's a ton of pressure and work that teams have to handle on a daily basis. Team members interact with each other, share information, and rely on others work. The same team members should be able to get together and share their joint successes too.

It always helps when team members can interact with each other in non-work settings like participating as a team in a volleyball tournament or going on a trek together.

In non-work settings, people get to see a more personal side of a person and, most times, realize that this person is a good human being to interact with (or the other way).

Group traditions that bring people together in informal settings help create team bonding and spirit.

Group traditions don't mean only team parties and lunches. Group traditions can also be work-related, for example every new team member should present their past projects in the very first week, everyone who goes for a customer meeting should present about the experience as well as talk about customers' products and services, and how the team's work is impacting the customer. The group gets together to question and learn. Group learning is another way of building team spirit, as the group gains in knowledge by virtue of being a group.

Don't forget the individual

Team spirit doesn't mean there are no individual needs. Every team member is a unique individual too, and has individual needs as well. Managers, as well as all team members, need to recognize individual needs and preferences of each team member. Each person is different in some way or the other. There are people who like to stand up and talk, and there are others who don't. Managers and the team can help individuals get better at stand up and talk, by being sensitive to their inclination. Managers have a special role to play and use the organizational support, in the form of training resources, to help an individual develop important soft skills.

While the team successes are to be celebrated, we must not forget to applaud the individuals who made it happen. Even if you have to recognize every individual that was part of the team that delivered, it's important to recognize people by their names. It's certainly important to recognize the key individuals who made a difference above and beyond the usual call of duty. Managers should not shy away from individual recognition, fearing that other team members may feel un-recognized. Individual excellence will also drive team excellence. Hopefully, these star individuals enjoy the peer recognition also, and the team may appreciate that the specific person has been given a special mention.

Rotate the champions

Every team has people who take more initiative than others. These are the people who arrange a picnic, find volunteer presenters for tech talks, and raise their hand up every time there's an opportunity to do so. These are some of the easily identifiable champions in your team. These people have the drive to contribute.

Many others may need some encouragement to contribute. They can even be assigned some of this voluntary work. It's perhaps just a personality trait that some people will take something on, when required to. When they see someone else taking the lead, they may be content to simply follow and be a participant. They don't necessarily wish to compete to take the lead.

Managers and leads can help rotate the champions, and create new ones by nudging people into some of these activities. The usual champions will always find ways to get involved and can be presented with other, perhaps harder, responsibilities to keep them adequately challenged.

The previous recommendations are not a complete list, but certainly a list that all managers must understand. Now, let's look at the issue from the other side and examine some key aspects on why teams fail.

Why teams fail

First let's answer the question: when is a team considered a failure? A team is considered failure when:

- It fails to deliver on promises.
- Path to delivery is difficult. Problems keep showing up all the time and no problem is easy to solve.
- It takes too much energy for people to work with this team.
- High turnover rate. Loses people all the time.
- Cost of delivery is high.
- Is unable to shake the perception of failure. Even though the team may do reasonably well, management and peers continue to see it as a failure due to past impressions.

Now, let's examine why teams fail. Many of the reasons are the negative contortion of the things that build a team.

Expectations, alignment, and team direction not clear

Teams fail when they don't know where it is going collectively and are unclear on its deliverables. This situation happens more often for brand new teams, and especially new remote teams. The management is unclear about the capacity of the team to deliver and end up with unclear or low expectations. The team members pull in different directions, not knowing any better. Management keeps adjusting their expectations based on how the team is shaping up. It's a difficult time for management and the new team, because neither is happy with what is happening and there isn't clarity for the future.

For existing teams, sometimes due to management changes, the alignment goes out of order. The top management sets new rules, new ways of reporting, and new success measures, without clarity on why these are being changed and sometimes worse, these changes aren't clearly communicated at all. People continue to work the old way and focus on wrong priorities. Line managers get into conflict with middle or top management. Finally, everyone loses.

Leadership deficit

This is usually the problem in many teams that fail. It's hard to find a good manager and a good leader. The rapid expansion of the industry has led to managers being made out of programmers and middle managers being in a hurry to set up a manager and delegate.

Ineffective leadership is like having a misfiring engine on your car, when you are just starting a long journey. Poor leadership shows up in many ways:

- Bad hiring in the team
- Imbalance in the team skills and experience
- Centralization of power and decision-making
- Low visibility of the team members and lower collaboration with other teams
- Low morale in the team and lack of team spirit

Once there's a lack of trust in leadership, team members don't see themselves going anywhere. The effort isn't 100 percent and productivity drops. Weak managers blame the team back for loss of productivity or set up tight rules of monitoring and reporting, which further lowers the morale. A vicious cycle sets in.

Confusion in structure

Team structures where team members get instructions from multiple places and have to report to multiple people tend to create confusion in teams. The **matrix** is one such formal structure where multiple reporting is formalized and is fairly popular in India. The local manager in India has only people management responsibility, while a different area manages from the headquarters and assigns and monitors daily work. In most cases, the lines of responsibility and authority between these two managers are not clear, and team members, as well as both the managers, struggle through the experience.

Conflict situations can arise and lead to loss in productivity as well as create difficult governance problems.

Not enough time for team dynamics to set in

Teams are an ecosystem, systems get set up, and people find their feet as they spend more time with each other. Sometimes, there isn't enough time for team dynamics to set in, but significant deliverables have to be met.

The team will end up going through a rough patch, unless the leadership roles are clearly defined. The task will get easier if standard operating procedures get applied.

If not, people will cross each other's paths and create confusion. Not knowing each other's strengths leads to everybody trying to do the same things. Miscommunication tends to happen a lot, and adds to the confusion. Milestones get missed and fire fighting begins.

Groupthink

This is perhaps the far side and the dark side of team spirit. The group takes an identity of its own and all action/inaction done as part of the group seems ok, although it is not. Groupthink occurs when team members start to avoid applying thought and common sense to a situation and don't raise a concern that upsets a group conclusion. Team members go along with a decision, just because the group is involved. It's a loss of reasoning with the assumption that the group (consensus) can't be wrong and a false sense of security that if people are in a group, then no harm can happen to individuals. It's a kind of mob mentality.

When groupthink sets in, the following things happen:

- Bad results are discussed in a team meeting and some reasons are found to justify the problems, usually blame is laid out to someone or some event outside the group
- Bad performances and bad decisions from individuals are not questioned
- People who question an agreed decision are looked down upon
- There's little focus on larger goals and just focus on any contribution by the group, however inadequate it may be
- People stop looking at learning from the outside and what other teams or industry is doing in general
- External inputs are not appreciated, and people tend to find solutions only within the group, thus limiting the use of organizational resources

Groupthink is as hurtful as a lack of team spirit, and sometimes leads to severe disastrous results like the management breaking the team down and firing the leaders.

Summary

Team building is a task that never really ends. Managers learn and re-learn as generation X gives way to generation Y, the communications models change, the organization's requirements change, the size of the team grows, the level of people changes, and team building continues at a different level. One thing that remains constant in any team for building is the fact that people want to learn and contribute and be treated with respect. These are just natural laws that apply to any human being. The team ecosystem will take care of itself as long as the natural laws are respected. The ether in this ecosystem is communication within the team and across the organization.

In the next chapter, we'll look at the communication aspects of an organization.

5
Communicating

Communicating is as natural to us as eating and breathing. This was very powerfully portrayed in a movie *Cast Away*. Tom Hanks is washed ashore a deserted island with no water, food, or shelter. He works hard to survive, to set up a shelter, find food, and make fire. Through this all, Tom spends his time talking to a basketball, Mr Wilson! We are so used to communicating that not communicating to the external world has become a form of meditation.

Communication skills are reflective of your personality, your attitude, your working style, and even your relationships. It is indeed a critical skill for a manager to succeed. In this chapter, we'll examine the key aspects of communication and look at some often-faced scenarios. Let's start with an example:

Amit walks into Rohan's room.

Rohan: What's the status of delta project?

Amit: Almost there. Ran into an issue.

Rohan: Ok. So another couple of days?

Amit: Yeah…should make it.

Rohan: Alright…let me know.

Amit: Bye.

What would you call this conversation? Is it clear? Is it accurate? Does it make any sense?

Here's another scenario, between Amit and Kannan.

Amit walks into Kannan's room.

Kannan: What's the status of delta project?

Amit: Almost there. Ran into an issue.

Kannan (looking perplexed), after a pause: What issue?

Amit (after a pause): Everything is working but the module performance isn't what we want.

Kannan: What do you mean, performance isn't what we want? How bad is it? What are we doing to fix it?

Amit: We are looking into it.

Kannan: What are we looking at?

Amit: Performance.

Kannan (throws up his hands): When will this be done?

Amit: Maybe, another couple of...(stops). A week.

Kannan: Ok.

Amit: (walks out)

Clearly scenario 2 is a strained, unsatisfactory communication. Both Amit and Kannan leave the room with a bad taste and without accomplishing much. Worse, it is likely that the scenario will be repeated.

Why did Amit's conversation take a different route with Kannan? It started pretty much the same way.

There are so many aspects that impact communication that each occurrence of communication tends to be unique. The same content when delivered to two different people takes a different route. The same content delivered via e-mail has a different impact when delivered in person. This is what makes communication such an important part of being a manager.

Elements of good communication

Let's look at some of the key characteristics of good communication.

Clarity

If someone can listen to a statement and understand what the speaker wants to convey, that communication can be termed clear. There's no fixed clarity that needs to be achieved. If both parties share a context and trust in each other, the communication will tend to be clear between them.

In a group situation, it's always better to add optimum detail in what you communicate that 80 percent or more of your audience can understand. Don't try to make the latest new hire understand everything.

Let's examine some examples.

Manager's e-mail to the team: "Please update all your bugs by the end of the day".

A new hire sees it as, "Update your bugs by 5 p.m. today" (given usual work hours of 9-5).

As interpreted by someone two years in the team: "Update your bugs before 9 p.m." (By the time most people on the US west coast get to work.)

As interpreted by someone five years in the team: "Update your bugs today sometime, if possible". He knows that there's no urgency in the communication, so he can give priority to something else as required.

Unclear communication leaves too much room for interpretation. If it is critical for communication to be interpreted one and only one way, be as clear as you can be to leave no room for confusion for your audience.

Caution: Some managers get into a habit of communicating with too many specifics. For example, "Update your bugs by 6 p.m. today, and make sure there's a clear description for each bug, and mark the priority no less than 3".

Such communication is technically very clear, but it is very prescriptive also. This kind of communication may be considered as challenging the basic intelligence of people in the team. Folks will feel stifled with little left to imagine.

Context

We have all heard film stars' and politicians' famous quote, "I have been quoted out of context". They are not always incorrect. In good communication, the context is either set before the communication starts or the participants are well aware of the context. Out of context communication is hard to understand and is another reason for bad clarity.

It's hard to understand if something is good or bad, if the context or the big picture isn't there. Consider the following conversation:

Rakesh: Ashish, after three days, we finally got it working.

If Ashish has a good idea about the context of the problem that Rakesh had been working on.

Ashish: Great job! This was a tough one to crack.

If Ashish has no idea or little idea about the context of the problem that Rakesh had been working on.

Ashish: Ok. What was the root cause?

If Ashish has the wrong context of the problem that Rakesh had been working on.

Ashish: Really? Why did it take three days?

Lack of context leads to assumptions and poor conclusions.

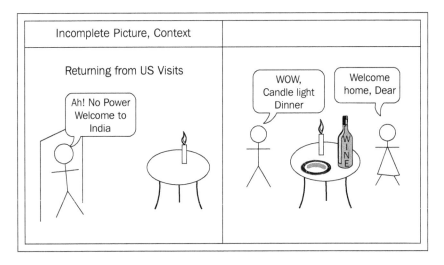

An incomplete picture will almost always lead to miscommunication. There are many discussions that start without setting the proper context, especially for managers. Many team members assume that the manager would know what exactly has been happening and start a discussion without setting the context, thereby prolonging the process or getting frustrated. This is one good reason why managers should spend time with the team and get to know the details.

Two-way

Good communication has two channels, one for speaking and one for listening. Good communication encourages both channels to be used but not at the same time. This is perhaps one of the most difficult things in communication, since it seems like humans can focus on only one channel. They can't listen well, if they are talking, and vice versa. That means you have two channels but only one can be used at a given point in time.

When you listen to someone, the mind races ahead of the conversation and you have ideas and opinions to express. It's hard to listen to what else the other person is saying, since you are still processing something that was said a few seconds back.

In good communication, the speaker and the listener give ample time to putting their thoughts forward and processing the same by the other person.

In a group situation, many times multiple people speak up, and chaos seems to happen. A team discussion looks like the political debates on national TV channels; nobody seems to hear anyone else and everybody is utilizing the speaking channel more than the listening channel.

Concise

Good communication is usually short and, hopefully, sweet. It doesn't require a two pager to say something. In fact, the less the amount of words necessary to say what you have to say, the better it is (necessary implies that the detail required by the receiver is provided). The level of detail required will vary.

Managers often try to over-explain things that don't require that much of an explanation. It's hard to reign in how much one thing can be explained and it's easy to go overboard.

Once again, how elaborate a communication needs to be depends on the situation and the two parties involved.

Often, the lack of feedback (two-way) leads to one person over-explaining himself. This is witnessed often over telephonic conference calls, where one person speaks and waits for a verbal signal to know if people got his point or not. In the absence of any, the choices are to continue or explain what was said in the last minute. People listening at the other end of the phone now roll their eyes and check their e-mail.

Rules of courtesy

Good communication follows rules of courtesy. Courtesy is about respect for the people and the institution. Communication is between people, and people don't like to be disrespected. A communication will go nowhere if the people involved do not show respect for each other.

Even between an adult and a child, the communication needs to follow simple rules of courtesy.

The whole atmosphere changes when people don't feel respected and even a communication in their best interest will tend to become a burden to carry on. Sooner or later, every manager will see a situation where something has not been done up to the expected quality or completeness. Even though the intention may be to provide constructive feedback, the communication needs to be respectful.

Watch out

Watch your e-mail communication. Since the other person may never have met you or may have no idea of your personal style, the communication may be construed as disrespectful. Some of this can be because of cultural influence also.

For example, do you start your e-mail with:

Hi Rahul,

There's a bug....

Or with:

Rahul,

There's a bug...

In India, a lot of people will find the 'Hi' very comforting and respectful, and it sets the tone of the e-mail.

Some people have a communication style where they respond in short words.

In Raman's e-mail: Help! I'm stuck with step 2 in order capture. Can you call me please?

In Anu's e-mail: I'm busy....Manual? <URL>

While Anu may have given a good pointer in the manual and replied promptly, the e-mail may seem discourteous, more of a 'buzz-off, I'm busy doing something more important'. The reality could be that Anu was replying using a phone, where typing long sentences is difficult.

In e-mail, try to use full sentences and assume that the recipient of the e-mail is an unknown person. Avoid verbiage and keep every paragraph at 3-4 lines. Always sign off, preferably with a greeting.

Timely

A communication happening at the wrong time, even when clear, two-way, and concise, will not be effective if it's timed incorrectly.

Rakesh is packing up for the day and thinking about which route to take home, given that it's a Friday. Rakesh's manager, Ashish, walks over and starts to talk about the ongoing project and some new information that he has come across. Rakesh understands the discussion is important but he has a commitment to reach home and take his family to the movies. He feels that the same discussion can be had on Monday morning and he's even willing to work over the weekend to catch up with the latest Ashish has to say. However hard Ashish tries, the communication will not be effective since Rakesh is not willing to be engaged. Ashish's timing is wrong. The fact that Rakesh should simply ask to be excused is a different aspect to be examined. However, that does not change the un-timeliness of this communication. Consider the state of mind of other people when you communicate. Untimely communication is not effective:

Delayed communication loses either complete relevance or most of its impact. For example, the information about a project delay needs to be communicated well before the deadline. After the deadline, it doesn't make any sense, since it's clear anyway that the project is delayed. Even if this information is communicated just before the deadline, there may not be time to do anything productive about it.

Similar vocabulary—apple means apple

A conversation between two people who have different vocabulary can go horribly wrong. This is a side effect of a cultural or generational gap between two people.

Anand (Network Administrator): Hey Rajesh, do you care if the database server db101 goes down for backup this evening?

Rajesh (Developer who uses db101): ...after taking a few seconds to absorb the statement, responds rather angrily: What do you mean? Of course I care about what happens to that server.

Actually, Anand did not question Rajesh's dependency or usage of the server. He knows this, hence he is checking if Rajesh will be impacted if the server is brought down this evening. However, Rajesh considers it as something completely different; perhaps Rajesh thinks that Anand is questioning his concern towards his resources or work.

When you talk to someone, especially young grads from different parts of the country, try to keep your vocabulary simple and in sync with what can be understood by your audience.

Now that we understand the elements of good communication, let's examine some of the key aspects of communication that every manager should understand.

What managers must know about communication

Often managers have trouble managing the communication within the team and with the rest of the organization. Here are some aspects to be aware of, in order to make the communication work.

Interpersonal communication is a process, not an event

Communication between two people is not a one-time event; it's a process that gets better or worse over a period of time. Communication is also reflective of the relationship between two people.

It's hard to say if communication is a cause of a good relationship or if a relationship is a cause of good communication. However, it's clear that each one feeds the other. Your most recent communication may have an impact on how your next communication with that person may go.

Rakesh: Kishore, can I take a minute of your time?

Kishore (in a hurry): I've got to go, let's talk later.

Rakesh: It's…

Kishore (cuts him short): Bye.

Rakesh's timing is not correct, but the end result is that the communication did not go well. Rakesh will feel short-changed, as he was not given a chance.

Two days later, Rakesh has to talk to Kishore again for something. Rakesh sends an Instant Message to Kishore, instead of walking up to him.

Rakesh: Are you there?

I am sending you the report over e-mail. Let me know if any changes needed.

Bye.

Kishore barely got a chance to type his response, and Rakesh already ended the conversation.

Rakesh is basically avoiding another let down interaction, and his communication shows that. If this pattern continues, the communication between the two will keep deteriorating until one of them changes the pattern or by some other co-incidence the pattern changes.

Understanding the communication needs of your organization

Every organization runs a little different. Information requirements change from sub organization to sub organization, and are usually driven by the culture of the larger organization and by the top management team of the organization.

Some organizations require a lot of communication to happen, most of it as reporting and broadcasting of data. The details required in the communication also change from organization to organization.

Some people need the data to be detailed, in order to feel comfortable that they understand and also ensure that they are getting the accurate information.

Each organization has a different expectation for communication. Figure out who needs to be included in the communication loop—key people who must acknowledge the communication versus the people who just need to be made aware. Figure out what the expectation is around day-to-day communication about the work being done in your team. Figure out which communication you need to acknowledge and respond to.

Each organization encourages a different level of inter-personal communication. In some cases, employee and manager one-on-one's may be expected to happen each month and in other cases, it could be every six months. I have seen a case where a manager was spending as much as two days in a week just on 101s because he found it useful. However, he ended up spending 40 percent of the week in an activity that wasn't much valued by his organization. The culture in the organization did not require such frequent 101s.

Understanding the communication needs of your role and work

The communication needs also change with the role you play. Of course, you are a manager, but if you are managing a small team of highly technical people, and the work is contained within the team, the communication required may not be as much. For the same team, if the work is dependent on another team or teams, your liaison role may require a higher level of communication.

In product development organizations, the role of the product manager is to liaison with customers and bridge the gap with development teams. One of the prime responsibilities of the role is to communicate the customer interactions, customer scenarios, and customer requirements. A good product manager can add a huge amount of value by simply communicating well. A common complaint from development is that product managers do not communicate enough or present only synthesized data. Development teams would like to understand the real customer scenarios. However, the communication is an analysis of the customer scenario. Soon development teams start to disengage with the product manager and a lower value relationship is created.

Communication needs will change from project to project as well. You may be working on two projects and the communication required may be high on one and low on the other, just because one is a high profile project and has higher interest from multiple parties, including your management.

Ask yourself the following questions:

- Is this a high interest project?
- Is this a high risk project?
- Who are the people whose success is also linked with this project?
- What am I supposed to do with the information that I have obtained?
- Would others be interested/benefit from information that I know?
- What level of detail is required?

Every time there's a role change or a new project started, re-evaluate the communication needs.

You set the communication model for your team

You will influence the communication models in your team, some of it explicitly and some implicitly. Based on your own requirements, you may set the communication expectation for your team; let people know how much detail you'd like to see and the frequency of updates.

Explicitly explain the boundaries of communication. Make sure people know common expectations and also know where to get more details when needed. Once explained, people should be able to make a distinction on the following kinds of questions:

- Can I send Santa Banta jokes on the mailing list?
- Can I send a link to an article on the web that talks about the greatness of India but also has references to other countries?
- Can I communicate to the world about my feelings towards my organization via a personal blog?
- What kinds of acronyms are ok in business language?

Your own communication style will also be a guide to your team, as they'll look up to you for a model to follow. If you engage in high pressure, abrasive communication, it'll start to take roots in your organization. Very soon the leads will be using similar communication with their own smaller organization.

Are you a manager who prefers to set up calendar meetings to communicate with the team or do you prefer just calling people as and when required and talking about stuff.

Do you call in your team members to participate in discussions which may not directly involve them? Just so they are aware of what's happening in other areas and can contribute in some way? Do you expect other managers or leads in your team to communicate among themselves on topics of interest?

Do you communicate your vacation plans to your team well in advance? Are you available to talk to even while you are on vacation?

Do you apologize when you ought to? Or are you defensive and try to explain why something happened the way it did, despite you trying to do the right thing?

Controlling unwanted communication, for example, salary discussions

More communication is good, but some of the topics are off limits from general discussion. The top item, on the off-limits list, is the **compensation** discussion.

India has a really bad reputation when it comes to confidentiality of compensation numbers. The impression isn't unfounded, but like all general impressions, it's a generalization that is hard to shake off despite things having turned around.

You must make it very clear that any salary discussion will not be tolerated (a simple message that needs to be delivered right when people join, and then reinforced at every one-on-one meeting for announcing a salary hike or a bonus or stock option).

If you see a salary slip lying around someone's desk, let him know that he needs to keep it away in a secure place. Anytime someone comes to you with a data point about someone else's salary, refuse to get into a discussion based on that data. It's hard to do so, but it'll set a good precedent and help in the long-term.

There may be other off-limit public topics that may be relevant in your scenario.

Cutting down the layers, shortening the channels

Communication will get distorted every time it needs to be repeated and through the many different people it passes through.

As a manager, you may have a hierarchy in your organization structure where a number of people will not be directly reporting to you. E-mail communication has been a great enabler where information can be quickly disbursed across the organization and with identifiable credibility.

Here's an example of distortion through the layers:

Create direct channels of communication to every level in the organization. You may not use these channels everyday, but the channels need to exist and be used on a regular basis. With direct channels of information, you will have the ability to get to the details and the happenings on the ground without having to wait for the information to bubble up the layers and get sanitized. You wouldn't want to make these channels primary channels; let the usual hierarchical channels be strong channels, or else you may have to deal with very detailed information. Instead, use these direct channels as additional channels to get deeper details and augment what you already have.

These channels will also keep you closer to your team and be connected with ground realities.

The grapevine—don't worry too much about it

The grapevine has been given way too much importance than it actually deserves. A lot of information coming via a grapevine may be correct, but there's no way of knowing which one.

People also use the grapevine as and when it works to their advantage. Here's one such incident during a salary discussion:

Rakesh: 10 percent? It's lower than what most people got in the other team.

Kishore (manager): Really. I don't know what people got elsewhere, but 10 percent looks like a good number given the recession we are in.

Rakesh: Yes, 10 percent is not bad but the grapevine number is around 15-20 percent in other teams.

Rakesh could have quoted any number here. It's possible, if Rakesh got 15 percent, he would have quoted the 20 percent number only.

The grapevine is a strong channel of information, but it can be given only so much respect, since it is indeed a **gossip channel**, and while it's almost a necessary social channel, business decisions don't need to be based on the grapevine.

Use the grapevine channel for figuring out the pulse of the organization. For example, getting to know people's reaction after a big announcement, people's concerns, in general, about work and otherwise.

When someone quotes any grapevine information, don't slam them into the ground for that. They are actually helping you in a way, but don't let the grapevine become the topic of central discussion.

Allowing people to vent

Everybody gets frustrated and overwhelmed it could be anything from a heavy workload, screaming customers, low salary, uncooperative co-workers, bad commute, bad time at home, and so on.

There are times when people will walk into your office and vent out their frustrations. Allow them to do so with minimal discussion. Everything that is wrong will get highlighted and a long list of complaints will be poured out at your desk. Most of the complaints are likely to be legitimate and some may be an over exaggeration.

Although your team member is complaining about something, he is not really expecting a save-the-world solution from you. He just needs to tell you these problems he is facing. That's the nature of venting.

You may feel like explaining something in a different light, or you may feel he is being overly negative, or that he doesn't have all the information around a particular issue. But you should simply hold your urge to make it too much of a discussion.

Very little needs to be offered back in this meeting. Be a good listener and allow the venting channel to be open with your team. It's better that they do this with you rather than with someone else outside the team.

There will be times when the venting is about a real concern, for example, someone venting about too big a workload. It's a real concern and needs to be addressed; however, the conversation may be in venting mode for sometime. Once the person feels lighter, having vented, you can start to have a more interactive discussion.

Scenarios

Let's examine communication in some common scenarios of communication in our work life.

Everyday communication

You'll have your own style of communication, and it'll be different from everybody else's. The way you communicate with your team on a daily basis will define your relationship with the team members and the team as an entity. Let's examine a few aspects.

Do the Hi exchange

Rewind your day at work and verify whether you pass by a team member and there are greetings exchanged or not.

Most people develop their own models of a pass-by-hello. Anything works like hello, hi, how are you, what's up? or just a smile, a nod, or a raise of a hand.

If you don't have any, consider adding one. Passing by people as if they are strangers leaves a bit of a bad taste every time it happens. In a way, saying hi to someone is like acknowledging their presence and it is a simple opportunity to make someone feel good.

Enagage in casual chat

Do you engage in casual talk with people around you? Casual talk is meaningless. Fore xample, "It's been raining so much the last few days, my house was nearly flooded". This has absolutely no connection to work, it isn't an engrossing discussion, it is not useful for anyone to know, and has no bearing on anything.

If yes, it's a good thing that you can have a casual talk with your team members. Casual talk allows you to unwind in the middle of a workday and allows two people to have a light conversation that is not exercising the brain much. It's the filler that is needed among all the heavy topics that get talked about.

Be available to talk

Are you available when people want to talk to you? Or do you have so many things to do that you find it very difficult to find the time to talk to your team members?

There are many reasons why your team members may wish to talk to you and it's very likely that you don't have any time slot left to talk to people in your own team. Making some time in your schedule for unexpected discussions with your team will help you be available when your team needs to talk to you.

Don't always keep looking for a status update

Are you always looking for a status update every time you meet a team member? Is your first question to them about where things are?

It is great that you know what each person is working on and can ask for more details. However, this should not be the only question every time you meet someone. Besides, there isn't enough time to complete the conversation. People will soon start waiting for the next elevator to avoid being questioned every time.

Don't keep telling them what to do

Do you add more work items to people as you walk over to the cafeteria for lunch? Some managers get so much into the manager mode that everything that comes out from them, sounds like an instruction.

"We should be doing….", "Try doing this…", "Go back and check this…", "Why don't we do the following…" become the standard instructions that team members hear all the time, and soon people will start avoiding spending time with you because nobody likes taking instructions all the time.

When someone just walks in with a problem

If you are a manager who is open and easy to talk to, you'll have people knock on your door and ask "Can I take a few minutes…?". Since you are open and a few minutes couldn't hurt, you invite them in. In a few seconds you have a question staring at you, "We mis-configured the customer environment. In about 24 hours, they may have a massive blow out".

Your first reaction maybe to say something like, "What the hell were you thinking?" or "You keep messing things up". Hopefully, you don't actually say it.

When someone walks in with a problem, he most probably wants to solve the problem and believes that you can solve it, help solve it, or simply help in some way. They may have been at fault; however, bringing the problem to you is a good thing.

Unfortunately, there is no way for you to know what to expect when a person walks in. In this situation, it's better to simply have no response to what you have heard; an acknowledgement like "Ok" or a simple "Hmmm" can be an appropriate response. You can also buy some time to think by asking the person to repeat what they just said or re-phrase what you heard.

Then focus on understanding the problem or getting someone else involved. Blaming the messenger doesn't usually help. What is needed is a cool-down of the situation, so people can think more logically. There will be plenty of time for a post-mortem after the problem is resolved.

If the person is agitated, make an attempt to calm down their nerves. The last thing needed is to have two people in the room who are agitated. A silence of a couple of minutes, while you think through the problem, will do wonders for the other person's nerves. So, a "Let me think…please take a seat", may bring down the level of anxiousness.

Sometimes, people walk into your room with a complaint, and you listen to them, and walk out to fix the issue or pick up the phone and shout at someone. Once again, as much as possible, don't try to take immediate action with a one-sided view of things.

It is also ok to evaluate the urgency of the problem and ask for another time to be set up to further discuss the topic.

Finally, there are situations when people walk in with problems that aren't yours to solve. They may be looking for help or simply to off load the problem to you. If you can recognize this, politely ask them to talk to someone else who may be able to provide better help.

When people share personal problems

A person sharing personal problems is not uncommon in India. In India, people are more comfortable with being personal than being formal. The personal network is one of the reasons of success for the Indian organization. People often cross organization boundaries or guidelines to solve problems using their personal network. Also, people come from very different backgrounds, and if you happen to be a likeable manager who gets along with your team members, you may hear more of their personal issues.

Hence, it's not uncommon that someone may walk into your office and discuss personal problems. It completely depends on the maturity of that person and his comfort level with you.

I have had people walk in and discuss their marriage plans, discuss personal finance, and even discuss honeymoon plans!

In general, managers should stay away from voluntarily getting involved in any personal matters. When someone walks in to talk about a personal issue, you can't really turn them down. It is possible that the person just needs to talk about it so you can understand the rest of the pressures on him, which may be impacting his work performance.

It's also possible, especially in India, that he may want to get some advice because he thinks you may know better. There's nothing right or wrong as such in airing your opinion, but it is certainly better to be very discreet and say the least possible. In any case, never be compelled to say something or put your thoughts out. It's OK to simply say, "It's difficult for me to say" or "I really don't know much about it".

In most cases, it may be just fine to listen to the person and let him say what he wants to, without providing any input as such. You can try to keep the conversation short.

Communicating bad news to an individual, for example, being denied a bonus

It's always easy and fun to deliver good news. However, there are times when bad news needs to be delivered, such as someone not getting a bonus or losing out on a salary hike. A manager tends to feel uneasy when these situations arrive and avoids these discussions altogether. However, it's part of your job to explain why someone lost out and, more importantly, how it can be avoided in the next cycle. Here are some things that can help:

- Don't delay delivering it till the last minute. Many a times, managers talk about it only after a team member approaches them.

- Prepare for the discussion. Make notes on what the key points are to be discussed. Schedule a time, rather than just calling people in the middle of something else.

- Pick a time that is not in the middle of action. An early morning slot may work better than noon. In some cases, an evening slot may work better, so the person can leave work and have time to sleep on the information.

- Since this is bad news, it's hard to tell people in advance about the topic of discussion. You can't have a meeting title called **bonus discussion**.

- Be clear about the event (what the bad news is), set the context, and don't mince words. "Rakesh, we have had the annual bonus cycle, and unfortunately, we were not able to allocate any bonus for you this cycle".

- Give it a minute to sink in, and then you can start putting the reasons on the table. It's the logical next step and you don't necessarily have to wait for people to ask "Why?"

- Keep the explanation crisp and objective. Let people respond to it, before you start explaining more.

- Be prepared to listen more. It's bad news and it's better if the employee can vent with the manager rather than with everybody else on the floor. Don't get into too much justification.

- You may also wish to talk about all the other good things that have happened for this person, and if there are performance concerns which lead to this, plan to discuss those in the same meeting.

Be prepared for all kinds of reactions including the blame game, helplessness, angry reactions, even threats of leaving, or personal accusations of favoritism. People respond in many different ways and you must plan to remain calm through it.

Communicating unwelcome news to a group, for example, undesired management changes

Managers are also messengers of decisions that impact the team, for example, change in the management structure or reorganization. More often than not, the team does not appreciate a reorganization as it brings about new uncertainties.

- Prepare: Get your facts right and talk to people who may know more.

- Before the group meeting, have another meeting with the key people and let them know what's going to happen. This will gain you the confidence of the key people and also understand the key concerns of the group.

- Set up a meeting, invite all the team members, and let them know it's important to attend it.

- Be the first one in the meeting room. Start a light conversation with people as they walk in, talk about other interesting work-related topics (Did we close that issue with the customer?) or otherwise (Great game last night).

- Tough news for the group is rarely grave news. More likely it's undesired or even unnecessary. It's more likely to be a business decision which impacts the individuals is new but not necessarliy bad news.

- Set the context by talking about a little history of the group, some achievements, and other good stuff.

- Then talk about the new decision that impacts the team. Talk about possible future scenarios and how the team will function in the new model.

- Explain the potential positives of the new model.

- Allow people to ask questions at any given point. You can answer them immediately or hold them to be answered a little later after you finish.

- Don't pretend there are no concerns. Recognize the new uncertainties and talk about why you think the team will do well.

- Provide the facts that highlight the business benefits of the new changes.

- As a leader, you need to show confidence towards doing well in future. At the same time, be honest and acknowledge a possibly uphill task.

- Finally, ask for group support for making it happen.

When a group has to face a tough or undesirable situation, the leader needs to stand up and be visible while navigating the course. Communicating with the team is a good start to the process of adjustment to new realities.

Difficult discussions—separate the person from the issue

With so many smart people in the team, any discussion tends to get long and heated. Here's an example: Rama and Kishore (perhaps some more people in the room) are talking about a solution to a problem. The problem impacts work for each of them, and the solution may also require each of them to do something.

Rama: We can do it easily by simply following what we did for customer X.

Kishore: Just because it solved the problem for customer x, doesn't mean it can solve the problem for customer Y.

Rama: Why not?

Kishore: I don't understand why you can't get it. It's simple logic. I just explained it a minute ago.

Rama: I heard what you said, but I still don't see how you can call it a different scenario. It's nearly the same as far as I can see.

Kishore: This is why we have so many problems showing up in this area.

This kind of conversation will be much longer and usually get to this point once people start getting frustrated. Sadly, the problem is nowhere close to a resolution because the discussion has turned personal. Instead of talking about the problem statement, scenario, and all things relevant, the discussion is turned towards what an individual is saying. Once people are put in the middle of the problem, they feel attacked and the natural instincts of defense will kick in.

Person	Statement	Thoughts
Rama	We can do it easily by simply following what we did for customer x.	I think we can solve this problem, I see a pattern.
Kishore	Just because it solved the problem for customer x, doesn't mean it can solve the problem for customer y.	The problem looks different.
Rama	Why not?	I need to hear more of an explanation than that.
Kishore	I don't understand why you can't get it, I just explained it a minute ago.	He's just trying to be difficult.

Person	Statement	Thoughts
Rama	I heard what you said, but I still don't see how you can call it a different scenario. It's nearly the same as far as I can see.	He's just trying to disregard my opinion. He is wrong, I am right.
Kishore	This is why we have so many problems showing up in this area.	What an incompetent fellow.

As soon as the focus shifts from the problem to the person, the thought process is focused more on self-defense and arguments rather than a problem solving process. If the focus is on the problem at hand, there's a better chance to solve the problem and people will be less traumatized by the discussion.

The same discussion can be different. For example:

Rama: We can do it easily by simply following what we did for customer x.

Kishore: Just because it solved the problem for customer x, doesn't mean it can solve the problem for customer y.

Rama: Why not?

Kishore (tries to provide more information): Well, as I said before, the end results are the same, but the platform works differently. Let's focus on the part where….

Rama: The reason why I believe the same approach can work despite the platform differences is because…

Kishore: Let's call another person into this discussion.

By keeping the focus on the problem, Rama and Kishore will be able to analyze the problem and apply their knowledge of the subject.

Many a time, it would be easy to blame people for their past decisions, but it can't help find the solution. In fact, it may be more fruitful to find the circumstances and the decision criterion rather than finding the person to blame.

If you do end up in an argument that is personally directed, try breaking the flow of the conversation and bringing the conversation back to the non-personal level. Avoid using words like me, for example, instead of "Let me explain…" use "Let's look at this…". Calm down your body language; pause for a few seconds, bring in a smile if you can. The idea is that you don't get provoked into responding the same way.

Communication in a distributed team

One of the challenges of today's world is the existence of distributed teams. For this discussion, we will consider teams where team members are located in different cities and perhaps different countries. While it's great that we can have talented people as part of the same team and work on a global product or process, we also need to focus on the communication in this scenario. We'll now look at some points to remember.

Extra communication required

More communication than usual is required in distributed teams. A conscious effort needs to be made to keep the flow of information across multiple locations. It could be in any form; e-mails will usually be the best method, but other models should also be used.

Check alignment frequently

Distributed teams can get out of sync very quickly and it may be a while before a misalignment gets detected. Managers need to set smaller checkpoints to make sure that everyone is aligned in their goals.

It's ok to have an accent

Distributed teams, especially across different countries, require people to recognize different accents and levels of proficiency in the English language. It's perfectly alright to have an accent that is different from the majority. Of course, if you happen to work in a call center where you are in a frontend consumer-facing role, it won't be ok to have an accent.

It's not just Indians who have a thick accent; most nationalities have different accents. Even within the United States, there are different accents. Irish and English have different accents, and French and Spanish have completely different accents.

Different accents and levels of English take time to adjust to. It usually gets better over time, but verbal communication in such a team will be a difficult experience. It's ok to ask people to repeat themselves if you did not understand them. Indians avoid asking people to repeat something, especially if the person on the other end is a senior person or a client.

Acknowledgement response

When you peep in any of the conference rooms, you can see people sitting around the speakerphone and listening intently, even nodding their head in acknowledgement. However, many a time, there's no acknowledgement given by the speaker on the other side. The speaker is left wondering if he is able to make his point or not.

More back and forth required, more questions to be asked

To avoid miscommunication, it's important to ask a lot of questions. Indians are not known to ask many questions. Although this aspect is changing with Gen Y, the perception in the global world still remains. This is perhaps a cultural dimension, given the fact that we don't usually question our parents or our teachers as much as folks in the western world do.

Different energy levels

An often forgotten aspect of global meetings is the fact that we end up with one person being fresh and starting his day and the other tired and at the end of his day. Most people have adapted very well to this aspect. However, it does make a difference when meetings start getting longer and more frequent.

Use a mix of methods to communicate

Don't let a distributed team use only one kind of medium for too long. They need to use e-mail, IM, audio conference, and video conference. Each of the mediums has its own set of problems and over reliance on any one medium creates issues.

Technically, video conferencing or tele-presence should be the best way, but the equipment and network availability is only in certain locations; that means if someone in India and someone in San Francisco have to be in a video conference, both the people have to be in their office location and at least for one of them, it'll be fairly late in the evening.

Create opportunities for in-person interactions

Till now, there has been no substitute for a face-to-face and in-person interaction. The vibe and rapport that is built when people meet is unmatched. The relationship will forever remain impersonal if people don't meet and spend time with one another.

Managers should try to create opportunities for people to meet with each other. There is a travel cost, but it'll be paid in itself by creating better communication and hence better productivity.

Finally, when to keep mum

There are plenty of times when a manager needs to hold the information to himself/herself and not communicate. This can be a temporary hold or a forever holding your peace kind of situation. Here are some examples:

- Do not talk about someone else's personal problems, definitely not in public and preferably not in private conversations either.

- Do not reveal what someone told you in confidence. For example, if someone came to you and told you that he is training in classical music, don't put them on the spot at the next birthday celebration at the office. Everybody has his or her own criteria of what to make public and it should be left to the individual.

- Do not announce the departure of another person before that person does. Even though you may come to know about another person leaving the company since you have access to a lot of information, it doesn't mean you are entitled to share it.

- Do not announce to the world about an employee leaving three months before the last day. In fact, make sure the employee doesn't announce it to the world either.

- Do not vent in public about anything. You may feel strongly about something in the organization, like a minimal training budget or uninteresting work, but venting in public will only spread negativity.

- Do not speak when angry. Period. You are likely to say something that isn't going to help anyway.

Knowing when not to communicate is as important an aspect as any other.

Summary

Communication plays a central role in your effectiveness as a manager. More importantly, good communication makes daily work life really enjoyable for the entire team. A daily dose of happiness is a key motivator for people.

In the next chapter, we will discuss what else causes people to be motivated to work, why people lose motivation, and how we can help keep motivation high for the team.

6
Motivation

Have you had a day when you wake up and say to yourself, "I wish I did not have to go to work today?" Maybe because there's something more interesting that you wish to do at home, or maybe because there are some issues at work which you don't want to deal with, or perhaps you just don't want to see your manager's face.

And then there are other days, when you have lots of issues to work on, but you feel all charged up to go and start working on them. It's the same job, but your willingness to be there is different.

Take another scenario of filing tax returns. Filing tax returns is not a fun activity, it's just paperwork since tax is already paid, and you don't get anything out of it as such. But you fear an audit by tax authorities and sooner or later you file your tax returns. You are willing to comply with the requirements because of fear of legal action.

In another example, you want to secure your future financial status. You know that one of the ways is to invest in the stock market. In order to invest, you need to research which stock or mutual fund you want to buy and allocate a part of your current income to it. Are you willing to spend the time and cut down on current expenses?

This willingness to act is the **motivation** every manager is so concerned about. The motivation (willingness to act) is different based on what's going on in the team, the kind of people you work with, how you are being treated, and several other factors.

The question is: how do we create a willingness in our team to work hard, work consistently, and give it all they have? In other words, how do we motivate our people, and keep them motivated? If you really wish to achieve great successes as a manager, you must understand: what is the motivation to work?

Understanding motivation

Now that we bring the long word motivation, closer to the simpler word willingness, it seems a little easier to relate to it. Motivation is not just to want something but also to have the desire to create the action in order to fulfill a want.

Motivation isn't just a business subject that needs to be analyzed in terms of work; it has always applied to all people in all situations. Go back to your college days and question: why were you motivated to spend time on certain subjects and not on others? You possibly scored well in those subjects. It's the same brain which needs to acquire knowledge of Subject A versus Subject B, and scoring well in each one is equally important, but you were drawn towards one more than the other. Do you think that certain teachers were so good that you always wanted to attend their class? Sometimes the subject was pretty easy for you but the class was so much fun that you wouldn't want to miss it. In another case, it was a subject that was a weak spot for you and even when the class was not really fun, you wanted to be there to get a better understanding. These are different reasons for the same action of being in the class and spending time on a given activity.

And then there were those people who you would want to spend time with; some of them became friends for life. There were movies that you didn't particularly want to watch, but went along to see anyway, and ended up enjoying some, and maybe slept through the others, but you went along anyway without much persuasion since you were motivated to spend time with your friends.

So the first thing to understand about motivation is that it isn't anything new. It's always been something you have dealt with every day of your life and it'll be even more relevant as you go through the stages of life; as you have a family and kids, as you grow older and the body starts creaking, and as you wish you could attain the same fitness level that you had a few years ago. Everything requires some motivation.

Desire is given but action is not

Desire is not motivation. Who wouldn't want to be awarded a big bonus for top performance? Who wouldn't want to be facilitated for hard work and solving a big problem?

Everyone desires to do well and create a name for himself or herself, and absolutely everyone desires to be paid higher. However, action is the hard part. Without action, desires have no real impact. In fact, there may be a negative impact when people want to achieve something for a long time and are unable to do so.

Positive and well-directed action is required in order to achieve those desires. Managers need to tap into this desire and create an action around it. Motivating people is all about energizing them to create an action, so people can realize their desires.

Everything takes some motivation

There is seldom a free lunch. Everything worthwhile takes effort, and every effort takes some motivation.

You may think that motivation is required for the harder tasks, but it impacts all tasks that a person has to achieve. Motivation or demotivation impacts a person on the job, and all activities related to that job may be impacted.

One can have lower motivation for one aspect of the job versus another, based on the factors that are driving the motivation. For example, a programmer who is not motivated to work on an outdated technology may find it hard to show good progress in his work around those outdated technologies, but he may be motivated on other aspects, like talking to customers and a requirement definition. In another case, when an employee is demotivated due to a lack of adequate compensation, he/she may not show enthusiasm in any activity.

Everyone's motivation is somewhat different

We know that no two people are the same. Even twin brothers, who grew up together in the same environment, tend to have different likes and dislikes. Clearly, each team member has a slightly different set of motivating factors, which will also be different from your own.

What appeals to you may not appeal to another person. Managers love to talk about, "once I did..." to refer to something they did. It may be interesting information, but it has little impact on another's motivation.

A person who is motivated by technology can't be motivated to work on outdated technology even when you compensate them extra. A person who is very attached to his family will be motivated to work in a town that allows him to be with his family. A person who is motivated to go for higher studies and earn a Ph.D. may give up on a very good MNC job, not for future money, but for the learning and to be part of the elite Ph.D. group.

Basic factors are common

Some basic things that are universal truths apply to any human being in any circumstance; for example, a clean work place, respect, safety, and so on. Almost everyone would want these to be present. In the knowledge industry, these factors are not as much of an issue. However, these basic factors MUST be met. Absence of them will create dissatisfaction very quickly and affect everyone. Beyond basic factors, each individual has a somewhat different set of motivating factors. Some find motivation in daily learning and some in the future glory that they are aiming for.

It's not just your responsibility

Keeping someone motivated is a shared responsibility, between the individual and the manager. It's not just your onus to keep motivating the employee. The individual employee also has to motivate himself/herself and create a positive action. If the employee is always looking for a stimulus to respond positively, it's not going to last very long. People need to make attempts to create conditions that work for them and help resolve the motivation issues.

There's such a thing as self-motivation

Self-motivation is the key to an individual's long-term success. Since it's your life and your career, you are the best person to take you there. This implies that you have to be your own cheerleader to motivate and help yourself move forward.

Self-motivation is what makes the world really go around, not the carrots and the sticks.

Demotivators are different from motivators

Demotivators are factors that discourage people from positive action. These stop or slow people down from achieving their goals. For example, a bad keyboard tray is a constant reminder of discomfort and will impact what people do on a daily basis. While adding a really comfortable keyboard tray will not create any extra motivation. Just like motivating factors vary with each individual, demotivating factors also vary from person to person.

Everyone is motivated to work

To begin with, it is fair to assume that almost everyone is motivated to work and certainly motivated to earn. That is the reason why one joined the workforce. It's part of a manager's responsibility to leverage this motivation and take the employee's performance to the next level.

Motivation theories

Motivation is an extensively researched subject and a rather large number of theories exist that explain the reasons for motivation and behavior of individuals and managers. Among these various theories, some have stood the test of time and have been widely accepted. Let's examine the basics of some of these theories.

Maslow's hierarchy of needs theory

One of the most basic and easy-to-understand theory is Maslow's 'hierarchy of needs'. Maslow proposed that human needs are to be satisfied in a set order: physiological, safety, belonging, esteem, and self-actualization. These were depicted in the famous pyramid:

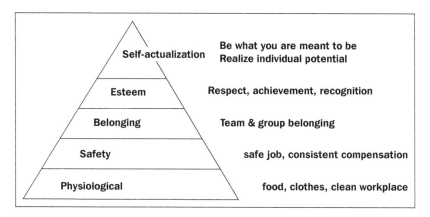

Physiological needs

These are the physical and the most basic of human needs. Food, water, and shelter were the basic needs of the cave man. Good food, a good and comfortable workplace, non-hazardous work, and a pollution-free environment are the basic needs of the knowledge worker. Maslow contended that humans would want to fulfill these first and there was little reason to doubt him. It's nearly impossible to do anything right if your body and mind are not in good shape.

A knowledge worker's basic food, clothing, and shelter needs are easily taken care of, and most don't really worry about them. However, in today's world, new basic needs have emerged: good sleep and low stress.

People are motivated to avoid stress and will work to avoid it, even change jobs. A case in point; Bangalore city traffic is one of the worst. Distance of the workplace from one's home is a key criterion for some people. Over the years, I have seen people changing jobs to avoid a long commute. Being in Bangalore traffic and wasting a precious 2-3 hours a day is a huge de-motivator for some people.

Good sleep is another basic need, which has become an issue in some of the industries like call centers or 24/7 support centers. Odd work hours create a difficult lifestyle, and despite a fair compensation and good comfortable surroundings, these businesses see a lot of attrition.

Safety needs

These are the next set of needs humans would want to fulfill once the physical needs are met. Safety in physical terms is a non-issue for knowledge workers, as most work in air-conditioned offices. However, safety in terms of keeping your job is the new need. Losing one's job is not unknown in the Indian industry now, and there is a fairly large population of employees who would stay with their current job because they are comforted by the security that the organization provides. Safety is still a very prime need for most Indians, and that is why we see brand name companies being able to attract a lot of talent, while startups or mid-size companies struggle to hire and retain people.

There are other safety needs like financial safety that employees will seek via good and consistent compensation being paid. In the initial years of employment, the job-hopping is partly the financial safety needs being met and partly the esteem needs.

Love and belonging needs

Once people have their basic physical needs met, and feel reasonably secure, they look for fulfilling the belonging and love needs. Team bonding and being part of an elite team or a group becomes something that people value.

Team spirit and team bonding have a huge impact on keeping people together and creating team successes. People wish to fulfill the group needs: they would like to support the group and the group goals.

Being part of a strong group makes people comfortable. You believe your opinions matter to those in the group, and other group members care about you as an individual.

Love is a big word, but one of the key factors in people giving their best for the organization is when they see that the organization cares — cares about the wellbeing of its employees, cares about their feelings, cares about them as human beings and not just as workers. The face of the organization is the direct manager of an employee. It works wonders when a manager really cares about the wellbeing of the individual.

Another aspect of love and belonging needs is the need to be with the family. Many engineers are open to taking a job anywhere in the country when they start their careers, and in a few years, once the safety needs are taken care of, that is, they are much more employable and can find a job elsewhere, they try to come closer to their hometowns.

Esteem needs

Once the physical, safety, and social needs are met, people aspire for esteem. As people grow in their careers, they get heavier titles and more visibility, which serves to fulfill their esteem needs, as titles indicate a higher or significant position in the organization.

Recognition and rewards help add to the esteem. Especially in India, titles mean a lot. Most folks want to be a manager as soon as they can. People attach different esteem values to different things. For some, earning more money is a matter of esteem and for others, a national award is the better factor.

Esteem also implies respect and praise, which is almost a basic need in the high education, high skill knowledge industry. However, respect and praise counts most from people who you have respect for. An appreciative word coming from a technical architect may be more valuable to you versus a kind word from your line of business VP or the other way around.

People also see social status as adding to esteem. Hence bigger, more expensive cars, luxury vacations, and fancy restaurants tend to get on the list as people grow and other needs are met.

Self-actualization

It's the final frontier of needs and Maslow contended that when all other needs are met, people will be motivated to do activities that fulfill their self-actualization needs. Self-actualization implies the need to achieve your potential; to be someone or something that you are meant to be. It's your calling.

When people grow and have taken care of their financial goals, have earned their respect, and achieved success professionally, they tend to look for something else. Something that can fill a gap they feel exists. Many people change careers, and many go back to school and several others think about what they can achieve in their remaining professional career. Many technology workers take the big plunge and start their own venture. They give up a cushy and secure job for the long hours and uncertainty of a startup. In Bangalore, there are several restaurants that are owned and run by an erstwhile techie. This need can drive one to very extreme decisions.

Putting Maslow's pyramid together in today's context

Maslow's pyramid of needs is as relevant today as it was 50 years ago. It applies to most people and situations and is one of the first theories to be taught at any B-school. However, a few things to be understood are as follows:

- The needs don't go away as you move up the hierarchy. The physiological needs don't go away once they are fulfilled and one moves to safety. A drop in meeting physiological needs will bring the focus back to physiological needs. As you move up the pyramid, the factors that satisfy the earlier needs must remain.

- In high education and high skill industry, like the IT software and services, the early needs are met very early in the career. Employees straight out of campus earn enough to feel financially secure and have little liability, unlike the previous generations. An employee joins and is looking to fulfill a love and belonging needs right away, even esteem needs in some cases. Hence motivating factors are already high up in the pyramid and that's where managers need to focus more.

- Increasingly, respect, love, and esteem are becoming as important as safety and physiological needs, all at the same time. In India, the significant change in economics as well as changing attitudes of generations has made the people value respect and esteem as basic needs. People are not motivated to work at a place that does not provide them with respect and a friendly environment.

- The priority of needs changes based on the situation of an individual. A person may have esteem as the primary motivation today, but safety can take over if circumstances change.

Many other types of needs can be categorized. For example, the need for knowledge, need for family and parenting, and it is possible to add more levels to Maslow's pyramid. However, Maslow provides a strong framework to understanding motivation on the basis that needs drive motivation.

Herzberg's motivation—hygiene and two-factor theory

As part of his research, Herzberg conducted a study asking people when they felt particularly good or exceptionally bad at their jobs. Using the data, Herzberg proposed that the factors which motivate people are different from the factors that demotivate people at work. Herzberg referred to the demotivating factors as hygiene factors. Herzberg contended that improvement in hygiene factors does not lead to motivation. However, it may avoid demotivation. This implies that a lack of good hygiene will cause demotivation.

For example, in most organizations in India, lunch is served at the premises and is usually subsidized by the employer. Almost everyone complains about food at the cafeteria. It's a source of much debate. Improving food quality and options often helps reduce heartburn (literally) for the employees, but it would not lead to motivation or higher performance on the job. If the food is made extremely well, like a gourmet chef cooking your choice at Google in Silicon valley, it'll be appreciated but it may not have a real impact on performance, as it doesn't really generate any extra motivation. If the food quality at the cafeteria keeps deteriorating, or leads to health issues, it will create dissatisfaction among the employees. If the organization takes away the lunch option entirely, and every employee has to either go out for lunch or arrange for lunch delivery himself or herself, it will surely lead to dissatisfaction.

Consider another case of additional responsibility, where responsibility also includes authority and more freedom. Additional responsibility given to someone often motivates them and can lead to better performance. Taking away responsibility will have the exact opposite effect. The employee will have a loss of power and this may have an adverse effect on performance.

Like one of the ex-managers once told me, "I'm not upset, but that doesn't mean I'm happy". Because an employee may not necessarily be dissatisfied, doesn't mean he is satisfied.

Herzberg listed the following factors in each category:

Motivators	Hygiene factors
Achievement	Company policy
Recognition	Supervision
Work itself	Relationship with your manager
Responsibility	Working conditions
Advancement	Salary
Growth	Relationship with co-workers
	Security

This list may not be completely agreeable, and the order of priority certainly does change, given a specific industry and nature of work. However, most of it holds true as it appeals to basic human traits.

For yourself, try the exercise and list when you were most satisfied and most dissatisfied at work.

In the last 5 years of work, I felt most satisfied when:
1
2
3
4
5
6

In the last 5 years of work, I felt most dissatisfied when:
1
2
3
4
5
6

McClelland's motivational needs theory

McClelland proposed that an individual's motivation is driven by his needs in three dimensions:

- Need for power
- Need for achievement
- Need for affiliation

All three needs will drive an individual with a different intensity level.

Need for power

Some people have a high need for power or being seen as a powerful person, being influential, getting their way through collecting symbols of power, and perhaps even seeing others being fearful of them.

Some others see power as a tool to create impact and strive for power that enables them to contribute to the benefit of the organization. These are typically good leaders, who share power with different people, so that they can deliver. They enjoy the fact that they have the power to share power.

Regardless of the usage of power, both kinds of people are driven by the need for power.

Need for achievement

In our industry, the need for achievement is generally very high. This is closer to the needs of self-actualization in Maslow's need hierarchy. The need for achievement drives people to learn and excel at their jobs. These people will usually be hard working and would like to leave no chance in order to achieve their goals.

In an extreme case where someone's drive for achievement is very high, it can lead to negative consequences. These individuals must win at any cost. People can become overly result-focused and lose sight of the bigger picture.

A person with low need for achievement is likely to be fearful of anything going wrong, and hence may risk achievement over safety.

A balanced need for achievement helps people achieve their goals without rubbing other people up the wrong way.

Need for affiliation

Everyone has the need for affiliation. Almost everyone wants to have friends, to be part of a group, and to have a family. Need for affiliation drives individuals to create life long relationships and abide by the rules of a civil society. How strong the need is depends on an individual.

People with low drive for affiliations will tend to have fewer friends and avoid networking. They should avoid jobs like sales and program management where your networking and group abilities are important to the job function. At the other end, people with an extremely high need for affiliation may become dependent on their relationships and groups. They go along with group decisions, regardless of whether they like them or not.

Indians, in general, are group conformists, and have a high affiliation need. It's a cultural thing, and you can find people in groups all over the place—groups of people at a tea-stall, groups of people visiting someone at the hospital, and even policemen standing in a group while they are supposed to be patrolling. One of the key elements of an organization's success at IDC is the strength of team bonding. Once a team starts to break and some key members of the team leave, more people follow.

All three factors

All of the previously discussed needs are present in each individual in varying degrees. The job function and level of experience typically dictates the balance of needs. A programmer is likely to have high achievement needs and moderate affiliation needs. A good balance of them makes a perfect employee for you. However, as we all know, perfect employees are hard to find. Managers need to identify the key driving needs of an employee and engage them in work that goes well with their key motivations. Once a match has been made at the motivation level, good performance becomes the automatic result.

What's motivating in today's workplace?

Now that we have a framework for understanding motivation, let's examine what's motivating in our environment today.

Success is motivating

Tasting success is like tasting blood. It's a high that you will want to experience again and again. The more successes people get, the better they are at creating more success for themselves. Not only because of acquiring better skills, but also because they are more motivated to get there.

Managers need to create systems that allow for more successes. For every project to be done, don't have only the final delivery as the success. You can create smaller milestones and success criteria. Once you get to a milestone, celebrate and compliment people on their success. This allows people to get their regular dose of success and they look forward to the next one. The ultimate success is extremely important too, hence at every milestone celebration, talk about how close or far you are from the ultimate success. This keeps people aware of the progress they are making towards the big success.

Beyond individual success, the success of the company also matters. In India, people prefer to work for large brand name companies. Besides safety, there is a certain esteem associated with a large brand name. People love to see their company in the newspaper for a big announcement and praise from the world. By association, they feel part of the success.

Team bonding is motivating

We all spend a very significant amount of our time at work and with our co-workers. When there is team bonding and a strong team spirit, every action that helps the team achieve its goals adds to the standing of an individual within the team. People get peer recognition when team bonding is strong.

Team bonding helps people get over problems collectively and people feel stronger and more capable when part of a strong team. A higher sense of capability, a sense of someone is watching my back, and a sense of I have people who care about me helps people go for their goals with a positive attitude.

Managers play a big part in facilitating and encouraging team bonding. Managers should feel ok to let people hang-out at the cafeteria a little longer than a coffee break, as it's a sign people like to spend time with each other. Encourage collaboration more than individual glory and let the team be bigger than any one individual.

Power is motivating: power to choose, power to shape the future

Power is very powerful! While power has different effects on different people, power is always addictive. People are motivated by the desire for more power, desire to exercise power, and the desire to retain power.

Power is not just authority over another person. The power that is most desired is the power to choose. In a high education industry, people love the freedom to do things their own way. While conformance is required in many places, there's always room for individual creativity and individual expression. Managers must leave that room there and allow people to apply their judgment and style to situations.

Power to shape the future of the product, power to shape the future of a client relationship, and power to shape the processes in the team and their own future is a big motivation for many people in the knowledge industry. Managers should allow team members to participate and contribute to future plans. Even if someone is new to the job, it helps to discuss the future and present future plans, seeking review and comments. Everyone should also feel that they have the opportunity to suggest improvements and make a positive difference to the team and the work itself.

A challenge is motivating

In the knowledge industry, easy is boring. People with high skills need to exercise the skills and stretch themselves. Without a challenge to stretch, people start losing interest and focus their energies on something else where they can find a challenge, rather than the primary job.

A challenge needs to be distinct from the usual work. Even when the usual work is hard enough, a challenge of a different kind is needed to allow for orthogonal thinking. The mind stops thinking during routine work. Just like driving is a challenge to start with, but ceases to be one after some time, unless you drive in a new terrain. The excitement to drive disappears after a few months of driving and then driving becomes a chore.

A sense of accomplishment comes only when a challenge is completed against a certain level of difficulty.

Managers need to keep the employees engaged in challenges of a different kind, from time-to-time. It's ok to create a challenge even when there's no immediate requirement for it from a work delivery perspective. It does generate extra work, and it may not be immediately valuable to the company, but it's valuable to the employee and hence will yield benefits for the company. It is best when these challenges can be directed to the future of the product and the team.

Challenges need not be just technical and can be process-oriented or training or planning.

A manager's confidence and belief in the individual is motivating

People value their manager's opinions, in most cases. When a manager shows belief in someone's ability, that person gets a boost of confidence. Confidence makes people believe in their own ability and encourages them to go for their goals.

Managers should show confidence in their team. Let people take charge and take ownership of various situations. Show that you believe that they are the best people to do it, even if it is a nearly impossible task.

Confidence and doubt are inversely proportional. When you show doubt, you take away confidence. The more confidence goes away, the less likely the chance of success and initiatives from the team.

Hope of achieving greatness is motivating

Everyone loves a hero, and there's no better hero than yourself, if only you could fly. Basic aspirations of a good, and perhaps expensive, lifestyle exist in the industry and the aspiration deep down is to achieve greatness. Not sure doing what will take you there, but you want a shot at greatness. That most difficult project, and the impossible chance that was against conventional wisdom, are actually attractive.

Glory is always individual. I bet, in M. S. Dhoni's dreams, he lifted the world cup and imagined taking the victory lap with the team in the background. He is of course a great team player, but that doesn't mean he doesn't value personal glory.

Managers need to allow people to think big and possibly help their team learn skills and values that can, hopefully, help them achieve the glory they dreamt about.

Hope of a better future is motivating

A car runs on petrol, but also runs on air. Without air the petrol can't be burned. Hope is like that. You need skills, proper compensation, and so on to do a job, but you need hope of growth, hope of more money, and the hope of better working conditions to keep you going everyday.

Hope of a better future motivates people to do better and get to that future. Especially when the chips are down, and the current situation dosen't look so good, people live on hope. People will work through the problems and try to solve them to make a better future.

Without hope of a better future, most people will end up quitting very soon. People lose motivation not because they can't handle a problem, but because they don't see things getting better.

Managers always need to show the future picture and how the future will be achieved by the actions of today.

What is demotivating?

Let us look at some of the factors that de-motivate people in the knowledge industry.

Uncertainty is demotivating

There are always some amount of unknown factors in everyday work (and life) and most people deal with them quite naturally. However, as the level of uncertainty rises, people get anxious.

When there is too much uncertainty, it gets harder to predict the outcomes of your efforts. If there's no real visibility of success, there will be less motivation to make an effort. It can be worse, based on an individual's capacity to handle uncertainty. Some people are too scared to make a mistake, and they will make every effort to validate before they move forward, losing precious time or not acting at all.

When uncertainty prevails for a long time, even the best employees find it hard to keep up the motivation.

You may not have control over factors leading to uncertainty. For example, a company is in the process of getting acquired but is stuck in a legal issue. Everybody knows that an acquisition may happen, and they don't know whether to move forward with the projects they have in hand. Some may fear losing the job they love and may start looking elsewhere and hence lose motivation.

As a manager, you can be an island of relative certainty, amid all the uncertainty. You don't need to fake stability, or give false promises. Instead, you can show the confidence that whatever the outcome, you are prepared to deal with it. Even when people fear losing their jobs, they should not lose the confidence in their ability to find another one. When the leader stands tall, people get a lot of assurance. Managers can help people focus on the task at hand; if things change, so be it. You can always deal with the change. Focus on work adds to confidence and reduces the threat that uncertainty brings about.

No social status is demotivating

There are a number of people in the team, and some have the status of a technical guru, some are very personable and hence have the status of a social leader, and many others are just worker bees.

In the knowledge industry, nobody wants to be a worker bee for too long. Everyone wants to be something that makes him/her distinct among his/her peers.

Managers can help facilitate these soft positions within the group. Everybody can't be a leader of the team, but they can be leaders in their own domain. Managers can create opportunities for people to display their expertise, such as seminars and training that the area-expert can deliver. Managers can acknowledge their expertise in various meetings and forums and involve them in discussions and decisions about their area.

Fear, threats, and disrespect are huge demotivators

No one likes being threatened in any condition. A threat or fear brings out the defensiveness in people.

There are many managers who believe more in the stick than in the carrot. There's a theory, by Douglas McGregor, Theory X and Theory Y. A Theory X manager believes that people inherently dislike work and will work only when pushed towards it. A Theory X manager believes employees are lazy and would work the minimum possible unless they are forced to do more. Hence all credit of work being done belongs to the Theory X manager, since work would not have happened at all if the Theory X manager didn't push it through.

The knowledge industry is just the wrong place for such managers, but unfortunately some do exist and sometimes they even flourish to reach senior positions. Such managers create an environment of fear where employees worry about bad consequences if they don't toe the line of the manager. They stop applying their best knowledge and judgment, and deliver on the lines of the prescription by the Theory X manager.

An environment where fear and threats run the system is highly demotivating for a knowledgeable individual.

Managers need to be Theory Y managers in the knowledge industry. They need to believe in the fact that every individual wishes to contribute their best, and a manager's job is to facilitate the team member to produce their best. Theory Y managers respect each individual. They understand that each individual's contribution is important and each person gets to contribute and deliver to the success of the team.

Lack of adequate and timely compensation is a demotivator

While we work for many reasons, at the end of the day, compensation is a big reason why people work and especially why people work for someone else. If one had a lot of money to spare, they would probably work for themselves and cater to their personal expression and learning.

When compensation is not adequate or doesn't show up on time, people feel cheated. It's a big word to use, but that's perhaps the closest way to describe it. It is a fact that people do evaluate themselves in terms of the compensation they receive. While compensation is not everything, it is a lot!

The lack of adequate compensation works a little differently in the knowledge industry. People don't really slow down in work, but they lose motivation to work for this company. So lack of compensation may not show up in terms of output loss of an individual, but as reduction in collective output of the team due to attrition and time lag of hiring and training new employees.

Poor working conditions are demotivators

In our industry, the air-conditioning and a clean office is given. These are easily met by every organization and are literally the hygiene factors. However, there are other factors such as a reliable, fast network, good hardware, and readily available support that are also part of the working conditions.

You may ask, "So what if the screen loads 30 seconds later?", how does it impact motivation? And the co-relation is not immediately visible but it does exist.

A few years back, a large company switched to a new set of technologies, and that made heavy demands on the network. As a consequence, every developer had to wait a few extra seconds for the application to load, as well as a half-a-second delay between a mouse click and the screen response to appear. It was frustrating to start with, but people had no choice, as they had to deliver, and while it didn't really make a difference in the overall time, it was annoying, to say the least.

In a couple of months, this half-a-second delay became the most talked about topic. Every conversation between a team member and a team lead had a mention of this half-a-second delay.

A person described it, quite dramatically, as: "It is as if someone blows a short trumpet, truuu....truuu....truuu, every 3 seconds into your ear while you are trying to concentrate on work".

Something like this kills the interest to work and it's repulsive to the extent that people would avoid spending extra time on the application.

Lack of opportunities to show their potential is demotivating

Having the potential and not getting a chance to utilize it is like having a million bucks and not getting a chance to spend it.

In the early days of a job, the focus is on learning. There are a lot of new things; new challenges in terms of just learning and getting comfortable with the requirements of the job. Through this learning process itself, people get to see a process, a product, and a system from a third person perspective. Almost always, folks have suggestions on how to make it better. Even campus hires that are working for the first time in a business environment have an opinion to share.

That's the nature of a thinking person, who not only absorbs what he/she sees but also analyzes at the same time and is not afraid to voice his/her opinions.

People need an avenue to realize their potential and stretch their imagination. When the job doesn't offer enough opportunities for people to contribute in multiple ways and try new things, people lose interest slowly but surely.

Lack of learning is demotivating

This is especially important in the knowledge industry, where the learning never really stops. Technologies change every few years and newer variations and enhancements show up almost every month.

Most teams tend to specialize in one kind of work, and that makes perfect sense for the organization as the quality and consistency of delivery gets better as people spend more time with the same kind of work.

However, the side effect of too much focus on one technology and one kind of work is that the learning curve becomes rather flat. It's more of the same every day, and every new project is only a small twist on the earlier one.

Individuals start seeing their technical growth as stagnant. Even when they want to spend some time on a new technology, there is very little time to go beyond tutorial-level knowledge. For some time, the non-technical growth, that is, growth in responsibilities or compensation, and so on, may keep a person motivated, but over time a technologist will get demotivated if learning slows down.

Managers and organizations need to invest in training infrastructure and make skills upgrade a part of the culture. Work rotation is another great way to create new learning opportunities. For example, a person working on pl.sql reports in project A can possibly work on high-volume data capture jobs or even a very different technology like Java.

Signs of low motivation

Everyone goes through days of low motivation, but prolonged low motivation will lead to lower productivity and attrition. Here are a few tips to spot low motivation in an employee.

Lack of attention to detail

Employees find it hard to focus when motivation is low. The mind and body aren't in a great state to pay attention to detail. Here's an example:

Sumit was a good Product Manager, but suffering from low motivation since he got passed up for a foreign assignment. Ritesh, his manager, asked Sumit to prepare a presentation for a customer visit. It was a fairly simple task of taking the screenshots and writing a few bullets about the features. Sumit had done this so many times before, and although he really didn't feel like doing it one more time, he quickly completed the task and went home.

The next day at the customer's office, Sumit and Ritesh set up the projector and started the presentation to an audience that had the top people in the customer's local organization. To their horror, all the screenshots had the Windows task bar as well as multiple tabs of Sumit's browser window from the previous day. It showed the titles of all the sites and applications Sumit was looking at the previous day. Some of them were downright embarrassing: a dating site, a free music site, a playing media player, and some others. Needless to say, Sumit got an earful.

This is an example of what happens when people don't pay attention to detail that is expected of their job function. Programmers don't handle all the boundary conditions and tests, process owners miss out on key pointers visible from the data, and there might be several others which are not killer mistakes, but incur a cost for the organization.

Absenteeism

This is an easy one to spot. Most people with low motivation will show up late to work or will frequently not show up at all. Any reason to skip work will be leveraged; sometimes it's too much rain, another time it'll be some friends visiting, and many a times of not feeling well. The frequency of absenteeism is relatively high and understandably so since the person really has no desire to contribute.

Many organizations have flexible hours, which are turned into lower working hours when an employee is not motivated. Since it's legitimate to work from home, employees can exploit the freedom. So they stay at home, but neither work nor claim a day off.

Managers need to watch out for frequent absence or working from home. If you suspect that an employee is taking undue advantage of the flexibility to work from home, you can assign specific tasks for the day and ask for a detailed status for them.

Dragging feet

When people have lower motivation, each task looks heavy, and hence it's hard to carry it. Simple tasks get delayed and this behavior is repeated over and over again.

You would notice that everything will take a little more time and will require an extra reminder. Sometimes, the employee will come around and inform you that something is delayed, and at other times, you will find out much later. Even simple tasks like setting up a meeting will be met with some resistance with something like, "can we do it next week" and will require some convincing to be done.

Managers should watch out when a little task requires a conversation and a reminder.

Dropped catches...too many misses at work

With low motivation, a lot of simple tasks will start to go wrong. More errors of all kinds will show up for no apparent reason.

You'll see a person who is very capable starting to make avoidable errors. He will always have some explanation and a complaint to go with it.

The scenario described regarding a lack of attention to detail is an example of a dropped catch too and there can be many more reasons for errors to happen.

Managers should watch out when capable people start to make silly mistakes.

No contest—passivity—low engagement

Another form in which low motivation shows up as is the lower engagement level of the employee. Given an assignment, a demotivated employee will just do it without much thought being applied.

Rakesh walked up to his manager's office, and he knew he was going to get some more work to do. Rakesh's manager, Sanjay, explained the new changes that the customer had asked in the module that Rakesh was working on. Through the conversation, Rakesh wanted to say something, but didn't. He wasn't convinced that all the changes were required and some of them looked downright incorrect to him. However, Rakesh simply listened to the whole explanation, took notes, and quickly walked out with an Ok. In the whole ten minutes of the conversation, Rakesh spoke for less than 60 seconds.

Rakesh's deep understanding of the module makes his opinion very valuable, but he is not really interested in discussing it with his manager. He prefers to just do it without applying his valuable judgment.

Low engagement is a slow poison, and sometimes hard to detect, as the work goes on and there is no protest, but at the same time, people are not putting in their 100 percent. Managers should always encourage 100 percent participation from their team in every activity; anything lower need not be expected.

Less social interaction

Another symptom of low motivation is that people start to spend less and less time with their team. The usual 4 p.m. coffee group starts to see one person not joining them for one reason or the other. Even when one joins, the interaction is limited.

People start to skip any team event, like a team lunch or team picnic or a launch event. Sometimes they'll sign up to avoid other people asking them reasons for the same, but have no real intentions of showing up.

Managers can take a clue from these behaviors and start observing an employee in greater detail. Motivation is a state of mind, and the earlier you address it, the easier it is to address. A simple and honest 101 can bring out some of these key issues and perhaps the tide can be turned.

Every year during budgeting and salary review sessions, one discussion is repeated with no conclusion. Is money a motivator? How much money is really a motivation in the current market? Let's examine the issue.

Is money a motivator?

Money certainly makes the world go around, but does it motivate people? Let's consider Maslow's needs pyramid.

Physiological needs: Food, good conditions, clothes, and so on, everything takes money. Without money, it's not possible to satisfy the physical needs of today.

Safety needs: The biggest need of today is financial safety, which is completely driven by money.

Belonging and love: It's true that this need isn't money-driven. Sometimes your financial status may determine if you can sustain being part of a particular group. Love is a big word and all I can say is that money can't buy love, but no money can certainly make it more difficult to be loved.

Esteem: While respect can't be bought, a lot of other esteem needs are fulfilled by money. Symbols of esteem, such as expensive bikes or cars and designer clothes, can only be satisfied by money.

Self actualization: Technically, self-actualization should not be money-related, but most people can take a risk and follow their heart only when future financial needs are secured. With a threat of future financial insecurity, it's very difficult to go on a trip to self-discovery and fulfillment.

Money essentially is part of every need and hence it is certainly a motivator, but when you look at it closely, there are two aspects of money and motivation. Firstly, the desire to earn more money is a motivator. Secondly, the fear of losing money or the desire to preserve money is a motivator by itself.

Money is highly-valued since it is such a great enabler. It helps satisfy multiple needs and is important in all stages of life.

What happens when money becomes a given?

Smart people reach a good career point pretty soon. They become highly employable and the economy supports an easy job switch to a slightly higher compensation. At this stage of a career, money is a given, and hence it'll cease to be a motivator.

An increase in salary of such an individual will have no real impact on his motivation. It would be seen as his/her right, and what he/she deserved anyway.

So what happens when you don't give someone what is theirs by right? By any chance, if this individual is denied a salary hike due to any reason, the employee will be demotivated.

Lack of good compensation will cause huge dissatisfaction, as it's seen as an employee being devalued by the organization. Unless there are other very strong motivators, the money demotivator will drive people to attrition.

Extra money may create an extra motivation only sometimes, but lack of money will almost always create demotivation. So while money is absolutely essential, it's a more powerful demotivator than a motivator.

Summary

Motivation is a tricky and a beautiful subject. There's no other subject that has been written about so much and it's the top agenda for all managers. Motivation is impacted by so many different factors, and many of these factors act all together while pulling in different directions. In essence, study of motivation is a study of human behavior.

All managers should spend time learning theories on human behavior and motivation. In case it gets too confusing, you can go back to the basics:

- Treat people with respect and fairness.
- Be an enabler and be flexible.
- Set clear deliverables and expectations.
- Be clear about compensation. Don't promise what you can't deliver.

At the end of the day, it's just people like yourself who you are dealing with. They are all individuals who have joined the organization in order to contribute, to learn, and to earn. They are already motivated when they join the company. What led that motivation to be eroded? Managers will have to work with each individual to help them find their way and keep the magic that was there since day one.

Every person hired in the team joins with a goal to contribute and grow, and it's best if the manager can keep him or her motivated. But what if the new hire is not really a good fit, technically or culturally, for the team? Whatever the effort from the manager, the returns will be marginal. In the next chapter, we will get into the details of various aspects of hiring and how we can avoid hiring mistakes.

References

The motivation to work — Frederick Herzberg

One more Time: How do you motivate employees: Frederick Herzberg: *Harvard Business Review*

Wikipedia — Maslow, Herzberg, McClelland

7
Hiring

Can one person make a real difference?

If the answer is yes, then each new person you hire is important since you want that person to make a positive, rather than a negative, impact. A manager is as capable as his/her team, and hence the emphasis is on team building, which we discussed in the earlier chapter. Hiring is step one of the team building process.

Technically, hiring should be simple—advertise the job opening, get resumes, shortlist a few candidates, interview the candidates, and select the best. However, hiring is tougher than it should be and each step has its challenges. Job postings on the Internet portals don't attract the right kind of candidates, resumes are incorrect and bloated with unnecessary details, the interview process is not structured enough to highlight the skills that matter, internal processes take long, compensation decisions are difficult and finally, the candidate may or may not join. There's a 50-50 chance that all the effort goes wasted because the candidate declines the offer and there's always a chance that the new hire doesn't perform as expected.

Although interviewing and hiring is a very critical activity, based on my observations of the industry, almost nobody has had any training in interviewing or hiring processes in general. It would be interesting for you to check if your organization offers any hiring/interviewing skills training. If yes, please go ahead and sign up and have some of the key members of your team also sign up for the same.

In this chapter, we'll try to get an understanding of the key concepts of hiring and look at specific ways of making the hiring process easier and effective at the same time.

Understanding hiring

Let's look at a few important aspects that we must understand about hiring.

Understanding your optimal requirements

When we hire, the mindset is typically to 'get the best out there'. So managers often start with a job description that has all the high standards listed. A top degree from a top educational institute, 'extensive' experience in technology of a specific kind, a number of years of experience in a specific domain, and so on.

Ask yourself:

- Do you need the top guy from a top school for the job?
- How is the rest of your team? Folks who are already doing the job. Does it fit the job description you are putting out?

While we put out a job description that usually specifies the top end of the spectrum, as hiring managers, we should also look at the optimum level of each criterion required.

Hiring for potential not just current skills

When we hire a person, we typically focus on what the candidate has done in the past. At every step, we look at their history; projects/work done in their previous job, academic performance in college, and even academic performance in school. We almost go with the assumption, "if he has done well in the past, he will do well in the future" and vice versa, "if he has done poorly in the past, he will likely do poorly in the future".

While it is indeed true that past performance is critical to look at, look for more than that. Of course, it is impossible to predict the future, but you have to make a call for the future anyway.

Some of the many things to look at are as follows:

- Look for enthusiasm to learn new things. Does the candidate seem open to trying out something different?
- Look for flexibility in approach. Is the candidate 'open' to considering multiple alternatives, even some that aren't outright applicable in the situation.
- Look for a candidate's approach in understanding the problem statement.

- Remember, if someone can learn one technology, that same person can learn another one too. Don't get stuck on specific technology skills. Look for application of skills. If someone can program well in Java, he can very easily become a good .NET programmer also.
- Don't outright reject a candidate because of multiple job switches in the past. Ask for reasons and look at the life-stage, which has a high bearing on people staying in a stable job.

Past performances certainly show that a candidate is capable of success, and the potential points to the fact that a candidate is likely to carry his/her successes forward and repeat them for you.

Hiring is a risk

Every new hire in the team may not turn out to be a stellar hire. Hiring is a matchmaking process and hiring managers are under pressure to hire quickly and staff their teams for delivery.

I have seen many managers try 'not to make a mistake' while hiring, and go overboard with the number of interviews to be done and the various kinds of testing, from technical skills to behavioral to simple communication to cognitive testing and what not. Managers must understand that hiring is a risky activity and some decisions may go wrong.

However, not hiring in time is also a risk, and these risks need to be balanced. Do the due diligence with every candidate and keep the process short and sweet, if possible.

Putting candidates through endless interviews only serves to delay the process and also makes the candidate frustrated. A good candidate, who is in the job market, is likely to be talking to other companies as well. You certainly run the risk of losing out on a good candidate if you are very risk averse.

Hiring is not an end to itself

Hiring is one step in the larger process of team building. I have seen many a manager spend too much time trying to hire that top profile candidate, rejecting any candidate, even at the slightest doubt, and offering much higher compensation than the market.

Hiring good candidates is very important, but it's not the answer to all the problems you may have to solve. Don't get focused on just hiring and miss the effort that needs to be put into team building.

Ultimately, it's what you and the new hires do 'post hiring' that will be important to the organization.

Be open—talking about challenges upfront

Part of the hiring process is to make the job you are offering sound attractive to a prospective candidate. It's a sell job. While there's no real chance of hiring someone if you paint a grim picture, it's important to paint a genuine picture without making it sound grim.

For example, working odd hours on a regular basis will be something that you may surely want to mention. In most software development companies, the late evening (say, 9:30 P.M. or 10 P.M.) conference call at least once or twice a week is a common requirement for the job. Make sure this is mentioned when you talk to the candidate.

A key aspect that I'm always upfront about is the 'on-site' assignments, that is, the opportunity to work abroad for long periods of time, say six months to a year. A large percentage of Indian IT professionals have the ambition to work abroad and it's great for someone to have that ambition. However, if your organization provides little chance of an on-site opportunity, be clear about it.

Any other issues, like constant high delivery pressures, expectations from customers, lack of foreign travel opportunities, local travel to multiple locations, or any other usual challenges, should be mentioned early on in the hiring process.

Pre-interview: knowing what you are looking for

One of the biggest problems I see is that the interviewer is not clear on the specifics of what he/she is looking for. So they end up looking for the 'best candidate' or a 'strong technical candidate', which leads to testing of technical skills and perhaps communication skills and not as much looking for a fitment into a position.

Hiring needs to be for a 'given position'. Before starting the hiring process, managers need to look at the current team composition and decide the ideal mix of technical and behavioral skills that are required in a candidate to fill that position.

For example, if you are expanding an existing team, take some time and evaluate the following:

- Key technical skills required:
    - Programming languages
    - Hands on expert for certain technologies or packages

- Related skills required, such as problem solving and analytical skills

- Kind of past experience required:
  - ° Is it important for the candidate to have worked in the same domain?
  - ° What kind of past experience will be ideal?
- Behavioral skills:
  - ° Desirable behavioral skills
    - Positive attitude
    - Team player
    - Flexibility in approach
    - Decision maker
  - ° Undesirable behavioral skills
    - Over aggressiveness

When hiring a replacement for someone, all of the previous points apply, plus a few more things to consider are as follows:

- Don't look for a direct replacement. Each individual is different, so in reality no one person will just replace another.
- A person leaving opens up the doors for existing team members to take on more responsibilities. Look to accommodate those first and then decide on the profile for the open position.
- Hiring takes time, so you'll need a continuity plan anyway that involves the current team members.
- Use the replacement as an opportunity to re-balance the team. For example, if you have a team where most members have more than 5 years of experience, look to add someone with 0-3 years of experience.

Advertising and sourcing

Each organization needs to build a good model for attracting talent. If your source market is not appropriate, you won't get good resumes to start with. Eventually, desperation will set in and you may end up hiring a not-so-great candidate and then dealing with the consequences.

Advertising in newspapers is not much of an option and doesn't necessarily generate the kind of good inflow of resumes that you may expect from that investment.

Internet portals are better options and cost effective too. However, these tend to generate a large number of unfit resumes. It is common to get job applications from a fresh out of college graduate although your job posting may clearly set the experience requirement at 5 years or more.

Most large organizations have their own recruitment teams. This team is focused on the market to generate leads and manage the online traffic as well. However, the size of the recruitment team is typically small and hence they are always under pressure to source better resumes. Essentially, a manager's capability to source good candidates depends on how well the manager can work with the recruiter. If the recruiter understands your requirements, he/she will be able to do a better job of filtering the resumes and he/she will be able to source from the right places.

The best source is always employee referrals. Almost every company offers a referral bonus incentive if a candidate gets selected via employee referral. Employee referral is also a great way to empower the team to build itself and for a team member to define the quality and shape of the team.

In large organizations, there are opportunities to advertise internally also to attract internal talent towards a new opportunity. Internal transfers are part of the policy for almost all large organizations and it helps in the long run to retain top performing employees by offering them a way to learn and work in different capacities and domains.

Pre-interview: resume screening

This is stage one of the screening process. Depending on the maturity of the hiring process in your organization, the resume may already be processed for some criteria match. Here are the key criteria to look for:

- Technical skills: Look not only for the presence of the skills, but into the projects where the skills are applied, the complexity, duration of the projects, and when the skills were last used. Very often someone may show their summary of skills as 'Expertise in C programming', but the project's summary shows that the candidate did programming using 'C' in a project five years ago.

- Relevant work experience: Look for the relevant work experience and not just the total. Candidates may have switched domains completely. For example, I have seen candidates who were teaching in a college for the first few years before they switched to working for a legitimate software services organization.

- Past projects: Look at the domain in which the projects were executed. The length of the projects is also an interesting criterion. For certain roles, you may prefer experience on large-sized projects, not 2-3 month quickies.

- Job switches: The number of job changes the candidate has gone through. Too many job changes is a warning sign. In general, an average of less than two years in a job is not a good sign. However, apply your understanding of the industry trends before you reject a resume. For example, a candidate may have held a job only for 2-3 months, as he may have quickly realized the misfit and moved on. Sometimes, a candidate's resume will show two companies but there may have been an acquisition, so technically it wasn't a voluntary job change.

- Broad nature of work: Look at the nature of work done in terms of the industry where the candidate worked in, for example, product development versus software services. The skills may match exactly in both cases, but the application may be different in each case.

- Exposure: Look for exposure that you may value, such as exposure to complex customer environments, or exposure to customer processes, or exposure to working on-site at a customer location in Europe.

- Add some points for resumes that are nicely put together. Where it's easy to find the details you are looking for, where there are no spelling mistakes, and information is not repeated.

Overall, a resume is a first impression of the candidate, but take it with a rather large pinch of salt. Look for details and not just keyword matches. Spend a little extra at this stage to avoid a lot of time wasted later on.

Pre-interview: phone screening

A phone screen has become a pretty standard step in the hiring process. It helps to avoid wasting yours and the candidate's time on detailed interviews, when there may not be a good match to begin with.

Primary goals of the phone screen are to establish the following:

- Is the candidate worthy of more detailed interviews?
- Is there a potential match between the candidate and the position?

Since the candidate is shortlisted, here's what you may know already:

- Several technical skills match
- Education summary indicates possibly good fundamentals
- Work experience indicates candidate has worked on interesting projects

What you'd like to know more of:

- Has the candidate really worked in depth on the projects listed?
- What was the candidate's role/responsibilities/contribution in the projects listed?
- Is the technical knowledge deep?
- How are the communication abilities of the candidate?
- Fuzzy abilities, like approach to a problem or being adaptive and so on, if you value these abilities.
- Can the candidate see the big picture, the 'why' versus 'how' of the project?

Here's what you may like to test:

- Test for resume versus reality
- Test for understanding of the problem and not just churning out code
- Test for the presence of basic concepts
- Test for the presence of depth in the required skills

Sample phone screen

Here's how a phone screen may be structured for a technical candidate.

Warm up (3-5) minutes

Introduce yourself and indicate a pattern of interview. Ask the candidate to talk about himself. There's no right or wrong answer in this case, but it may tell you "how a candidate sees himself/herself". One candidate may start with "I'm the project lead of …" and another with "I have been working in C++…". This also gets the candidate loosened up a little bit and lowers the anxiety level.

Recent significant projects (10 minutes)

Pick one, it doesn't have to be the latest, but rather a project which is of a significant duration and that the candidate feels he has contributed most in.

Understanding of the project: Can he provide a good summary of the project at a high/big picture level? Set your expectations according to the career level.

Candidate's role in these projects: Look for a specific contribution.

"I was involved in overall design and was responsible for detail design of the module…"

"I coded modules A, B, and C".

Ask for explanation of key features and design elements where the candidate was deeply involved.

Check if the candidate knows the design goals. Where would the design fail?

Domain experience (5 minutes)

Ask candidates to describe the usual problems in the domain they are working in. Or ask them to describe the workflow in a specific function.

Basic technical questions (10 minutes)

Sometimes interviewers don't want to ask very basic questions, perhaps because the candidate has good experience or most candidates would have prepared from the 'common interview questions' from the web. However, there's absolutely no harm in starting with easy warm up questions. You'll be surprised how many candidates are unable to answer basic questions with clarity or go beyond the bookish examples. Make the questions interesting and contextual by asking where they have applied this in their recent projects. Add a twist if possible.

For a Java interview: instead of asking what "interfaces"are, ask "What is an interface, how does it help?" Explain one situation where he/she used interfaces in the project. How would they implement the same functionality, if they were asked NOT to use Java interfaces?

Limit the basic questions to about two to three only.

Code writing capabilities (10 minutes)

One aspect that is very difficult to test during a phone interview is code writing ability. You can leave this for more detailed interviews later on. However, if coding is core to the job function, it would be prudent to test some coding ability.

In general everybody can write code, so it's fine not to test for syntax. However, what is more interesting is how the overall solution is implemented. For example, you can ask the list of classes and interfaces needed in order to implement a browser history manager. Ask for definition of data structures that are required and the relationship between classes and/or interfaces. In my opinion, syntax is not really important. A smart guy will figure it out very quickly but the approach to a problem, the structure of the solution, and choice of data structures are very important.

In case you do want to see some real code written, it is possible to e-mail a question during interview and ask the candidate to write code and e-mail the solution. You can also explore the possibility of using a virtual meeting or desktop-sharing software, so you and the candidate can look at the same screen. This is similar to a white-board during a face-to-face interview.

 Have a question bank that can be used. It'll surely become stale, but it's better than nothing.

Closing (5-7 minutes)

Allow the candidate to ask questions. Usually, the questions would be around what the product does, what will I work on? And so on. Avoid long winded responses. A crisp and concise explanation is all that is needed. You can point the candidate to interesting websites about your product, and e-mail links if possible. Finally, let the candidate know the next steps.

How to conduct an effective interview

Now that you know the candidates that you are looking for and have identified a few to talk to, let's look at some strategies to conduct an effective interview.

Interview plan

For each position that you hire for, you need to decide how many different interviews you'd like to conduct and in which areas.

Here's a sample interview plan:

1. Interview 1: Let the candidate explain the high-level details of the recent work and the role played in it. Explain challenges that need to be overcome.

2. Interview 2: Core technical skills focus. For example: Java - Multithreading, J2EE-EJB's concepts, programming fundamentals, and application.

3. Lunch with the hiring manager: Get to know the candidate more at a personal level—interests, likes, dislikes, and so on.

4. Interview 3: Problem solving using puzzles and program design problems.

5. Interview 4: Open-ended questions and answers with a fairly senior person in the organization for assessing behavioral aspects and big picture understanding. Explain about the company, position details, and any other questions that the candidate has.

Based on the level of the position and profile of the candidate, the questions and interview plan can be tailored.

Reading and analyzing the resume beforehand

"Hey Vishnu, can you conduct an interview for me?", said Rakesh.

Vishnu, "Sure, send me the resume".

Rakesh, "Already sent a few minutes ago. Candidate is waiting in meeting room 6M001".

This conversation repeats many times. What follows is that Vishnu prints the resume, picks up the printout, and walks over to the meeting room. All this takes about ten minutes, while the candidate sits and gets a little more anxious.

It seems such an obvious thing to do, but it is quite amazing that most interviewers look at the resume of a candidate only a few minutes before the interview, or worse. There's no preparation whatsoever, and Vishnu will ask the candidate to explain 'a little about himself', while he gets familiar with the resume.

The problem compounds itself, as the next interviewer and the one after may end up doing the same thing, and with little feedback from the earlier interview, each interviewer ends up wasting time to 'know the candidate' and then ends up asking similar questions.

If interviewers spend a little time beforehand, they can enter the discussion with a plan and a set of questions that will suit the candidate.

Analyze the resume and pick questions beforehand that will fit the candidate's experience and the requirements of the position.

Interview tips

We will not go into 'how to conduct an interview', since I believe you must know how to already. Instead, we'll look at some factors to consider while interviewing.

Listen to the candidate

Don't make the interview a stage to demonstrate your technical abilities. The interview is about the candidate's abilities. Try to leave as much as possible, nearly 99 percent of the time, for the candidate to talk.

Try not to interrupt the candidate when he is presenting his thoughts, even if you think it's pointless to go down that line of thinking. You may be surprised by how different people reach a solution for a problem. Besides, breaking the candidate's line of thought may throw him off his thought process.

Don't ask the same questions to people at different levels

Interviewers tend to develop a style, and unfortunately, a beloved set of questions. Often interviewers ask the same kind of questions, no matter who they are interviewing. This is probably a side effect of no preparation for the interview. Not only does one need a different set of questions at each level, the expected answers should also be different. Someone straight out of college may have a to-the-point solution to a problem, while someone with a few years of experience will have a more thoughtful answer that may consider the usage and other dependencies to the given problem.

Warm-up questions

Sometimes interviewers are running against time, once again a side effect of not planning prior to the interview, and start the interview with some massive problem to solve. Sometimes this is done to engage the candidate in the question, while the interviewer takes the opportunity to respond to some e-mails.

There is a reason why the first few questions on 'Kaun banega crorepati' (the Indian version of 'Who wants to be a millionaire?') were very easy to answer. Success at answering correctly acts as a warm up to the candidate, and he/she may do better in the rest of the interview.

As interviewers, we do want the candidate to do well; after all, a successful hire is the success of the hiring process.

Talking about the candidate's past work is a good way to get him/her warmed up too. This way, the candidate is quizzed about what he/she has done in the past, and the details will be a good pointer to know how well the candidate was involved in that work.

Basics plus deep drill on key areas

For a given position, you must identify the set of basics that should be adhered to. For example, even though you may hire a guy for J2EE skills, the basics of data structures and design principles must be tested for.

At the same time, define some key areas where a candidate must be strong in. It may not be exactly the technology that you work on, but can be a related technology or a platform that the candidate must demonstrate expertise in. For example, you may have a high usage of EJBs in your project, but it's possible that a candidate does not know EJBs that well, so drilling on EJBs will not take you anywhere. However, the candidate must be good at a related J2EE platform and areas where he has worked earlier.

Also, if you define that EJB expertise is a must for your area, then you probably want to check this at the pre-screen stage itself, and deep drill on that during interviews.

Look for application and not just theory

In the technical world at least, there are a lot of people who prepare well for the interviews, that is, they have read up on all the theory with examples. However, what is important is the application of theory. So frame your questions more on the application of theory, rather than just the theory.

Define problems where a certain theory can be applied and let the candidate come up with a solution. You can also tweak the problem and test how the candidate re-fits the solution to the changed problem description.

Look beyond technical skills

Technical strength or domain strength may be a key requirement for a job position, but there are other factors too, which make a new hire a great hire. Managers need to spend some thinking time to define the desired soft skills for a job position.

Increasingly, the success of an employee is a factor of softer aspects. Unfortunately, it's hard to test for soft skills. Here are some examples that test certain skills.

To test communication:

- The communication during an interview is a good pointer.
- Evaluate how easy it is to explain the questions. Does he/she get the questions? Does he/she follow-up to get a better picture?
- Evaluate how easy it is for you to understand the responses.

To test the bigger picture:

- Ask the candidate to describe the business proposition of his/her last job.
- Why was his/her job important to the organization?

- What is the impact of him/her leaving the job?
- Ask him/her to describe a situation where the big picture understanding helped him/her do a better job.

To test for relationships:

- Ask the candidate to identify a colleague that he/she holds in high regard. Ask him/her to describe why he/she has such high regard for that person.
- Ask him/her to talk about his/her manager and management in general.

To test for ethics and integrity:

- Ask 'what will you do...' if you were in a situation where ethics may be tested.
- Ask his/her feelings towards his last organization.

Managers can work with their HR department to formulate a set of questions that can test for softer skills. Caution is required so that such questions don't overstep personal boundaries.

Past work is important

Although we hire for the potential to deliver in the future, past experience is a significant pointer to future performance and to the refinement of key skills. Remember when you first learnt cycling, every pedal push was accompanied by anxiousness of falling or bumping into someone. As you did more of it, you got more confidence. However, the first time you went onto the main road, in the middle of high traffic, the same anxiousness returned. After a few times of being in high traffic, you could navigate with ease.

This is a result of conditioning. A fast oncoming car doesn't make you nervous because you have the confidence that you will cross the road before any contact happens. The mind is conditioned to make the right responses, and you have better decision making in that situation.

The biggest impact of prior work experience in similar situations is the conditioning it gives you. It makes a person more confident, reduces anxiety, and leads to better decision-making.

When testing for past work, don't just focus on past technical work but also situations, processes, and systems that the person worked in.

Using behavioral interviews

Behavioral interviews are becoming increasingly popular in the industry, especially at senior levels. In traditional interviews, we typically present a scenario: what will you do if you have a very complex technical problem to solve? You may even provide a hypothetical situation, like you published a design document and received very poor feedback from the chief architect and some others. What would you do?

The candidate will typically explain the approach to solving this problem, such as "I would analyze the feedback in detail with my team members first. We would analyze the comments and create a list of further questions and some alternative solutions where required. Then set up a meeting with the chief architect and discuss in detail".

The idea behind this question would be to understand the way a candidate approaches a certain situation at work.

In a behavioral interviewing model, the same goal will be achieved differently. The interviewer may ask, "Describe a situation where your technical design/decisions were not well received. How did you handle the feedback? What did you do?"

The candidate is supposed to dig out one significant incident that fell into this category, and describe what happened back then. A specific real example is expected in this case. The candidate may start with, "This was 2 years ago when we started the project 'Delta X'…".

The idea behind behavioral interviews is that past performance is an indicator of future performance. Since these are supposed to be real examples, a candidate having gone through these critical situations will probably be able to do better than someone who hasn't. For example, if the candidate says, "I have never had my design being challenged by anybody in the organization, not even the chief architect". This may mean that the candidate is either gullible or that the candidate has not worked on projects that a chief architect may be interested in. Sometimes the candidate may pick a situation that isn't quite as complex as interviewers may expect, and that may also be a warning sign of exposure to complex contentious issues.

Organizations can define the required competencies or behaviors for a given job position, and devise behavioral interview questions around that. For example, if "conflict resolution" is something that you value for a position, some of the questions could be as follows:

- Describe a situation where you disagreed with your direct manager. How did the disagreement get resolved?

- Describe a situation where your key team member was in conflict with someone outside your direct team. What was the conflict about? How did you resolve it?

While behavioral interviews work great, the technique also suffers from obvious flaws such as the following:

- Candidates may find it difficult to articulate the problem and the context. Hence candidates who are good storytellers may stand a better chance of acing the interview. Especially with technical candidates, communication isn't always the top skill.

- Since hindsight is 20-20, candidates may have ignored some situations in the past, believing them to be simpler problems solved.

- Interviewers may find it hard to capture the context in which a certain problem occurred and may not be able to appreciate the complexity.

- Each response can be long, since each response requires some context setting and descriptions of problems, possible solutions, and outcomes.

- Past performance is not the only indicator of future performance. Just because someone hasn't been through a situation doesn't mean they can't handle that situation in future.

Overall, behavioral interviews are being heavily used today in the knowledge industry, especially at senior levels where soft skills like collaboration and communication are as important as the technical skills.

Feedback recording

This is another rather neglected area in the hiring processes. The interview feedback is often verbal and even when it is written down, it is unstructured with short sentences like the following:

- C programming – good
- Problem solving – average
- Good communication

Often interviewers talk to each other and exchange the details verbally, but those details aren't often captured on paper. This makes it difficult to recall the interview if you need to do so at a later stage. Most of the time, managers like to interview three or four candidates and take their best pick among them. Unfortunately, a couple of weeks later the interviewer has only a vague impression of the interview and the feedback sheet doesn't provide enough information.

A simple format can be developed based on the requirements of the position. The template may provide a list of dimensions that could be tested, and a rating scale from 1 to 5 or 1 to 10. Besides, it also needs to have space for unstructured comments.

Any mandatory requirements can also be added to the template, for example, "Did you inform the candidate about the mandatory background check required?"

Here's a very simple template sample:

Criterion	Rating (1-10)	Comments
Programming in C		
Data structures		
MVC architecture		
Data structures		
Understanding of past work		
Communication		

A format forces structured thinking and will help in adding structure to the process without having to explain it. As a simple measure, the feedback sheets, along with worksheets used by the candidate, can be scanned and uploaded into a system.

A rating system, in general, will have the issue of subjectivity. Different people will rate the same response differently. There aren't many surefire ways of getting around it, but simple things may help:

- If the hiring manager knows the interviewer well, he may understand the interviewers style and inclination and can normalize the feedback from different people.

- Many times, people from different teams may be asked to interview, and the manager may not have a good idea of the style of interviewing. The hiring manager should spend some time with the interviewer before the interview and explain the expectations from the candidate. The hiring manager can also discuss with other hiring managers who may have used this interviewer's services earlier to get an idea of his/her rating style.

- It will always help, if the hiring manager looks for details of the interview – a quick two minute phone call with an interviewer to understand the kind of questions asked and how the candidate responded.

Regardless of its subjectivity, a rating system is still the best available way to capture feedback.

Hiring decision

Once the interviews are over, the manager has to make a decision. Is the guy in or not? While you collect feedback from all the interviewers, the hiring manager holds the power to make the final call.

If you have done your pre-screening well, it's unlikely that the candidate is a complete misfit. What you are most likely to get are the impressions from different interviewers, and some of the feedback comments might look like the following:

- Good with Java servlets and JSPs – 4 on 5 but hasn't worked on EJBs
- Can explain the projects in detail but missing the larger picture
- Starts well but stumbles when it gets to details
- Could solve problem 'X' but didn't even get half way with problem 'Y'

The empirical ratings on various subjects will give you good guidance on what interviewers think in more absolute terms. However, the ratings may also have some low scores and some high scores.

Here's how to analyze the feedback:

- Focus on the core skills first: For every job function, there are a set of core skills. For example, if you are hiring someone for a programmer position, then coding proficiency will be a core skill. If you are hiring someone to be a web designer, then expertise with web designing tools will be a core skill. List out the candidates' performance in the core skills. It's best to not make the core skills definition too narrow, so instead of EJB coding, it can be just Java coding proficiency.

- Identify the skills gap: Analyze the feedback and carefully read through the comments from interviewers to list out the gaps in skills and competencies. For example, a comment that says, "Can explain the projects in detail but is missing the larger picture", points to a gap in the desired set of skills. Another example would be, "Good with Java servlets and JSPs – 4 on 5 but hasn't worked on EJBs", which points to a technical gap.

- List out the non-technical aspects such as communication, exposure to working in a distributed team, working in customer production environments, and so on.

- List out the softer aspects that stand out: It's not easy and measurable, but it's a key aspect of a hiring decision. Was the candidate too nervous? Was the candidate forthcoming? Look for comments like 'looks like a smart guy' and 'seems confused about many things'.

- Look at the reasons for leaving the last few jobs, is there a recurring theme? Look for statements like "I did not want to work client server " or "I desperately wanted to learn Java but my manager kept refusing to send me for training" or "It did not seem like there was a future for that product".

- Take a shot at listing out a candidate's "attitude" based on feedback and your interview of the candidate.

  ° Attitude towards learning

  ° Is the candidate open to new learning?

  ° How does the candidate pick up new technology? By asking for formal training or by starting with an Internet tutorial?

  ° What has the candidate learnt in the last one year that may or may not be part of his job?

- What were the candidate's feelings towards his previous company, job, peers, and manager?

  ° Look for statements like, "I was working very hard, much harder than everyone else…"

  ° "Every time I went with a good idea, my manager turned me down…"

  ° "Even after working in that organization for 5 years, I was not given my due…"

- Does the candidate defend everything that he said?

  ° Is there defensiveness and a resistant attitude?

Finally, here are some rules you can apply to arrive at a decision:

- No compromise on key core skills. If a candidate does not match the minimum criteria for core skills, it's better not to hire. However, be sure you have not defined core skills too narrowly.

- Look at gaps in core skills and how large that gap is. Ask yourself: can this gap be filled up later as the job progresses? Can another function fill in for this gap, till it gets better?

- Look at the gaps in skills and evaluate if these gaps are really important or not. Ask yourself: can we live without this? Can the candidate be an effective contributor even without this skill?

- Analyze the softer aspects and attitude:
    ◦ Does the candidate seem confident of his abilities?
    ◦ Does the candidate show a positive attitude?
    ◦ Does the candidate show respect towards his peers and the organization?

Finally, all this data is for making a decision. Listen to your gut feel and make one.

Compensation

Regardless of why someone is looking for a new job, compensation will be an important factor. It is one measure that can be applied across all organizations and all industries. Applying basic economics, a job seeker would like to maximize the compensation while an organization would like to minimize compensation. However, the incentive to minimize compensation is reduced, if lower compensation leads to lower productivity and higher attrition. Cost of attrition is high. Hence, to minimize the cost of attrition, an organization would need to increase the compensation beyond the minimum. Of course, the desired quality of work force must be ensured.

Key questions are as follows:

- Should you pay based on the compensation of a similar profile in the team?
- Should you pay based on market data?
- Should you pay 20 percent on top of the current compensation?
- Should you negotiate?

Let's examine the problems and dilemmas of each one given a scenario:

Murali is in the process of expanding his team and has finalized on a candidate; Raman has four years of experience, a CS degree from a good college, has relevant experience, and did quite well in the interviews. Now Murali has to make an offer to the candidate; let's look at Murali's options.

Option 1: compensation on par with a team member with similar profile

Murali feels this is the right approach, so people with similar capabilities are paid the same. However, the existing team member, Aditi, is productive right now and has been working with the team for the last three years. Murali feels Aditi should be paid a little higher than Raman as her contributions are higher and she should be rewarded for loyalty.

The problem with this approach is that the offered salary may not match Raman's expectations. He is already in the job market, and may have seen better offers for his 'friends' (in India, almost every candidate has a friend who he would have consulted with to set his salary expectation). Offering him a salary that is much less than what he is expecting may lead Raman to reject the offer.

Also, Aditi has her own career graph, and maybe her salary is 'compressed' (that is, lower than market). Murali will end up penalizing Raman for no fault of his, if he sets Raman's salary based on Aditi's salary.

However, Murali fears that Aditi may come to know Raman's salary and then she may feel she is being paid unfairly, given all the effort from her.

Option 2: new compensation = previous compensation + 20%

Another approach Murali can take is to set Raman's salary based on what Raman was earning earlier, that is, Raman's current salary plus a 20 percent jump on it. This way, Raman gets a jump in compensation and the organization doesn't overspend on salary.

Murali is worried that this puts Raman in a lower end of the salary range at the position they are hiring him for. He also knows that Raman will not be eligible for a salary increment this year and it may be more than sixteen months before Raman gets a hike. Murali worries that he may have another salary issue by next year if he hires Raman at current plus 20 percent.

Also, Raman is expecting a 40 percent hike, so it's possible that Raman may reject the offer.

Option 3: compensation based on market data

Murali wonders if Raman's salary should be based on what he can get in the market. After all, that's what the market economy runs on. Raman will join where he can get the best compensation for what he brings to the table.

Murali checks with the HR manager and gets the market numbers available. He wonders how the data is arrived at and asks the HR manager. The HR manager tells him that the data comes from one of the HR consulting organization that maintains a database that is updated by member organizations.

Murali is even more confused looking at the market data. The range is very broad, the companies participating don't exactly overlap with what Murali's organization does, and he feels it's not justified to set Raman's salary by market data while rest of the people in the team are not really paid based on market data.

Option 4: compensation by negotiation

Murali also wonders if he should enter into a negotiation process with the candidate, so Murali can possibly start at the lower end of the salary range and then negotiate with the candidate to arrive at a mutual agreement. This way the organization doesn't pay more than it needs to, in order to get the guy and the candidate gets what he asked for eventually. This also fits well with market economy principles.

Personally, Murali doesn't like the negotiation as the process rewards candidates for their negotiating skills and not on job essential technical skills, but it also depends on the urgency of filling the position.

Truth about compensation

Some universal truths about compensation that every manager should understand are as follows:

- New hire compensation will usually be higher than the current employees at that skill and experience level. It is very common to have a new hire at a higher salary than his/her peers at the same level. Over the next salary revision, this gap will become shorter. Also, existing employees may also be compensated by other forms, like stock options, additional leave benefits, and bonuses.

- Usual yearly salary revision percentages will be less than the usual hike percentage when switching jobs. This implies that in order to get a bigger jump people will necessarily need to switch jobs. Hence bigger compensation is one of the key drivers of a job switch.

- It is NOT possible to provide large percentage hikes to all existing employees to bring them on par with the market ranges. Since the number of people to be considered is usually very high, the cost of such a hike is very prohibitive. The company is usually better off letting salary-driven attrition happen and finding replacements at market salary.

- Compensation is confidential. In general, nobody besides the candidate and the hiring manager should know the compensation being offered. However, in India, this may not hold true. Candidates (especially in early stages of their career) are likely to talk about their compensation with their friends and family.

  - Hiring managers need to very firmly indicate that compensation is a confidential subject and that the organization does not take it lightly when this confidentiality is breached.

- However high the compensation may be, it has only so much effect on productivity and retention. However, an inadequate compensation (highly compressed) situation will lead to loss of productivity and attrition despite other good factors.

What is the answer?

Every business has a different model to decide the salary when hiring from the market. Any one of the previous options or a combination thereof may be applied and may work best in the given scenario. Hence, managers need to first understand the usual policies that are applied. If they don't necessarily agree with the compensation policy in this regard, it needs to be discussed as a separate thread. In any case, it's best to stick with the usual policies until a new system can be put in place. Managers also need to find the discretion/flexibility that they have when making compensation decisions, so they don't just follow the book, but can also apply their judgment. Policies and books can't capture the sensitivities of the market and usually allow some avenues of flexibility.

Here is an example of a very objective model of compensation setting that combines some of the previous options:

- Candidate interview results in a rating of technical strengths
- Candidate experience is considered and rated on a scale
  - Most relevant experience – high rating
  - Partially relevant experience – a percentage of the highest possible rating
- Rating for any other criterion can be added

- A final rating arrived at using all of the previous points
- A mathematical formula can be applied to arrive at the final compensation number
- The hiring manager may have room for some adjustment, based on the candidate's expectations or any other consideration
- If there is urgency to hire, more flexibility in compensation may be required
- Similarly, if the position requires some unique skills, once again the usual compensation rules may not work and a higher compensation may be required

Compensation policies differ widely from one organization to another. Compensation is one of the biggest cash outflows for the company in the knowledge industry and organizations must ensure that compensation policies are clear to every manager.

Closing the hiring process

The ideal result of the hiring process is an offer being made to a candidate or a rejection. In a positive result, the hiring manager and the organization does a good job of reaching out to the candidate and keeping him/her informed. However, in the case of a rejection, it is unfortunate that a large number of people get no clear response or any response whatsoever from the organization they were interviewed at.

Also, some organizations have a rather long process of interviewing. It may take several weeks before the entire process is completed. At times during the process, a candidate is often left wondering where he/she stands. A candidate in such a situation may continue to interview in the market and with the confidence of already having a job offer, may actually be able to get a better offer. Managers need to keep the candidate engaged and warmed up during this time.

A good practice for hiring managers and their supporting recruitment organizations is to treat the candidate the way they themselves would like to be treated. Treat everybody with respect, regardless of the interview result and keep them informed of what's happening. Besides, this is a small world, and you may wish to hire the same guy again, or worse, you may find yourself being interviewed by the same person.

Campus hiring

In India, Campus hiring is one of the most significant hiring activities for a company in the Software/IT/BPO sector. Here's a snippet from Indian IT services bellwether Infosys Technologies, conference call:

From 2009-2010 Q3 Results:

(Reference: `http://www.infosys.com/investors/reports-filings/quarterly-results/2009-2010/Q3/Documents/transcripts/evening-call.pdf`)

"…We are also in the campus doing campus recruitment. Our plan is to give 15,000 offers. So far we have given 9000 offers."

From 2010-2011 Q4 Results:

Reference: `http://www.infosys.com/investors/reports-filings/quarterly-results/2010-2011/Q4/Documents/transcripts/evening-call.pdf`

"…We are planning to hire 45,000 people next year, 6500 in Q1. Our lateral hiring is about 20-30 percent of that approximately".

Campus hiring is essential for some of the companies to sustain the business model. India Inc. relies on a good supply of talent from the campuses every year and most top organizations in India have a significant infrastructure to hire and train freshers.

Here are some of the key aspects of campus hiring.

There is a shortage

While there are a very large number of colleges that offer education, sadly the industry preparedness of the young graduates leaves much to be desired. A few top' colleges in the country and the state end up being the target of all campus hiring.

This has resulted in a shortage situation, where each hiring company wishes to be at the campus, as early as possible so they can attract the best of the students from that college.

Campus day 1

Since a large number of companies visit a campus and as early as possible, the campus placement teams typically set a short window within the academic year to invite companies to the campus.

In most campuses, students decide which companies should show up in which order. Based on student voting and discretion of placement officer, companies are invited to the campus on day 1, day 2, and so on. Multiple companies can be present at the campus on each day. Some campuses have a day zero now for the companies that are very attractive to the students.

The most important goal of the placement office is to get 100 percent placement, hence companies offering more positions may get a better slot on the hiring calendar.

Only one offer

Campus placement officers typically allow only one job offer per candidate. Once a student gets an offer from a company, he is not allowed to apply to any other company visiting the campus.

This ensures that the same top students don't hog the large number of jobs and other students get the same opportunity. It also ensures that companies will see less of attrition, since a candidate can eventually join only one company.

Some colleges allow students to appear for a second job, if the compensation being offered is much higher than usual. This second chance is called the **dream job offer**.

Compensation rules

The biggest attraction for the students is the compensation being offered. Branding of a company is very important too, but since branding gets confusing with several companies claiming to be the 'best employer' and 'technically challenging work', ultimately compensation becomes the top criterion for the students.

Some companies create confusion around compensation by offering a range in compensation, that is, students will be offered a compensation package between Rs 5 Lakhs (five hundred thousand rupees) to Rs 8 Lakhs. This creates a possibility of a compensation of Rs 8 Lakhs that may or may not be offered. This may work for a year or two, but soon enough the students figure out the average number being offered.

Elimination process followed by selection process

Some companies are popular at the campus due to high compensation or branding or opening up the hiring for a large number of branches. There may be hundreds of students who are interested. However, companies have only a day or day and a half to complete the entire process.

Hence the process becomes a process of elimination first, before it becomes a process of selection. Different strategies can be followed for elimination:

- Only selected branches are allowed; for example, only computer science and telecom engineering students may be allowed
- GPA cutoff
- Written test – typically aptitude (including mathematical aptitude, cognitive ability, reasoning, and more) and in some cases, a programming test may be conducted

This narrows down the field to a certain size. After this the selection process starts, which typically includes in-person interviews.

Interviewing on campus

The interviewing on campus needs to be thought through a little different than lateral hiring. Students have only basic skills and theoretical knowledge and the focus of interviews needs to be on applicability of the knowledge and understanding of the basics.

Interviewers sometimes get lost on what to test with candidates who have only theory to talk about. I have seen interviewers ask obscure questions to test theory understanding of the student, but in reality they are not prepared for the answer and possibly can't ask more than a few questions that they remember from their theory days. Here's an example taken from a real situation:

Interviewer: "How does the ….. happen in a single phase induction motor when ….. "

Student: "Sir, do you mean…"

Interviewer: (Now confused, since he can't understand the student's question…)

OR

Interviewer: "How does the ….. happen in a single phase induction motor when ….. "

Student: (after a little pause) "Sir, we did this paper in second year. I can't really remember."

Interviewer: (Now gloating) "What do you mean…I did this 15 years back, and I can still remember it."

Unfortunately, this was an interview for a programming position. Even if the student could provide a good answer that the interviewer accepted, it does not establish if the same student would be able to do well in programming. There's little point in testing the student's knowledge on this subject in the interviews as you can just as well look at the marks in that paper and get a better measurement.

Campus hiring – allocations

Campus hiring is typically done for a common pool, that is, it's not known which exact project the candidate will work on. The final allocation to a project may happen much later.

Usually, each company will have its own model of allocation and allocation to a project may happen months after joining. In the interim, the students may spend time in training.

Pre-join attrition

Campus hiring happens when the student is in the middle of the final academic year or even earlier. There is a 6-10 month time period by when the student will join a company they got selected for at the campus. Things can change during this time period. A student may decide to go for higher studies or may get another offer.

A fairly high percentage of attrition happens even before the student joins and this is called **pre-join attrition**. Organizations need to have a counter strategy in place to handle pre-join attrition. This may involve hiring more in anticipation or a special drive off-campus to invite students who have been placed in other companies.

Campus hires boot camp

Once on board, campus hires spend a good amount of time learning relevant job skills. Unfortunately, the education system in India has not seen the introduction of newer courses that are more relevant to the industry. Hence, every company spends a significant amount of time and resources on upgrading the knowledge and skills of campus hires. Some have a rather elaborate setup of a training center that can accommodate hundreds of students and impart training to make them job-ready.

Overall, campus hiring policy of these large IT Services and BPO companies has added to the uplift of the entire society. The education sector, obviously, got a boost because of high demand for engineering and management courses. Parents were ready to pay higher fees and other charges, which lead to larger fund availability for the educational institutes, and attracted more investment in the sector. A larger number of colleges increased competition among colleges and lead to better infrastructure. The society at large saw the immediate returns of better paying jobs and added to the desire for engineering seats at good colleges that could offer placement at a well-known company.

Campus hiring has truly been wonderful for India Inc. and Indians. It can only get better as focus on quality education increases, since capacity has been built up already.

Summary

Hiring continues to be on the agenda for every manager today. Every manager needs to understand that hiring is a part of the larger process of team building. In order to truly get the returns of the hiring process, managers need to continue their investment into team building and helping a new hire become successful in the organization. Managing performance is the next goal. In the next chapter, we'll discuss performance evaluation process in detail.

As of this writing, the Indian knowledge industry continues to grow at a healthy rate, keeping the hiring managers busy. Besides, there is significant new hiring that needs to be done due to higher rates of attrition. We will discuss how to manage attrition in *Chapter 9, Attrition*.

8
Performance Evaluation

In India, the Republic Day parade is quite a spectacle. It is a show of India's mighty military strength as well as its diverse culture. Every Republic Day parade has one contingent that's very different from all the others, that is, the kids who are awarded the 'bravery award'. A group of kids sitting on top of an elephant, some waving enthusiastically, and others seeming a little lost looking at the hoopla around them.

Someone saved many other kids from drowning in a river, someone fought a leopard to save another child. Each story is inspiring and makes us proud to be Indians. Each one of them went through a very extraordinary situation and performed an extraordinary act of bravery. One day the kid was like any other kid in a group of kids who played together every day, but now this kid stands out.

It takes an extraordinary situation to exist for an extraordinary performance to be demonstrated.

So when we expect our team to produce a 'top rating', we must also provide them with an opportunity that demands a performance higher than usual. It must have that extra level of difficulty in terms of one or more of the factors such as the technical challenge, tough market conditions, difficult collaborative scenario, or tough customers to manage, and so on. If no such opportunity exists, then consequently the employee should not expect to get the top rating.

Coming back to the brave kid's story, it's difficult to imagine how an individual kid would be picked out. Nowadays it's usually the media, perhaps local media, which would broadcast it and even go deeper into the details and perhaps the story caught the fancy of some government official or a politician, who submitted the application for a bravery award. This brings us to another key aspect: visibility.

Performance should be identifiable in order to be rated high, and it should be visible to the right people.

Among the many stories of bravery, there are always a couple of incidents where a kid would have saved another kid from drowning. The feat is usually very remarkable and makes us proud. Now imagine if the kid had pulled out a suitcase from a raging river, instead of a drowning kid! The level of difficulty may be higher, and the suitcase may be very important to this kid, but it simply would not qualify.

Performance should be applicable to something of value to the organization, in order for it to qualify for a top performance.

Let's understand how we define performance.

Understanding performance

Performance is work done that meets a certain set of criteria. So every 'good performance' must have 'work done' plus meeting or exceeding other criteria about the work done. If either the work is not done or other criteria are not met, it would be hard to consider it as good performance.

Depending on the task, there are different levels of expectation. Consider this scenario: the task is to deliver a package from point A to point B.

The work will be considered "done" if the package is delivered to point B.

Basic expectation: the package is not broken and it's delivered in the promised time. If it's a next-day delivery, it should be the next day.

Basic plus expectation: the package is delivered in much shorter time than expected. An intimation of delivery is made to the sender.

Enhanced expectation: the package is delivered in a much shorter time. An intimation of delivery is made to the sender. The courier person is really nice.

Blow away expectation: all of the previous expectations plus the package are delivered despite a riot in the city and the contents of the package were very critical to the receiver.

Now consider another aspect:

Can the courier guy deliver on basic expectation?

Yes. He knows what he has signed up for. He knows it's a next day delivery. He knows that anybody would expect careful handling of the package.

Can the courier guy deliver on basic plus expectation?

If he really wants to, he can push himself to deliver in the fastest possible time.

Can the courier guy deliver on enhanced expectation?

If he really wants to, he can be a nice personable guy and treat his customers very well. He can ensure a personal call or SMS to the sender is made after a stellar delivery time is achieved. But why should he really do so?

Can the courier guy deliver on blown away expectation?

No. He's not going to create a riot in the city and neither does he know how important the contents are to the receiver and sender.

Looking at the other side, what would cause the performance to be poor?

Any delay beyond the promised delivery time:

- Damaged contents delivered
- Rude delivery guy
- No response or intimation to sender on delivery

Some key aspects are well illustrated by the previous example:

- Performance always includes the completion of the primary task
- Performance includes the quality of work being performed
- The performer must understand the criteria for completion and quality
- Higher performance depends on the person who is performing the task
- Higher performance requires some extra work to be done
- Highest performance depends on the opportunity available
- Higher performance perception depends on how important the task is
- It's easier to have poor performance than good performance

The three most important aspects about performance are understanding expectations, opportunity for stellar performance, and perception of performance.

Now that we understand performance, let's look at the performance evaluation process.

Purpose of performance evaluation

Performance evaluation is an important process for the employees and the organization. It plays a central role in talent management within an enterprise. Every organization needs to have systems in place to identify the best and the worst talent within the organization, and then create rewards, recognition, and development systems around the same.

Let's now enumerate some of the key objectives.

Reviewing and reflecting

In general, everybody is loaded with enough work that one moves from one task to another. In most cases, the next task starts even before the current one is completed. This provides little time to review what went well and what did not.

The performance review process forces the step back from the daily priorities, so employees and managers can review and reflect on the past year's performance.

Feedback

One important aspect of the performance review is the feedback that a manager can provide to the team member, as well as feedback that a team member will provide to the manager. Also, this feedback will have elements of both positive and negative feedback, which allows people to take a larger view of things and makes it easy to accept the feedback.

Alignment

Performance review also serves as a time to align the employee goals and the organization goals. It's a powerful tool to set expectations and set the stage for the coming year for employees and the organization to achieve their goals. Employees get to discuss their aspirations, such as learning a new technology or growing into a different role and also understand the opportunities available to learn that new technology or move into another role.

Looking ahead

The performance evaluation process allows an employee and his manager to look ahead to what's coming up. This is not a detailed planning session for next year's tasks, but a high level look to what's coming up for the next year and the success criteria for the same. In today's dynamic world, it is almost a given that plans for the year will change.

Personal development and career planning

Performance evaluation time is perhaps the best opportunity to discuss an employee's personal development and career planning. All other aspects such as a review of last year, discussion of successes and failures, factors that led to each one, and so on, are being discussed anyway. This creates the ideal condition to discover the development needs and perhaps also discover the best-fit tasks for an individual.

Tracking progress over the years

Performance evaluation becomes part of the employee's HR record and the default way to track progress of an employee over the years. This is the only reliable account of an employee's performance and will be referred to for various reasons.

Positive side effects

Performance appraisal forces managers and team members to have a one-on-one and look through the details. It forces introspection and creates an opportunity for employee-focussed discussion. This is motivating for employees and beneficial for the overall health of the organization.

Used in reward calculations

Performance rating, which is an end result of the process, has a relationship with the rewards that flow to an employee. In some organizations, it serves as 'inclusion factor'; for example, only employees rated 7 and above are eligible for a bonus. In some organizations, the rating may have a direct impact on the 'quantum' of the reward; for example, an employee rated 'N' and in grade 'Y' will receive a bonus amount of 'X'.

Some organizations may also look at historic ratings for promotions at key positions. If there are inconsistencies in ratings, that would be a cause to investigate further.

Used in layoffs

Performance ratings, current and historic, may play a crucial role when an organization needs to let go of people. Layoffs are very complex and have many different aspects than just performance ratings; however, the ratings may also have a role to play.

Organizational improvements

Performance evaluation data can also be used to measure the effectiveness of organizational systems. For example, if performance ratings of folks hired from campuses are lower than expected, the processes for campus hiring may need a review, or the training provided to the new hires may need to be reviewed for effectiveness.

Similarly, performance ratings can also be used to evaluate if employees recently promoted are able to excel at their new role and responsibilities. If not, the process and criterion of promotions may need to be reviewed.

New policies may also need to be formed to prevent further hiring or promotion mistakes.

Performance evaluation process

The performance evaluation process is fairly standard across most organizations. Also, it has not changed much over the last decade and a half. Let's look at some key aspects of the process itself.

Appraisal form

The appraisal form is the primary artifact used in the performance evaluation process. Most of the process steps will revolve around filling out a section of this document. The document is designed such that it acts as the guide for the process and adds consistency to it.

An appraisal form is designed for a particular job definition or a job code; for example, the form used for a software engineer would be different for a development manager or a product manager or a technical support engineer. A single form usually applies to multiple job functions, which may be closely related (perhaps because the HR folks don't want to spend too much time developing one that is unique to a job function).

An appraisal form has a set format with some fixed and some open-ended sections. We'll now look at the typical sections of an appraisal form.

Competencies

This section lists out the typical competencies and behaviors expected from an employee in that particular job function. The competencies section is objective type and with a rating scale of 1 to 5 and possibly the 'not applicable' option.

Since the same form applies to multiple related job functions and does not take experience into account, many items may not be applicable.

Typical competencies are problem solving, results orientation, continuous learning, customer orientation, and honesty.

Typically, there are a couple of lines of explanation for each competency.
For example:

Problem solving explores various ideas and alternatives, contacts relevant sources to resolve the problems.

Goals from last year

The goals from last year are the objectives that the individual was assigned as part of last year's goal setting process. Some of the set objectives may be invalid due to various changes such as a project ending too soon. Also, some new objectives will need to be added to reflect the work done in the past year.

Some organizations also add 'development objectives', like 'Java 7 Certification' as part of the yearly objectives.

These goals are typically rated on a set scale, usually of 1-5. The rating here is completely subjective as there's no standardization.

Open-ended questions

Most appraisal forms have a few open-ended questions such as the following:

- List the key accomplishments of the last performance year
- What were the top pain points of last year?
- What were the most successful customer initiatives? What were your contributions to them?

Employees get to write free form responses and capture key accomplishments and issues from the past year.

Key dimensions

Some organizations define some umbrella dimensions to be evaluated. These typically combine demonstration of competencies and achievements on common grounds. For example, build high performance teams. This dimension encompasses a lot of different achievements, such as hiring, retention, delivery, collaboration, and so on.

Development plan

Part of the appraisal is to look forward to the coming year and come up with a plan for skills advancement. Some of these would be based on feedback from the competencies section; for example, someone who is rated average or below in the communication competency should spend some time taking trainings for the same.

Other feedback from the manager or employee's own career goals can also result in some actionable items in the development plan.

Goal setting for the coming year

A key part of the appraisal is to set the objectives for the next year. The manager drives these based on the project plans for the coming year. The often-used model for setting goals is to define them as **S.M.A.R.T**. goals. These are:

Specific: A goal should be specific and well understood by manager and employee.

Measurable: The completion criteria and the progress on the goal should be measurable. This is one of the biggest problems with most of the goals being set.

Achievable: A goal should be achievable by the employee. The tools required and other supporting ecosystem must exist.

Relevant: The goal should be relevant to the organization and to the individual. An irrelevant goal will hardly be attempted, given all the priorities.

Time-Bound: Goals need to be achieved in a given time frame. In general, anything that does not give a timeline tends to get pushed forever.

Final/overall rating

Finally, an overall rating is set for the employee. This rating is supposed to summarize the overall performance considering all the aspects mentioned in the appraisal form. After all is said and done, this is the most important rating, as it'll be the only one that may be referred to later on for any purpose whatsoever.

Usual appraisal models

In HR theory, there are many models for performance appraisals; many of them are irrelevant to the knowledge industry. Let's look at some that are often used today.

Employee – manager review

The typical evaluation process involves only two parties: the employee being evaluated and his direct manager.

Additional external reviewers

In some cases, organizations recommend additional reviewers to be added to the appraisal process. This is most relevant in India where a matrix structure exists. A matrix structure has multiple lines of reporting, a technical line and one around functional lines. The primary responsibility may still lie with the direct local manager, while the dotted-line manager provides the evaluation on certain relevant lines only.

Additional peer reviews

Some organizations encourage peer reviews to be included in the performance appraisal process. The peer reviews may be done more frequently and can be less structured. The idea is to get feedback from the peer that may help an individual tune better with the people he works with, while having no direct control over them. Usually, only a small set of questions are asked, so it takes only 15-30 minutes to complete the review.

360 degree reviews

These are very popular today and are usually done in addition to the regular appraisal process. A 360-degree evaluation includes the following reviewers:

- Direct manager
- Dotted line manager or other superiors
- Team members – direct
- Team members – beyond directs
- Peers – from different teams that one frequently works with
- In certain roles, including feedback from customers, partners, and so on

A 360-degree review can be done more frequently and is generally very effective in getting feedback from various aspects. Typically, 360-degree reviews are done online and there are various agencies that provide services to design and conduct 360-degree feedback.

The usual once-a-year appraisal process steps

The appraisal process is pretty much the same in most organizations. Here's the basic structure of the process:

	Steps	Description
1	Self evaluation	Self evaluation is an important step in the process and allows an employee to express his/her understanding of his/her own performance.
2	Manager review and rating	Manager gets to review employee impressions and attach his/her ratings and impressions of the employee's performance.
3	One-on-one review meeting	A meeting to discuss an overview and specific items, especially those where a gap exists between manager rating and employee self rating.
4	Feedback	Any positive and negative feedback and development plan for the employee should emerge out of the process.
5	Goal setting	Goals for the next year set. Ideally, this should drive the next year's performance. However, in today's fast changing industry, things change too frequently and hence yearly goal setting is not completely effective.

The entire process may take two to six weeks to complete.

Using the bell curve in performance evaluation

Many organizations prefer to fit the performance ratings distribution into a bell curve.

What's a bell curve?

The **bell curve** represents the normal distribution in statistics. Performance ratings fitted into a bell curve looks as follows:

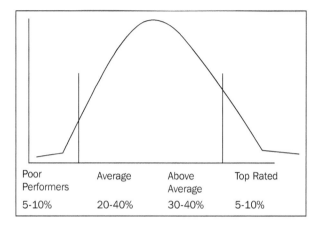

The normal distribution implies that when considering a large number of data points, most values will tend towards the average and a small percentage of very high and very low numbers. For example, if you conduct a poll of people to capture their physical fitness, you might find a large number of people will be averagely fit, while some will be very fit, and some will be very unfit.

It's quite commonly used in statistics and also makes good common sense. After all, most people in a large sample should be closer to average, and as you move away from the average, the number of people in that category should reduce.

Many organizations mandate that the ratings awarded to people should fit into a bell curve, that is:

- A small percentage, say 5-10 percent should be treated as top performers. On a scale of 1-5, these would be rated 5.

- A significant percentage, say 30-40 percent, to be rated 'above average'. On a scale of 1-5, these would be rated 4.

- A significant percentage, say 30-40 percent, to be rated 'average'. On a scale of 1-5, these would be rated 3.

- A 5-10 percent may be rated below average, that is, rated 1 or 2.

The percentages mentioned can vary as the organization designs the system, and the bell curve shape will change to become leaner or fatter in the middle.

The folks at the highest rating will get the best rewards and will be expected to grow faster in the organization. The folks who fall in the bottom 5-10 percent may not survive the year. New hires will be brought in, and hopefully can deliver at a higher level.

The bell curve fitment forces managers to consider a strong differentiation in performance and not overload performance evaluation towards higher ratings. It also forces managers to identify those who are not able to keep up with the rest of the team. Eventually, as better performers survive and are rewarded, the overall level of performance in the team will go up.

The bell curve model works well in situations where there is a sizeable population that can be evaluated on similar parameters and is assigned comparative work. It will not work when there are small teams of five people working on projects of a different nature. While the basic principles of the bell curve should still be applicable, that is, a majority of people should be in the middle, it's possible that there aren't any poor performers who deserve to go. Replacement has its costs too and blindly following the bell curve model may not help.

Bell curve fitment may also lead to a different problem, where a person may be rated average in a high-performance team, while the same person may get a much higher rating in a somewhat lower-performing team. In some cases, this situation will lead to a healthy attrition where an employee can move to a different team if he views his prospects to be better.

The bell curve is a good guideline for all to follow, and when applied at a macro level, it'll help improve the overall performance of the organization.

Problems with the performance appraisal process

The appraisal process is full of problems and sadly most of these problems are repeated every year. These problems never go away, since performance appraisal is seen as a once a year activity, and hence the problems are forgotten before they are solved.

Let's look at some typical problems and possible ways to get around them.

It has become an event

The performance evaluation has become more of an event than a regular activity. For most organizations, it happens only once a year, hence feedback can get delayed and problems may remain hidden for a long time.

In a more ideal world, performance appraisal needs to be a continuous activity. It should get attached to every delivery. For any project that takes about 3 months, employees should be given feedback. For non-project related work, evaluation should be done every 3 months.

Once the duration is reduced, the time it takes to evaluate will also reduce and a better alignment should result from the activity.

Always done in a hurry

Since performance appraisal is essentially a look back and does not have an impact on the most immediate deliverable, it'll always be pushed over current work. It's a classic battle between the urgent and the important, where the urgent always has a priority. Besides the fact that filling out the appraisal form isn't really exciting.

Performance appraisals aren't planned like a usual project. Most employees or managers don't allocate enough time for them. There are delays at every step. Employees fill out the self-evaluation a day before the extended last date. Since most of the self-evaluation comes at the same time, managers are not able to plan and give each one enough time. Managers don't plan one-on-ones and end up calling people at random to complete the process.

Only when the appraisal process is linked to incentives and employees see it having an immediate difference will there be an attempt to give it priority.

There isn't a good solution to this problem. Some suggestions that you could try are as follows:

- Organizations can be strict about keeping deadlines for various stages, as mentioned in the appraisal process.
- Automated systems of reminders every morning, based on progress of the appraisal form.
- Create a warm up phase of trainings, seminars, and so on, to catch employees' attention and help them get more information about the process.
- Managers can proactively and diligently set individual timelines for folks to submit their appraisals. That way, there will be enough time and attention paid to each appraisal.

The hurriedness is one big reason why performance appraisals are not an enjoyable activity.

Hard to remember the details – especially for a manager

Since the appraisal is essentially a look back into the past year, it's always hard to remember all the key happenings and how one felt about those at that point in time. Especially for a manager who manages 10-15 people, it's nearly impossible to remember the details around events of the past year for all team members. Hence impressions tend to become generalized and lose accuracy.

One technique that smart managers use is to keep their own personal journal on each employee. Every time there is a significant event, with either good or bad outcomes, the manager makes a journal entry. Personally, I have used my PDA – Notes section or a password-protected document. While making an entry, remember that this will be used to recall the event later and note down the appropriate context of the situation and not just the impression.

A better solution for this problem is to have a shorter cycle for recording employee accomplishments and activities that a manager can comment upon. This can be used for quarterly feedback and during the annual appraisal cycle.

Disconnected managers

Here's a situation you don't want to be in during an appraisal process:

Vikas (manager): Hi Suresh, can you talk a little more about this objective you mentioned, 'Solved high impact customer escalation for Company_X'?

Suresh (being appraised): Oh, sure. This was last year in August when....

Vikas (thinking to himself): I can't remember a thing, and he is making it sound so big. If it were such a big deal, I would surely remember.

Suresh (thinking to himself, while talking): How is this guy supposed to know what I worked on. He is busy sending reports and chatting on Facebook while I worked on key issues.

It is actually quite common for a manager to become disconnected from the team and team members. Sometimes managers stop spending time on getting know the details and are happy with the status.

The only cure for this issue is for managers to be detail-oriented and allocate the time to spend with the team. If the manager has a lot of responsibilities that keep him away from the team, it is good to meet with the team in sync-up meetings, every two weeks or so. Also, managers can plan a review meeting at the end of each project and capture the details.

Proximity effect

It is natural for people to remember more of the most recent happenings, as they are at the top of their mind. Let's consider the following situation.

Suresh had been working on a customer deliverable, and at first, it was delayed and then after delivery the feature did not work for the customer. Not surprisingly, the customer sent a stinker back to Vikas (Suresh's manager) and his manager on the quality of work being done. Vikas got an earful from his manager and is supposed to send a report of why the deliverable did not work and the corrective measures.

Next day, Suresh and Vikas have the appraisal one-on-one.

Would it be possible for Vikas to ignore the current happenings at the customer side and rate Suresh's performance for the last year? Would it not make Vikas skeptical of Suresh's work in the past year? Would Vikas focus deeper on failed tasks for Suresh, trying to find a pattern and not so much on the successful tasks?

The performance appraisal process demands that Vikas should forget what's happening at the current point in time and rate Suresh with a clear, open mind considering only the past year. Vikas can take some time to review his notes on Suresh and all the other activities that Suresh was involved in over the last year. Vikas can consciously remind himself that the appraisal is for a certain time period and the latest happenings should not impact it.

Only Vikas can tell if he was able to do so or not.

Halo effect

Here's a situation of another kind. Suresh plays a major role in handling customer issues. He is so passionate about working with customers that he frequently gets involved to help others solve their customer issues as well. He is the customer champion.

Vikas, his manager, values the role Suresh plays. Customer issues are really important to the organization. Vikas makes it very obvious that he likes Suresh's work and acknowledges that at every opportunity in a team meeting or with his management chain.

However, there are some deliverables that Suresh did not do so well. In fact, one of the assignments was in real trouble last year and required contingency measures to bring the situation back under control.

While reviewing Suresh's appraisal, Vikas finds it very hard to call out the problems around the botched up assignment. The 'halo' from Suresh's customer work impacts his ratings in other objectives.

It can work the other way also; managers sometimes have a 'set impression' of a team member. I remember, many years ago, my manager gave me feedback of 'lack of initiative' during my first performance year in that team. The following year, I purposefully took several initiatives from writing documents to process improvements to hiring to leading design discussions. However, the next year my manager told me the exact same thing, 'you lack initiative'. Three months later, I moved on.

Managers shy away from disagreements and having a hard discussion

Most managers (in fact most people) tend to avoid a conflict or even an argument. It is common to see that most self-appraisal ratings and manager ratings match or are very close to each other. There is nothing wrong with that, except that when there is a case of disagreement, the manager shies away from it.

Managers also know that some employees will argue more about a rating difference. Just that knowledge itself makes some managers assign a rating that will not generate that much of an argument.

The rating model is a very subjective model. This makes every rating susceptible to being argued.

Needless to say, a manager needs to be consistent and fair in rating his/her team members. If you are being honest and believe in the rating, then you must be open to answering a question on that rating. If you can't, then work at improving your own reasoning. Also, if there is a rating that will require a discussion, it's better to be prepared. Jot down points and reasons why a rating needs to be that way. An employee has a right to question and understand the rating being assigned to his work.

Some managers also fear becoming 'unpopular' or disliked by a team member. Sometimes, there may be a personal relationship or friendship that might also influence decisions.

Managers should attempt to keep a distinction between personal and professional relationship. Strong managers can always be friends with someone, but must be able to have an open, honest but sometimes difficult discussion with the team member. Don't let your friendship become a hurdle in your affectivity as a manager.

Subjective ratings – depends on interpretation

The rating system is largely subjective. Everything needs to be rated from 1 to 5 or any other similar scale and is largely dependent on the individual perception. In organizations where HR practices are well established, there's an explanation of each rating. For example, in **Customer Orientation**, the ratings are explained as follows:

- 1 – Does not have an understanding of customer needs.
- 2 – Needs to improve the understanding of customer needs and usage of the product in a customer environment.
- 3 – Understands the customer needs and helps solve customer problems.
- 4 – Understands the customer needs and application of the product in the customer environment. Focuses on solving customer problems. Pro-actively engages with the customers.
- 5 – Has an in-depth understanding of customer needs and customer domain. Actively works to solve customer problems. Anticipates customer issues and requirements and works to build this the product. Engages with customers on a regular basis.

With a detailed description like this example, it becomes much easier to rate. However, it's completely dependent on the manager to assign a 3 or a 4.

The problem starts with the manager never actually reading through these explanations. Even when they do understand them, they rate people based on their 'impressions', but fail to validate the impressions against real work done. Managers can look for real examples where a team member demonstrated these competencies.

Rating some competencies makes no sense

Some of the competencies make no sense to be rated at all, for example, 'ethics' or 'honesty'. How do you rate 'ethics' on a scale of 1 to 5? What will make a person top-rated in 'ethics'?

If someone is in fact rated low in 'ethics', should this employee be immediately fired?

I'm not sure why such competencies exist, but one way to deal with them is to refrain from evaluating these and simply assign the same rating to everyone in the team, unless there is a clear case of non-ethical behavior. If such a case exists, managers should also initiate an HR inquiry.

Inconsistency in ratings by different managers

Since the nature of the performance evaluation is subjective, each manager has an impact on how the ratings are done. Some managers are 'strict' and have very high expectations and tend to rate people between 2 and 4 and with great difficulty, 5, while others are 'generous' and tend to rate people between 3 and 5, heavily loaded on 4 and many in the top rating of 5.

In organizations where rewards like bonuses and salary hikes are directly linked to performance ratings, this situation can lead to different rewards, which will make the 'strict' manager unpopular. In most companies where there's a direct linkage of performance rating and financial rewards, there's likely to be a 'bell curve' policy as well.

In any case, ratings differences may have unknown effects over the long term. Since ratings are historic data and preserved forever, it's impossible to know the long-term impact of average ratings. While it may not be an issue right now, it can become an issue if HR policies change to account for ratings while considering promotions or layoffs.

One way to deal with this issue is to train managers on performance evaluation. This will not take away the personality traits of being 'strict' versus 'generous', but it'll create awareness in the manager community about the expectations and issues around ratings.

Consistency across the larger organization is not easy and is rarely achieved. We will probably continue to live with this problem forever.

High self-appraisal

Many self-appraisal forms have a top rating for almost everything. This is likely a result of a lack of training on performance appraisal. Even simple tasks, like creating a simple design document, which is easily accomplished by an employee at a given level, can be given a top rating.

I have personally seen many such appraisal forms, and the simple solution is to educate the team member on how to do a self-rating and criteria to be applied, and ask for the appraisal form to be filled out again.

Besides just training on how to rate, what works is a simple rule, "Any task which is given a top rating must have justification as to why this task or competency deserves a top rating". This will force an individual to think through and write down the specifics. Once again, if you see appraisal forms with top rating, '5', but no justification, you are well within your rights to send it back until all justification has been provided.

Remote manager

This is a fairly common problem in India where an employee has a remote manager. In many cases the manager is perpetually remote, and in some cases, either one of them is traveling on an assignment to another country.

A performance appraisal discussion is as personal as it gets in a professional environment and is best done face-to-face. A long discussion over the phone is difficult to manage and may lead to unnecessary dissatisfaction in the team member or the manager.

In some organizations, it is encouraged that people travel specifically to participate in performance appraisal discussions, but the costs and time are usually prohibitive. If possible, you can also leverage webcams or video conferencing, which is becoming increasingly popular.

Performance management and appraisal as a two-stage system

The primary purpose of performance appraisal is to review and reflect on employee performance with the aim that employee performance will improve in the next appraisal cycle. However, in order to ensure performance improvements, we really need to manage performance in a more proactive and continuous basis.

Looking at the issues with the annual performance appraisal cycles, it is clear that many of the issues are due to the long nature of the cycle. Managers and employees simply 'forget' a lot of detail. Most people are also susceptible to the proximity of the events. More importantly, in the current knowledge industry, setting specific goals for the next one year is a futile exercise since things are almost guaranteed to change from what can be planned at this point in time.

The answer is really in taking a holistic view on active and continuous performance management and putting it in the larger umbrella of annual performance appraisal.

Performance management is a continuous activity for a manager to evoke good performance from each individual's daily tasks, his behavior as a corporate citizen, and his contributions to the product, team, and the organization.

Ongoing performance management

On almost daily basis, managers help team members perform to their potential and beyond. Almost everything that a manager does with respect to an individual team member will fall into this category. Here are some examples:

- If someone is having trouble completing a certain task due to lack of information, the manager is supposed to show him the way on how to get the information or perhaps connect him with the right people who can help in moving forward. You could just give the information to the guy, but equipping him in the organizational ways of getting to the right information is a performance enhancing activity.

- Someone is stuck trying to debug a problem and asks for help, while you help the guy get over with the problem you realize that you have seen them getting stuck in similar problem earlier. You suggest the team member to enroll in technical training in that area. Skills enhancement in the required area is performance management.

- A team member walks into your office and unloads his frustration on you. He is unhappy with the work responsibilities, he feels concerned that he is not growing in the organization, and other career growth related issues. You listen intently to him and thank him for raising his concerns. You may do nothing at this point in time, but promise to discuss the issues in detail later next week. Listening to your team member's career concerns and hopefully, working to address them is performance management.

- In your weekly review, you notice that a deliverable is in danger of slipping the due date. You know that the due date is important to meet for contractual purposes. You explain the importance of meeting the date and also call in another team member to help out with the work. Actively ensuring that the required performance criteria is being met is performance management.

- You have the authority to reward a small cash bonus to five employees every quarter. After completion of a critical delivery, you announce the reward recipients. Timely reward and recognition is performance management.

- A new task shows up. You assign it to one of your team member based on the skills requirement and also personal interest of the team member. Work distribution and providing the team members, opportunities to work in desired areas is performance management.

- Program management in your organization rolled out a new process, but a certain team member does not follow the required steps. Program management team points out that your team is not adhering to the necessary process and this may cause delays in product release. You call in a general meeting to emphasize the importance of the new process and call the specific individual to set the ground rules. Ensuring process alignment and the individual's commitment to required processes is also performance management.

- After the product release, you ask your team to plan a celebration. You invite people to share their experiences and also 'goofy' mistakes. Allowing people to learn from each other is also performance management.

In general, a lot of what you do every day to encourage and support team members to meet the required organizational performance criteria and deliver high individual performance are all part of performance management.

Short cycle and long cycle performance evaluation

There's a clear disconnect between the performance management activity and the performance appraisal cycle. While the organization usually mandates the performance appraisal to a one-time activity every year, each manager has to manage performance on a daily basis. How can a manager do justice? What if there is a change in manager?

The obvious answer would be to do the performance appraisals more frequently, perhaps every quarter. However, the cost of performance appraisals would become prohibitive as the entire organization, especially the manager will spend a large amount of time completing the process.

There is a middle ground that managers and perhaps organizations can adopt in order to do more effective performance management and appraisals too. Let's call it a two-stage process consisting of a short-cycle appraisal and a long-cycle appraisal.

Short cycle

This is a shorter format appraisal done on completion of a significant assignment, such as a project delivery or around the three-month boundary. Proposal is to have 3-4 short cycle appraisals in a year.

The focus in this cycle would be on task completed recently and goals set for the recently concluded quarter:

- Review the recent challenges and performance of the employee in those tasks.
- Focus on key aspects that are important to the organization, such as collaboration and innovation in context of the tasks completed.
- Review of progress on development plan, as discussed in previous review. Has the employee and his manager worked to address the items listed in the development plan, such as technical or process trainings?
- Goals and tasks for the next three months.
- Discuss all concerns of the employee with regards to any other aspects of the job, such as 'working from home'.
- There may be no numerical rating given during this cycle, only feedback is provided.

The short-cycle review will keep the context current and will likely be a more informed discussion. It will also be more objective, as it is focused on a small set of tasks delivered in the immediate past. Employee dissatisfaction or disengagement may show up in the short-cycle review, hopefully triggering a corrective action before things go beyond repair.

In my opinion, a short-cycle performance evaluation will lead to better evaluation and satisfied employees. Even when the organization does not mandate a short-cycle review, managers can do this on their own initiative as a simple one-on-one discussion that is better structured. Enterprising managers can also create a criteria list of their own, which can be used to guide the discussion. The time spent should be around 25-30 percent of what is typically spent in annual appraisal.

Long cycle

The annual performance appraisal cycle will happen at the designated time of the year with the entire organization mobilized to participate in it. The annual appraisal form will be a comprehensive form with multiple sections as described already and will be a more holistic discussion. Short cycle details and feedback can be used during this annual cycle, and managers, as well as team members will be better prepared for it as the facts and previous evaluation are clearly visible. Managers and team members should discuss long-term career goals, improvements, and strategize for better performance during this cycle.

Overall, a combination of short and long cycle may lead to a better evaluation and would increase the employee engagement. The additional costs of short cycle would be easily recovered through enhanced performance of the team.

Summary

Performance evaluation is not an exact science and by nature it is subjective. As such, it will continue to deal with inaccuracies and bad evaluation. However, performance evaluation is essential for talent management in the organization. Top talent needs to be recognized formally and rewarded accordingly. A differentiation must be created between good performers and otherwise.

The solid performance evaluation system is a must for any organization today. In India, most organizations inherit the systems that are in place in the parent organization, somewhere in the United States or Europe or East Asia. These systems need to be tuned to the requirements of the Indian organization. Also, a strong system needs to be supported with training and awareness, so all employees can leverage it effectively.

In particular in India, the knowledge industry has grown rapidly and a huge amount of hiring happens every year. With mass hiring, there would be many 'unfit' candidates who will enter the organization and strong and consistent performance evaluation systems should be able to weed out such cases.

Poor talent management and no significant differentiation leads to top talent leaving the company. Attrition is one of the biggest issues in today's Indian organizations. In the next chapter, we will examine the issue of attrition in greater detail.

9
Attrition

It was fairly early in my career, but I was already leading a small team of interns and fresh programmers, building a rather cool product. Life was exciting as we worked hard and enjoyed being together as a team. But good times can't last forever.

It was as if a bomb dropped on me. Jagdish told me he was going to leave and join a large Indian software services company. I honestly thought he was making a mistake and was misguided and should really stay with the team to make a good career for himself. I couldn't stop thinking about the impact of him going away and didn't understand how we would manage without him. That evening, I drove over to Jagdish's house in a little rain and terrible Bangalore traffic. He was clearly surprised and invited me in. Almost immediately, his father offered me coffee. We had a good conversation and he told me that he liked working in the company and was very happy to work for me, but he really wanted to work on an international project and eventually go to US and work there. I felt consoled and somehow agreed with his goals and didn't actually ask him to stay.

I could not sleep that night. It was my first attrition experience. I had seen many other people leave around me in different teams, but someone leaving from my team was like a personal loss to me. I was clearly immature and worked in a rather small software company in a tight knit team. Over the years, I have learned and have been tempered to manage attrition as it comes. But even today in large MNC setups, I have seen many young managers go through something similar, despite all the exposure. Thankfully, today most managers are able to handle this fairly well.

Attrition is a pain and essentially creates unnecessary work for all concerned — the manager, the organization, and other team members. Even the person leaving has more work to do: He has to move his accounts, Provident Fund, and so on; needs to deal with multiple tax forms, fit into a new place, learn new things, and prove himself all over again.

No individual will take all the pain of moving, unless there's enough incentive to take the pain. For a manager, understanding the incentives and motivations of an individual is key to creating a team with low attrition.

Understanding attrition

Let's look at a few facts about attrition.

It's going to happen

Attrition is a reality waiting to happen. It's only a matter of time before you see attrition in your team. Just the way people came in for a reason, they will leave for a reason. Despite the fact that you have been very nice to them and treated them well, people will still find a reason to leave. You and the organization may do everything 'right'; timely raises, good treatment, good work, and good working conditions, but still people will have their reasons to leave. Some of the reasons could be as abstract as 'I need to do something else', and some very simple like, 'I need to earn more money'.

The goal for a manager is to 'minimize' attrition and 'manage' attrition. As long as a manager can do that, especially through critical phases of execution, the manager would be considered successful in this aspect.

Multiple reasons, but one driver

It's not that the people who stay like everything about the work, team, or organization. They too might have a lot of avenues of dissatisfaction but they still decide to stay on, since there are enough reasons to stay as well. For people who leave, it's usually one (or two) key driver(s) that 'tips them over' into the danger zone where they actively start looking and sooner or later will find a new job.

In many cases, the key driver will be money. In another case, it may be safety of the job.

Attrition can be healthy

Attrition is helpful for the team in many situations. Sometimes it helps people unlock their potential in a new team, and may lead to more collaboration between the two teams. At other times, it relieves the team of an employee who isn't performing well, and at many other times it helps balance the team structure and growth opportunities for others. Attrition also creates an opportunity to get new people, thus a flow of new ideas and perspectives helps the team.

Don't take it personally

To be honest, a team member, especially a top performer leaving the team, does feel personal at some level. You may have invested in training that individual and perhaps allocating a bigger share of rewards for him/her. You may have some future plans that will get impacted and more of your time and effort may need to be re-invested.

While it does feel personal, it's not a statement on your abilities. At least the employee is not trying to make a statement on your abilities. He/she is more likely trying to do the best for himself/herself.

Top 3 reasons why people quit: 'money', 'career growth', 'manager'

The exit interviews rarely show that as a reason, but in reality money is usually a big driver that leads to attrition, especially in the early career stages. It's one factor that is common to almost all exits in the organization; even when there are other primary reasons, money will always play a part. It's always debatable the kind of money a particular individual should earn, thus the market economy model applies. Pay someone below the market value and watch him/her leave soon, if the job market is in good shape.

Career growth is very important to any professional today. Learning and skills development are important to today's knowledge worker and lead to long-term career building. Position and responsibility are indicative of career growth and very important as well. When people stop seeing themselves grow in the team, they will start to lose motivation and will soon look for better avenues.

The cliché 'People leave managers not jobs' is certainly true. Managers have a huge influence on an individual. Not only are the rewards and recognition highly controlled by the direct manager, the quality of work, and more importantly the day-to-day experience is highly influenced by a manager. A bad manager can literally drive people insane and drive them out of the job.

Rarely does the decision change

Once someone has put in his papers, it's pretty much a done deal. Over 95 percent of employees will not change their decision. Managers (and organizations) try and reason and sometimes bend backwards to accommodate certain requests like a promotion or a compensation revision, but the promise of a change is too exciting to give up for most people. This is perhaps due to the fact that most employees have multiple reasons to move on and they would have gone over the scenarios in their minds many times, before sending out the resignation.

If you have a really good team and you are a good manager (as per your team), you'll make the decision hard, and people would have done their thinking before they come to you. If you aren't exactly viewed as a 'good manager' (as per your team), then the decision is easy anyway.

In any case, as a manager it's part of your job description to spend time with the employee to understand his concerns and what led to the attrition. You may offer solutions where possible but with very low expectations of success in turning around the decision.

While the decision rarely changes, there are times when a manager is able to influence and retain an employee who has resigned, mostly when some of the desires (or demands) of the employee are met by the organization.

Categories of 'quitters'

People leave for a reason, but the mindset can be possibly slotted into a few categories. Let's examine the list:

Growth Oriented	Jump jobs to grow
Dissatisfied	Dissatisfied with work/career/money
Mismatched	Skills or personality mismatch. Will get frustrated.
Whimsical	Just jump just because there's another job available.
Still Searching	Haven't found their groove yet.
Purposeful	Got specific objectives that aren't met
Fearful	In-secure, safety fears

The growth-oriented

There's a large percentage of the working population who believes that switching jobs is the best, if not the only way to achieve growth. The threshold for a 'need to change' differs from one person to another, so some look for growth in two years' time and some in four to five years' time.

Switching jobs is a rather easy way of getting a jump in one's salary. If someone has the right skills that are wanted in the market, it would not be difficult to find another job. Any job change, within 2-3 years of last change, will certainly get at least a 20 percent jump in salary, especially in the knowledge industry in India. In the current job too, folks will get a jump in salary every year, but it is a known fact that the market moves faster than any single organization.

In terms of learning (and hence skills advancement, which implies future career growth), there's stagnation after the first couple of years. While responsibilities may get enhanced, the technical learning stalls and more of the same kind of work is allocated to the individual.

In most interviews, I have heard the candidate say that they wish to learn more and they always have a target salary in mind that is more than 25 percent and sometimes more than 40 percent of what they are earning currently. Growth is mandatory in a voluntary job switch.

In some cases, switching a job also allows an individual to get enhanced responsibility or role, which is equated to career growth. Someone working in a large MNC as an individual contributor may get to a lead position in another organization where those skills and experience may be in shortage.

Most attrition is driven by growth aspirations of the individual.

The dissatisfied

This is the second most common mindset. A number of people are simply dissatisfied with the current job. It's a manifestation of growth orientation, but they don't leave due to lack of growth; instead this set of people hang around till the dissatisfaction sets in. The performance is possibly dipping sharply by the time they take a decision to move on.

There's another category of dissatisfied employees, namely, the ones who are 'generally dissatisfied'. These are the people who constantly complain and disregard everything that the organization does. This set of folks has a negative mindset and they look to make snide remarks at every opportunity.

Sam was one from this category. He had spent two years in the organization and had been 'not happy' for the past one year. However, he wanted to spend at least one more year in the organization, so he could possibly get a promotion and the next hike before looking for a new job. Clearly, Sam was not motivated to work hard, although he hoped for a promotion to happen. Of course, the performance wouldn't justify the promotion and Sam's frustration would only increase.

Jaydeep was another dissatisfied employee. In the past, he had contributed a lot to the organization and was growing well, until he got re-organized into a different team. Although the work was not bad and the people were a fine lot, Jaydeep felt somewhat 'discriminated' since his earlier product was not merged into this larger, much more established product. Technically, Jaydeep could have easily made a place for himself, as he was a good contributor, but he couldn't get over the re-organization. He disliked the new processes and felt them to be a strain. He thought the decision-makingwas taking longer and worst of all, he felt he wasn't given enough weightage in the decision-making process. Jaydeep's inability to adjust to the new realities converted him into a dissatisfied employee.

A bad manager will quickly lead many people into the dissatisfied category and then it'll only be a matter of time before people quit. Bad managers or poor management in general has a big impact on the individuals in the team. As we discussed in the earlier chapters, a manager plays a big part in what the team members' experience will be in the organization.

There could be any number of reasons why an employee becomes dissatisfied with the job. Usually, the dissatisfaction brews for some time as people may try different measures to correct the situation or make peace with the situation. If things continue to slide for them, attrition will be the next step.

The mismatched

The third category contains the people who are woefully mismatched. Usually this mismatch may be in one of the following categories:

- Skills mismatch
- Role mismatch
- Culture mismatch
- Thought process mismatch

A skills mismatch is fairly common in most organizations. People are hired for proficiency in certain technical skills and a fair past record. Beyond that, it is assumed that the individual will learn and catch up with whatever else shows up. However, at times, individuals are not able to match up to the expected technical level. Most organizations will allow a little time for things to settle down, but when they don't, the situation gets tricky.

Role mismatch is another difficult situation. Here's a classic situation: Amit was a good technical guy and a driven individual. Once given a task, he was able to deliver with minimum instuctions or help. At times he was a little 'rough' on other people who weren't as technical as him, but it was not a big issue. He was the darling of the manager. In a year's time, Amit was made a manager. Now, as a manager, Amit was supposed to co-ordinate and collaborate, provide status updates, and explain delays and many more functions that he didn't have the patience for. Amit's performance started to fall and his team's assignments frequently ran into trouble. There could be many other reasons for role mismatch, like someone expecting to play a larger role while there is no scope for it.

Culture mismatch is also a difficult issue to get over and mostly happens when someone moves between companies of different size and scale, or from Global product development MNC to an Indian Services company. Suddenly flexible timings are replaced by time sheets; working from home becomes difficult since product access to client systems may be an issue. At times, formal attire is mandatory and systems are more formal. There are a significant number of people who are unable to adjust to the new culture and leave fairly quickly.

Thought process or philosophy mismatch is another reason why people get uneasy in their current jobs. This can happen for a person new to the job or role and not agreeing with the philosophy of execution. For example, Tarun came from a rather process-oriented company and was used to doing things in a specific sequence. However, in his current company, many of the process steps that he valued were skipped as a matter of routine. Tarun believed that those steps are necessary always, and not doing them leads to problems. However, his current organization considered those to be 'future problems' that can be easily handled in the future within a reasonable cost. Every time Tarun started a project, he would be in this dilemma of following his own philosophy. Many times, the 'future problems' showed up fairly quickly, and while he was able to handle them easily, this solidified his faith in his philosophy.

Similar philosophical issues happen between people all the time, but when someone feels very strongly opposed to a certain thought process, it hurts them at a personal level to work in an ideologically opposite environment.

The whimsical

Some of the attrition happens without a strong reason. It's rather whimsical and based on arbitrary reasoning or the absence of any reasoning.

This is seen mostly in the early career in industries with an acute shortage of skilled manpower. At this point in time, it's the BPO industry in India or 'sales' function in the Indian retail industry. There are a number of exits that can be attributed to these 'whims'. These are folks who leave, just because "they can".

If you happen to see the resume of a call center professional with three years' experience, it will probably have five jobs already on it. In some cases, every job function and the role played may look very similar to any other on the resume. There may be small salary jumps, but not significant ones. A wide range of reasons may exist, and here are some that I have heard:

- I didn't like it
- I needed more money (got an 8 percent jump and a Rs. 10,000 sign-on bonus)
- The new job is closer to my home (it saved about 5 minutes of extra drive)
- My friend also joined there
- They have a better social scene

To a serious professional, these reasons would make no sense, but to some of the Gen-Y BPO professionals any of these is a good enough reason to move jobs.

The still searching

There is a small percentage of people who leave their job because they are 'still searching'. The individual may be doing 'just fine' in the current position, and took it up because it sounded exciting at that point in time, but after a few months he/she realizes that this 'isn't it'.

Ambar studied in a top college in India and secured a job in a top MNC in India, right from the campus. He had a great personality and was technically very strong as well. Right after he started working, he was introduced to the CFA course by one of his seniors at college. Ambar joined the CFA course because it sounded interesting. Before long, Ambar found the finance domain much more interesting than anything he had ever done or his current job. He also found he had a flair of understanding and relating to the financial intricacies and soon found himself doing well in all the exams. Two years into his job, he figured he had to leave, giving up a big salary and a top MNC job to pursue higher studies in Finance.

A 'still searching' mindset may sound like a fickle mindset, but it's actually the other way around. It takes courage to follow your dreams and give up your job because working there isn't your calling.

Another kind of 'still searching' can be seen in resumes of some of the Gen-Y professionals. These are young professionals with about 3-4 years of experience in completely different kinds of jobs. The first job may be in a BPO, the next one in retail, the third one in a software company in a recruitment role, and the fourth one in a blue-chip company doing some business co-ordination role. A clear 'still searching' pattern. The individual is likely to be very confident about his abilities and while he loses a job in one year, he also manages to get another one quite easily.

Some of it stems from the fact that India is a rapidly growing job market and the need for manpower supersedes the focus on specialization. General belief in the organizations as well as employees is that a smart guy can work in any capacity. The academic knowledge and degree is only a pointer to a 'smart candidate' and everything else can be learned on the job. Therefore, we have 'metallurgy engineers' (or any other for that matter) working as programmers, sales execs, electronics support, networking, business development, and every possible job definition. We have students of 'journalism' working in business development or software sales.

The 'still searching' is a different lot from the 'whimsical', as they are strong in what they do, usually have a stellar background, and make very thoughtful decisions. They are NOT serial job hoppers.

The purposeful

Many thoughtful exits happen because people embrace a specific purpose that cannot be achieved in the current organization.

My friend, Bala, worked in a very large German company for almost ten years. He was very comfortable in his job and was satisfied as such. Bala is very different from most software engineers. He learnt Sanskrit and spends time deciphering Indian mythology and religion. He has little craving for money and is a rather enlightened kind of a person. He gives his 100 percent to the job, 100 percent to his family, and 100 percent to his own interests. Bala quit his job of ten years to join a large Indian Services company because he wanted to work abroad at that point in time. For him, the timing was just right, given the age of his kids. Bala had a purpose that had a much better chance of getting fulfilled in the new job.

Many of my friends and team members have taken the start-up plunge and quit their jobs to follow their dreams of building a new product. My friend, Rajiv, had over a decade of experience working in India and the US for one of the largest software product development companies. He was growing in his current organization and things looked in great shape. However, he took the start-up plunge once he was convinced that the time had come for him to do so.

The fearful

Fear of losing your job or losing out on a promotion or salary hike is a very real fear in today's business environment.

The moment a company reports a few bad quarters, many will start preparing their resumes. There may not be any indication of impact on their business unit or team, but the fear of getting 'laid-off' drives people into 'action'. They feel it's necessary to be actively responding to the situation. First of all, this will give them a feel of the market and just in case there is a lay-off in a few months, they will be prepared to handle it.

Indians, in general, can't imagine being in a lay-off situation. It's as close to personal and professional degradation as one (Indian) can imagine. In the United States, there were 'pink slip' parties organized during the dot-com bust to network and to have a good time, usually at a bar. To an Indian, talking openly about being 'laid-off' is just not right. For most people, the fact that they got laid-off will remain a secret. Pink-slip parties remain a rare occurrence in India.

Until a few years ago, most Indians were very particular about 'no break in service'. People would get relieved from their job on Friday and join in the new position the following Monday. Thankfully, the trend has certainly changed now and people do take a break between two jobs, which is perhaps one of the best times to enjoy some time-off. This says a lot of the Indian mindset though.

People change a job, when they see themselves getting in an unfavorable position with their manager. This perception may come from the interactions with the manager, like getting a tough e-mail directly addressed to the employee or an occasion where the manager praises someone else in the team but not this person. A repeat of these interactions will lead to making the individual believe that he/she is out of favor and the fear of losing out of rewards or the job itself will force attrition.

Cost of attrition

We all know that attrition is costly for any organization. Like any other cost, every organization wishes to reduce attrition also. In the knowledge industry, attrition costs are magnified due to the people-centric nature of work. However, most people do not understand the real costs of attrition. Unfortunately, the real cost of attrition is many times higher than what it seems to be to the manager on the floor. Let's break the costs down.

Direct costs

Some of the costs of attrition are straightforward to see.

Administrative costs of an exit

There are a bunch of simple administrative costs associated with every employee who leaves:

- HR – Exit interviews
- No-dues process that requires signatures from various departments
- Financial work to pay out the 'full and final payment', other settlements like PF (Provident Fund) transfer, gratuity, balance vacation, and so on
- Other admin work to disable access to various places including network and buildings

Admin costs are generally not a significant cost, but nevertheless contribute to the costs.

Hiring costs

These are the costs related to hiring the replacement candidate.

Finding the candidates

Finding the right talent is one of the most challenging parts of the recruitment process. Many organizations engage external agencies to 'hunt' and find people who would be interested in the open position.

Interviewing costs

Once a candidate is identified, he/she will be put through the process of interviews. Usually there are three to four interviews for a given position. Mid-to-senior employees in the team conduct interviews. If the usual hit ratio between interview and selection is 1:5, that is, interviewing five people before one offer can be made, the total time spent on interviewing alone would be about 25-30 hours. There's a significant cost to this time spent.

Cost of background check

Almost all organizations have a background check process that is conducted by a third party. Even smaller organizations that work with MNCs are mandated to do background checks for employees who would be working on projects outsourced by the larger organization.

Relocation cost for a new employee

Many candidates may need a relocation, which includes the travel of the candidate and family, cost of moving household goods, and stay in a hotel for two weeks. The total costs can be substantial.

Induction and on-boarding costs

Once a candidate joins, there are initial costs to the on-boarding process and induction trainings. Induction training can last from one to five days, depending on the organization. In some organizations, there's a mandatory off-site program where the company culture, team building, and so on is emphasized. The induction costs can be small to large, based on how much emphasis the organization places on these processes.

Training costs

A new employee will usually need training of various kinds. Sometimes in technologies being used in the products, development, and execution processes; the actual product and code need to be worked at in the case of software companies.

In the case of campus hires, this training can be anywhere from one month to three months. Some organizations like Infosys have set up very large facilities to train campus hires for up to three months before they are assigned to any project.

Indirect costs

Direct costs are just the tip of the iceberg when it comes to attrition costs. The indirect costs are much more significant. Here are some of the indirect costs of attrition.

Loss of productivity

This is indeed the biggest pain that the team and manager have to bear, while a new employee catches up on the job.

Learning curve

Every new employee will take a fair amount of time to deliver at the same productivity as the previous employee (assuming the last employee was not a poor performer).

For the first four to eight weeks, the new employee will probably operate at 25 percent productivity of the pervious employee. A lot of time is likely to be spent in training.

In the next four to eight weeks, we can assume the productivity to be around 50 percent, as the new employee starts to deliver more but needs some hand-holding and extra work monitoring is required to avoid errors.

In the next 10 weeks, the productivity may rise to 75 percent, as the employee becomes more confident and independent.

Finally, after nearly 6 months of joining, a new employee may be able to deliver at 100 percent of his/her own potential.

Loss of tacit knowledge

In our industry, knowledge is everything. Tacit knowledge is different from formal or explicit knowledge that can be written down. **Tacit knowledge** is the knowledge that a person possesses by virtue of possessing formal knowledge, experience in the system, knowing the environment, and putting all of them together. For example, tacit knowledge will allow one person to make co-relations between different details. Hence, tacit knowledge is very difficult to transfer over to another person.

Loss of tacit knowledge leads to errors in decision making. Software programs take longer to stabilize and older problems that were fixed months ago surface again.

It is impossible to measure the impact of tacit knowledge.

Loss of personal network

People work with people and so many things happen well because the two parties involved have some kind of a business or personal connection. Every time an employee leaves, he/she takes away that personal network along with himself/herself.

It is obvious that the impact of this in a sales situation is very high, but even in other jobs like programming, the personal network helps in getting people to talk and reach decisions and accept solutions from each other.

A new person will take time to establish a personal network and trust relationship within the organization. Until then, there will be some amount of productivity loss.

Loss of efficiency in teamwork

The collaborative environment within a team is disturbed every time a team member leaves and a new member comes in. People are a little cautious with the new person. They will likely be a little formal as well and the speed of execution slows down a little.

Also, while the new person takes over the full set of responsibilities, the rest of the team members may have to handle extra work. This extra work is unlikely to be accounted for in the earlier plans. Hence the team members feel even more pressure.

Loss of morale for the rest of the team

Productivity will be hit if the team member who leaves has a high influence within the team. The leaders of a team are usually the people who have a high impact on the team. A leader quitting creates doubts in the rest of the team and a loss of morale and motivation may be seen.

Loss of customers due to inefficiency

Customers may also feel the pain in case they have to interact with the new employee who is still catching up on the job. This will certainly happen in a call center scenario. A new call center agent may create an unsatisfactory customer experience due to his/her own lack of experience with the systems. For example, a simple query may take unusually long to complete. A repeat of this experience and the customer will look for another service provider if there is a choice.

In software services, a loss of a customer may mean losing the client because the quality of service drops and delays happen due to attrition led inefficiencies. Today, customers of large services' organizations keep track of attrition within the team that is dedicated to them.

Opportunity cost

With every minute spent on bringing up the new hire and every rupee spent on the new hire, there's an opportunity lost in spending the same time, money, and resources on something else.

Copy cat attrition

Attrition also induces the thought in other team members. The 'notice period' is a rather dangerous time, where a lot of discussions around leaving the job may happen. Most other team members are interested in knowing the 'market salary' for the position by comparing against the offer of the employee leaving. Sometimes, more detailed discussions around what is wrong in the current organization can start to undermine the confidence of the rest of the team.

Benefits of attrition

Although it is hard to imagine, attrition isn't always a bad thing. In many situations, attrition can be of good benefit.

Attrition may get rid of deadwood and misfits

A non-performing employee, whatever the reason, is a problem for a manager. It's almost always better to have a shortage of people than to have individuals who aren't performing. Managers may be asked to take on more responsibility, given that they have bandwidth, but in reality, the output will be lower than expected. Ultimately, managers are responsible for delivering and performance management. However, in most organizations, it is not easy to 'let go' or 'fire' an employee. The legalities ensure that there is a fair chance given to the employee to perform and these efforts need to be documented.

Managers are actually relieved when a misfit or underperforming employee leaves the team.

Attrition creates space for new perspectives and new energy

As people leave, new people are hired and they bring in new thinking, new experience, and new perspectives to the team. While the organization processes and systems are to be learnt by the new employee, there is also an opportunity for the manager and the organization to learn from the new employee and his/her experience in the industry.

New employees also bring more enthusiasm and energy into the team as they are on a mission to make space for themselves in the team. A new employee may put in the extra effort that may also inspire others to raise the level of their contributions.

Newer perspectives from the new employees may also help the product to grow. Sometimes the team is so much into their own world and work within a set system that they miss the developments in the world outside.

Attrition may help achieve a balance in the team

Attrition helps create opportunities to balance the team composition. Sometimes teams become 'top heavy' with multiple people with relatively high experience for example, a team of five where three members have more than 8-9 years of experience. In most situations, there is not enough opportunity for all three to shine. Instead, one or even two of them can move to a different team within the larger organization. This internal attrition helps the talent to be utilized better and creates a balance in the teams.

It can work the other way round also. Sometimes, due to some stroke of bad planning, a team of five gets staffed with all low-experienced employees. This creates a high load of mentorship and managing on the manager. Attrition in such a team creates an opportunity for a more experienced and skilled person to be hired, thus creating more balance.

Internal attrition is very healthy

Most large organizations have a policy of 'internal transfers', where an employee is allowed to move to another team in a similar role or sometimes in a very different role.

This movement of talent to different teams is great for the larger organization. Employees get to work in newer technologies and areas, thus getting a variety of exposure. New teams get the required support. Networking within the organization helps in achieving results faster.

Many employees, who have had a long career in one single company, would have moved around within the organization.

Attrition may lower total costs

At times, attrition may also serve to lower the average costs within a team. Say a person with four years of experience leaves the team and is replaced by a campus hire or a person with two years of experience; there is a direct cost benefit. Sometimes these benefits can be significant. There's obviously a difference in the expertise level of the two; however, there are many situations where a higher level of expertise is not required anymore for the job in question.

Attrition may create space for growth

Attrition also creates growth opportunities for other team members, as they can take up more responsibilities. In my opinion, attrition creates the 'best' opportunity for others to grow.

When a key person leaves the team, the manager is under tremendous pressure to keep the motor running while the replacements come in. In most organizations, the replacement will not show up well after 3 months of the employee leaving. Clearly, someone has to pick up the extra responsibilities. When another employee stands up at such a crucial juncture, it means a lot to the manager. Taking on new responsibilities allows the employee to be part of many more forums and discussions and create his/her own network. Performance delivered in tough times is the one that stands out and helps an employee transition into a higher position.

Attrition helps a manager expand the network

Another positive side effect of attrition is the expansion of the business network. When one employee goes to another organization, essentially a new connection is made between the two organizations.

A strong business and personal network is essential in today's business environment and one more reason why managers should make a transition out to be a pleasant experience.

Attrition—watch out

Here are some situations where managers need to watch out for the beginning of attrition in the team:

- The usual time of attrition:
    - Watch out for certain points in an employee's career where an individual may think of a new job. For example, a campus hire may look for a new job or higher studies after two years of experience. Also, there's a big difference perceived between one year of experience and two years. Two years of experience is valued much more by the industry, giving an individual more leverage.
    - When engineers complete six or seven years of experience, they look for another job to justify their entry into a new league of engineers.

- The usual signs of low motivation:
  - When employees display lower motivation signs, like absenteeism, lower involvement in team activities, missing out on deadlines, and so on, it is also a slow slide into the next step of attrition.
  - As discussed in detail in the chapter on motivation, managers need to understand and work with individuals to get them motivated.

- Low overall compensation for an individual:
  - Watch out for individuals who are being paid below average. If you aren't paying your best employees, then someone else will. Even if the person is happy with other things, it'll only be a matter of time before the guy comes around to the realization that he needs to make more money. As a manager, you will know the usual salary range for a person in a certain grade. If an individual in the grade is under the half way mark, review it closely. If the individual is indeed 'compressed', you can proactively engage the person. Provide opportunities to grow in technical abilities and other exposure as a professional.

- Poor salary hike:
  - Poor hike numbers are sure to start trouble for anyone and some people may not be able to put it in perspective. Some folks may take it as a negative vote on their capabilities. Any individual in this category is at risk. They know that the next hike opportunity is about one year away.

- Someone's peer gets promoted:
  - Not many people take it easy when their peer gets promoted but not them. People feel vulnerable in this situation, as they see themselves being left out, perhaps under appreciated.
  - Managers can proactively discuss this with the individual and attempt to put things in perspective. Perhaps go over what it will take for this individual to get to the next level like his/her colleague.

- When there's a layoff in another division:
  - A layoff creates a general feeling of insecurity in the organization. People think that their organization may be next on the block and may take defensive action to seek out a job elsewhere.

- ° You can actively address this as a general message to alleviate fears. You may need to discuss the right kind of messaging with your higher management and deliver the same for the team. As a bare minimum, you can give your vote of confidence to the team's abilities. If needed, you can get someone from higher management to address the team and re-iterate the message.

- Increased networking activity:
  - ° It's a sign that is not always the right indicator, but it's better not to ignore it, although I wouldn't recommend actively monitoring it.
  - ° When people start building their online profile on LinkedIn ©, seeking recommendations, adding more links, and putting out an impressive brief of their profiles, it's fairly clear that the individual is building an external image. Many a times, this is for the purpose of getting a better job as well.
  - ° Other networking activity within the company that is not work-related may point to explorations of an internal move.

Managing attrition

Given that attrition will happen sooner or later, every manager is expected to be able to 'manage attrition'. This means, every manager should be able to reduce attrition as much as possible and ensure business goes on as usual, even when the team does face attrition. Here are some ways to manage attrition.

Expect it: anybody can leave

As a manager, you should expect that anyone can leave. Here are some of the cases I have heard:

- Employee who joined two weeks ago can leave
- Employee who has been around for 1,2,3,….n years can leave
- Employee who just recently got a promotion can leave
- Employee who just recently got a big salary hike can leave
- Employee who was given a lot of support by the organization in times of their personal difficulties can leave
- Young, married, unmarried, men, women can leave

Essentially, it is a given that people will leave and no amount of motivation, rewards, help, or support will ensure no attrition.

Expecting attrition to happen doesn't mean being 'fearful' that attrition will happen; instead the manager's attitude should shift to the other side, that is, not to be constrained by the thought of attrition and to manage fearlessly.

Know your people

The most basic thing each manager can do to manage attrition is to connect with each individual in the team. Do you understand the aspirations of each individual? His/her life goals? His/her strengths? What gets him/her excited and what doesn't?

Spend time and energy in getting to know each person on your team. Set up formal one-on-ones and also hangout with people to understand them at a personal level. Engage in a serious technical discussion and also in a passionate 'go green' kind of discussion.

Knowing your people will help you understand their aspirations, their working model, their habits, and values. This will help you manage them well and appeal to their strengths and also avoid situations where they may not be at their best.

You may be able to find a better match between their skills, aspirations, and assignments available.

Manage expectations proactively

Expectations mismatch is an 'attrition starter'. People expect something and when the reality is not close to expectations, disappointment sets in.

For example, Roshan was a smart engineer with six years of work experience. He had been performing well in his current role as a senior engineer and had spent two years in the grade already. In Roshan's mind, he was ready for a promotion to the next level of technical lead. He expected that two years in the grade with good performance should get him there. In reality, there were more criteria than that to make the grade of technical lead, besides in a given team you could only have so many technical leads. Roshan's expectations need to be managed proactively, so he can understand the reality and set his expectations in line with what is achievable in the given organizational scenario. Roshan's manager can also direct Roshan's energies towards other tasks that allow him to take on more responsibilities.

Salary hikes are another time where expectations need to be managed well. Employees start expecting numbers that are unreal or not possible in the current organization. For example, in at least one of the recession years, most organizations did not give a salary hike (in fact, some even cut down on several perks). The following year, the hike was on the cards and many employees expected the hike to be substantial, almost twice the usual amount. However, that was clearly not going to happen. Expectations needed to be managed to stem disappointment and subsequent attrition thoughts.

Team members get frustrated with the speed of processes that impact execution of the project. Large companies working on large products have a latency in the system, some of which is actually necessary and some of it is size-related. Young programmers get very frustrated and very bored working on a large release. Managers can manage the expectations around these aspects and perhaps, create other avenues of technical excitement and accomplishments.

Enhance team capabilities

Managers need to invest in and encourage 'team capabilities' and not just work with a few 'stars' of the team. Eventually, the collective strength of the team determines how the team will react to people leaving.

While 'stars' are very important in any team, the manager needs to ensure that the entire team is improving at a collective level.

In the chapter on team building, we have already discussed many strategies to develop team strength and effectiveness.

Encourage cross-area awareness

As teams mature, the specialization sets in, that is, each sub team tends to develop deep knowledge of their areas. Also, as the work pressure grows, there is less and less time for team members to take a peek at what is happening in other areas.

As a manager, this is something that needs to be systematically avoided. Managers need to encourage and reward cross-area awareness and contributions, especially for senior technical folks in various teams.

Cross-area contributions are healthy for the team as more technical strengths can be applied to each area and also because people get to contribute beyond the boundaries of their own little areas. As a side effect, this helps in managing the impact of attrition. Senior people in other sub-teams are quickly able to handle the extra load and transition or temporary management of the area becomes much easier.

Promote openness and be accessible

Another way to deal with attrition is to 'avoid it' before it happens. If managers were open and accessible to their team, it would be possible for team members to come over and talk about any issues. A good open discussion not only leads to a solution to a problem but it'll also create a better relationship between the team member and his manager.

Several times, I have had someone from my team come over and discuss their intent to move on because they had a certain goal or career ambition to be met and sometimes because they were unhappy with the way things have been in the team. In each of these conversations, we discussed the issues, the constraints, and the possible solutions.

As a manager, you'll be able to put out a lot of attrition fires, even before they began.

Create documentation and trainings

Lack of documentation is the number one complaint from a new employee. There is so much knowledge, so many details, and so many relevant meeting minutes that never get documented.

In general, there is a lot of scope for improvement when it comes to documenting the relevant details about a project, process, or decisions. While the organization processes may already make sure there is documentation, managers can create additional documentation that can help in future support and transition. Documentation that is created keeping a new team member in mind will be very helpful.

Create a fun work environment

Employees spend significant amount of time at work, and a fun working environment makes a significant difference.

Managers can proactively promote an environment where people spend time socially with each other and help each other in non-work related activities. For example, helping each other out in the tax season by sharing tax saving tips.

Managers can also be gatekeepers of stress and may create an environment where folks are not unduly exposed to stress factors that they don't need to. For example, a manager can avoid multiple late night meetings by dividing the responsibilities so lines of communication are optimized.

Managers should also take advantage of the support from the organization to indulge in other fun activities like team lunches, adventure outings and picnics.

Summary

From the day Jagdish gave me my first experience of dealing with attrition to today, attrition still gives a feeling of 'loss' and a chance to look inward and all around to make improvements. It's a constant challenge to keep the workplace attractive and exciting for a variety of people and to be able to create an environment where everyone can meet their goals and deliver for the organization at the same time.

The key to dealing with attrition is really in creating a workplace that people will not want to leave. In the next chapter, we will discuss some more aspects of managing like work life balance, working with Gen Y, working in remote teams, and diversity.

10

Managing – Remoteness, Work-Life, Gen Y, and Diversity

Many team-building excursions include a game called **Minefield**. The objective of the game is to lead a blindfolded team member across the room with only verbal commands, such that the person does not step on randomly thrown around, obstacles and reach a certain 'mine', which is then considered 'cleared'. Two teams are created and while one team is 'clearing the mines', the other one can create some distractions to confuse the minesweeper. Sometimes, two blindfolded people can be directed together.

The emphasis of the game is on 'trust', 'communication', and 'co-ordination' among different players, blindfolded and others.

While regular (with eyes) players know that the instructions are for the blindfolded player, they continue to use hand gestures to explain and communicate. With a combination of unclear instructions (at least to him) and noise around the floor, the blindfolded person stops in his tracks and slows down to avoid stepping on obstacles. At times, the blindfolded player gets frustrated enough to just step forward and 'get out' of the game.

The game is very appropriate to describe a remote management situation. The 'visual' sense is lost as the team member and manager are unable to see each other on a daily basis. The communication medium is reduced and noise creeps in. People slow down and frustration can set in. If the models don't improve and stabilize, the remote worker will soon get out of the game, creating another set of challenges to be managed.

Managing is a challenge on a daily basis and we have discussed several aspects of managing, such as hiring, team building, performance evaluation, and attrition. Certain situations that are very relevant to the current environment add a new dimension to each of these aspects and require some special thought.

Managing remoteness

Dealing with remoteness is part of the design of the Indian knowledge industry. After all, the initial models of the industry itself were based on the cost effectiveness of the Indian team versus the team in the US or Europe.

There was a point where every team of 5-10 people had to deal with a remote manager or remote 'parent' teams in the US. The Indian management chain was thin and there was a high dependence on the US team. Over the years, the Indian teams have grown in strength and skills and have less dependence on the remote parent for day-to-day operations.

As the Indian organization has matured, several organizations have expanded into multiple cities to leverage the local incentives and talent. It's fairly common now to find an Oracle in Bangalore, Hyderabad, and Delhi or an Amazon in Bangalore, Hyderabad, and Chennai or an Infosys in Bangalore, Hyderabad, Delhi, Chennai, Chandigarh, and more.

As a result of the maturation of the Indian organization, the span of management has become more and more location-agnostic; that is, as a manager, you may have a team that spreads to one or two or any number of locations.

A different kind of remote situation is also emerging, where the Indian center acts as the 'parent' organization to the new centers coming up in China, Malaysia, or Singapore. These new centers are facing the same growing pains, and managers in Indian centers are able to play a big role in lending support to them with the added advantage of sharing a large part of the working time zone.

Remote employee means

We will now look at some implications of what it means to manage remotely.

You can't see him/her – visual observation is lost

The first thing that happens when you get a remote team member is that you feel the loss of one of your key senses. We rely on visual clues for everything and take it for granted. Just as observed in the 'Minesweeper' game, every conversation has a visual element to it.

With no visual communication, the rest of the senses need to pick up, but many managers fail to recognize the fact and do not enhance their verbal and written communication.

You only see results, not efforts

Once a team member is remote, the visibility into their efforts becomes nearly zero, unless the remote employee tries hard to make that happen. What would always be visible are the results, since results are always tracked.

Rakesh got an e-mail from Amit, his remote manager, to urgently fix a bug reported by an escalated customer. Rakesh read the e-mail when he logged in from home and started early for the office to have enough time to work at it. He spent the whole day trying to reproduce the issue and then making various code changes and testing them. However, even by 7 P.M. in the evening the bug fix was not really working in all scenarios. Rakesh went home at 7 P.M. and started working at it again by 9 P.M. After another 2 hours of work and no luck getting an acceptable fix, Rakesh got frustrated and called it a day. He sent an e-mail to his manager Amit, stating: "Have worked at it but no luck. Plan to get back at it tomorrow."

Amit was livid with the lack of action, despite him sending an e-mail and expressing the urgency of the issue.

While Rakesh did everything right, his efforts are not visible to Amit. Perhaps Amit and Rakesh do not have a long, trusting relationship. Even in a trusting relationship, it would help if Rakesh could be more descriptive about options tried out and problems faced.

Distrust creeps in – wonder what he is up to

As long as the results are as expected or better, the remote relationship works well. However, the moment results are not as expected, it would be natural to think beyond results and into the process or action behind the results.

The manager wonders, what is the employee up to? Is he really making all the effort necessary? Is he even in the office long enough?

The manager will ask simple questions like, 'Did you try this?', which may actually offend the remote worker if 'this' happens to be a natural simple thing. Remote employee starts to think that the manager doubts his/her capabilities and the relationship becomes sour.

Relationship becomes very 'black box'

As a consequence of limited visibility into what is happening remotely, the relationship becomes very 'black box' like, that is, the manager sends out some work that gets done by the remote employee and the results are communicated.

If both are very efficient, this black box relationship will happen very quickly. This leads to a loss of the personal touch and warmth within a relationship. For a long-term, fruitful association, a good relationship between manager and team member is essential. In a remote scenario, this can be very challenging.

In daily management, a lot of 'small stuff' happens that creates a great relationship. Getting together for coffee and chatting about the cricket match last night actually creates a one-to-one relationship. Passing by and exchanging a 'Good Morning' has a certain value. These little things are completely lost in a remote relationship.

Out of sight, out of mind

If you can't 'see' some people on a daily basis, you tend to reach out a little less to them; after all it's easier to just ask the guy outside your office to help out. Very likely the larger team is local and invariably the remote employee will miss out on being part of a team lunch or a birthday celebration.

Managers sometimes have some 'pet' projects or key work, which is important to them but isn't exactly an organizational deliverable; for example, working on creating a prototype of a new reporting system or a software product feature. Since these kinds of activities are highly interactive, it is natural for managers to go to the guy who is local, sometimes even though the remote worker may be more technically adept at that.

Everything becomes harder, requiring extra effort

In a remote worker or team situation, everything becomes harder. The effort required to accomplish most of the tasks goes up a notch. Even simple things like one-on-one meetings are not the same as being present in the same room, extra effort is required throughout the process, and the scope for doubts increases.

Growing a remote team is another difficult task, as a telephonic interview has much less impact than an in-person interview. It is often seen that candidates end up going for multiple interviews and still the outcome remains inconclusive. This is very frustrating for the manager as well as the candidate.

Daily work, that is, the usual collaboration, back-and-forth discussions and reviews, reporting, and so on, also takes a little more energy from the parties involved.

A remote leader becomes very important, just for being remote

Over time you will become successful in setting up the remote team and finding a good leader to manage the remote team. The remote leader soon becomes much more important than his peers for just being remote and not exactly because of better delivery or execution.

Making remoteness work

Remote working relationships become so much easier when an interaction becomes personalized — when individuals can visualize other people, get a feel for their voice and even mannerisms. Putting a face to a name is the very first step in that direction. Encourage people to put their pictures on the corporate directory. Create a physical meeting wherever possible and use all available tools. Here are some strategies that help in managing a remote team.

Indulge in chitchat

Indulging in chitchat sounds a little frivolous, but it's one of the easiest things to do and has great intangible returns. One of the biggest problems of remote working is that you lose 'touch', especially the 'personal touch' with people.

Engaging in small talk is part of human nature, and especially so for Indians. We love to talk, comment, and engage with other people. Chitchat allows the manager and the remote worker to feel connected and only an instant message away.

Embrace new technology to get closer

While there is no parallel (yet) for being physically present in the same room, technology provides the next best solution, which is very workable.

Video conferencing has really come of age and the bandwidth available on the corporate network makes it a very viable solution. Imagine calling a remote person via Skype© - like corporate software over a video call. It may be weird in the beginning, but soon everyone gets used to it.

Cisco TelePresence© is an absolutely amazing technology, but is not available everywhere and hence can be used only sometimes. If you have access to it, use it at least once a month to meet the remote team.

Web conferencing is widely used by everyone today and besides corporate standard software, there are several free and pay-and-use versions available.

There are various team collaboration software packages also available which are designed for project management across a spread out team.

Set expectations with the remote employee to communicate more

A good start to better communication is the setting of the expectations around communication. Given the remote nature, the communication requirements for a remote worker will be higher. Start by calling out the communication requirements, that is, the amount, detail, and frequency of communication. Call out the kind of communication required by you, so employees know what to communicate and what not to communicate. Too much or too less communication is equally frustrating. Over a period of time, a stable system will set in as remote workers and managers figure each other out.

Formalize some of the communication

It is fine to set up some formal systems of communication, such as weekly reports that employees need to mail to the manager. If there is team collaboration or project management software available, make sure you leverage those.

However, when you create formalized structures for communication, don't make them overbearing only for remote workers. The local team should also be using the same systems.

Make it two-way

While you set up models to get information, also work on models to provide information for remote workers.

Make sure you consciously provide information to the remote team members, in formal and informal ways.

Drive by setting clear goals and success criteria

Having clear expectations and goals are important for any employee, but these are absolutely a must for a remote employee. Be clear on what the tasks and goals are and, very importantly, what the success criteria are. Work getting completed without quality or work getting done with quality but delayed, may or may not be acceptable based on the situation.

More frequent checkpoints

Plan for more frequent checkpoints with remote workers. There may or may not be a higher chance of things going off track, but if they do, it's definitely more difficult to correct.

Especially during the early days of remote team setup or a new remote worker, plan for as many checkpoints as needed.

Checkpoints also serve as an opportunity to provide your feedback and support back to the remote team. Hearing more often from the manager, reassures the remote team that the work is on the right track and helps move ahead with confidence.

While you set up additional checkpoints, be acutely aware of the balance required, so the frequent checkpoints don't become overbearing.

Open sessions

Another way to improve inclusiveness is to conduct open sessions, where team members from all locations can dial in and participate. The nature of these meetings is a free form introspective discussion for post mortem and improvements. This allows a remote team to listen in to the troubles of other team members and realize that others share the same pains and hopefully find solutions that work for all, local as well as remote team members.

Get into detail rather than just 'everything is fine'

This is true for all status updates, and extremely important for remote workers. Status updates tend to become a formality if no serious follow up or discussion happens around them. Getting into at least one more level of detail creates a much more meaningful discussion and will greatly enhance the value of a status update.

Evaluate if it's working

While remote working is very common today, not everybody is cut out to be in a remote situation. Many employees sulk when kept away from the key action and for some, their personalities are such that they are most effective when surrounded by their co-workers.

Every 3-6 months, evaluate the effectiveness of the remote worker and remote relationship. If it isn't working, look for alternatives. It's better to lose the employee by helping him/her move to another team local to him, than to drag out the pain.

Don't become the only face of the remote team; let them have their identity

In some cases, the remote team becomes completely invisible to the rest of the organization. Every touch point with the higher management or external teams gets fronted by the manager. Eventually, this leads to a situation where the remote team will lose the sense of ownership on the work being done. Once people lose ownership of the work, the enthusiasm to work and the quality of work will suffer.

Managers need to consciously promote the visibility of the remote team in the rest of the organization. Meetings may need to be set considering the time zone for the remote team and some discussions may take a little longer. But that's a small price to pay for treating the remote teams the right way.

Don't overdo it – excessive reporting

As discussed earlier, in order to get a better connection with remote teams, formal communication and more frequent status updates are required. However, there is a real danger of overdoing the reporting. When a remote worker gets appreciated for good reporting and the manager feels in control because there is good reporting, it is possible that there is more focus on reporting than on real work.

In particular, when the remote team is doing critical work, the managers wish to run a 'tight ship' and try to get into a lot of detail about the work and time spent by remote workers.

Leverage the 'local' for the remote employee

Being remote may have its own advantages. For example, a remote worker may be closer to certain customers or may have specific geographical advantages that may be leveraged for the greater benefit of the team. It will also provide a certain added value to the remote job itself.

For example, a remote team located in Delhi can own the hiring from that region. They can also be responsible for creating and managing programs with local educational institutes like engineering and management schools. The remote team in Delhi can be leveraged for working with key customers in that area, including the Indian government.

Provision for travel – make it economical

Travel budgets may need to be enhanced to allow for regular travel for managers or remote workers to travel. As the remote team grows, make sure these budgets move in tandem.

It is also understood that no organization likes to spend money on travel and hotels. Even though it may not be in your job description, explore avenues to make the travel and stay as economical as possible without being 'cheap'. Explore the usage of company guesthouses or boutique hotels, usage of existing cab services at the company that are several times cheaper than usual 4 or 5 star hotels, but provide extremely good service and quality accommodation and food.

Make travel meaningful

Whenever the remote team member travels to your location or you travel to the remote location, make sure you spend the time connecting with people 'personally' and over work discussions.

For example, be connected personally by spending time over a cup of coffee and talking about the Indian cricket team and kids' schooling. Also, spend a significant amount of time on work discussions, such as about design reviews and process improvements. As a manager, spend one-on-one time with each remote person you meet and discuss performance. Every travel opportunity should be leveraged to foster stronger personal relationships and get some good work done as well.

Remote working scenarios are absolutely necessary in the current global model. While you may be tempted to not venture into a remote relationship, it is nearly impossible that you'll be able to avoid them forever. In fact, the earlier you get into managing remote teams, the better it is. As you grow as a manager and the span of control grows, remote teams will certainly be part of the equation. Making mistakes then would be much more costly. So, like with all other things, work your way to managing a successful remote team.

Work-life balance

Here's a question for all working professionals:

What is important to you?

a. Success at work – money, recognition

b. Time spent with your parents

c. Both

Don't be in a hurry, and take a minute to think it through. Wait for the sand to flow down.

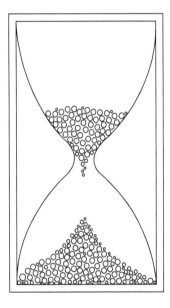

Very likely your answer is c) Both. If you have spent too much time thinking about it, you probably want a fourth option d) It depends. It depends on the time and place and priority of things.

Today's professional wishes to have "more of everything"; more money, more recognition, more vacations, more family time, and more time for themselves. We don't really see a need to compromise on one or the other and there's an inherent belief that all can be achieved.

However, option a) Success at work – money, recognition will certainly demand a lot more time from an individual at work, and hence there will be a lot less time left to be spent with parents or family.

Understanding work, life, and the balance

Let's try to establish what it means to have a work – life balance.

What is work?

Common understanding of 'work' is: work that we get paid for, something done, using our skills to get money.

There is other 'work' that we do, such as voluntary work in a community centre, that is not being counted as 'work' in this definition, because that work is not done to earn money. That work has a different meaning for the individual.

What is life?

We are not about to get into a deep philosophical discussion about 'What is Life?' That's certainly not something I can explain.

Life, in this context, is 'personal life' — the activities you do for your pleasure, as part of your social obligation or to achieve personal goals. These include activities that you undertake while playing all the other roles in life, a friend, a spouse, a brother or a sister and for your own growth, like going on a vacation or spending time at the gym or going to the temple.

What is work-life balance (WLB)?

Work – life balance is the balance between activities that earn you a living and activities that are important to you as a person, such that you find a sense of fulfillment in both.

WLB is NOT an equal number of hours

It is important to understand that work – life balance is not a balance of time. So you don't necessarily have work – life balance if you spend equal hours on each. Time management, to ensure that there is 'enough' time for work and life, is very important for achieving the balance.

There are no formulas to find out how much time should be spent at work or on personal activities, and it'll be different for each individual's work conditions and personal preferences. So you shouldn't look at a friend of yours who has a lot of time for personal activities as a role model for WLB; he may be slacking off at work and it'll soon catch up. What matters is the quality of work and personal time and how much energy you have for each.

Achievement and fulfillment are key

We find balance in work and life when we get a sense of achievement and fulfillment. Achievement at work is measured in terms of satisfaction of doing a task well, getting recognized, getting paid well, getting the respect of all around you, and more. Achievement and fulfillment in personal life usually come in the form of being able to spend time and energy on things that are important to you, like being able to help your kids with homework, or going out with friends in the evening, or taking an evening class in Salsa, or even visiting back home to take care of your family.

Enjoyment test

A simple way to test if employees are getting fulfillment from work is to do the enjoyment test, that is, does an employee look like he/she is enjoying the work? Does an employee enjoy being at work place? If yes, then the employee is likely to be getting a sense of achievement and fulfillment as well.

Work is NOT life, but work IS life too

Now that we understand fulfillment as the key word in finding WLB, it becomes easier to understand why work and life are intertwined. The dissatisfaction at work will spill over to the personal life and similarly, the dissatisfaction in personal life will impact the work. Essentially, you are one person with goals to achieve and many roles to play. As much as the roles are different and distinct from each other, the performance in each role is impacted since it is delivered via the same person.

Balance now is better than balance later

In general, striving towards a balance at all times is better than making a mad dash in one area and then trying to play catch up on balance.

You may lean towards maximum achievement in work, by spending a huge amount of time, working smart, and taking care of your responsibilities and more. You may actually get that extra recognition and another promotion that was important for you at work, but you may get a dissatisfied family or disconnected kids. Although after the promotion, you may try to come back to spending more quality time with the family, things may be too bad already or the family has figured out their balance without you in the picture; besides, the higher demands of your new responsibilities (that you worked hard for) may not allow you to come back and spend more quality time with the family. If you really care about the family relationship, the situation may lead to guilt and mental disturbance that will impact the work and the person that you are.

At the same time, you can possibly work hard and spend quality time (not a lot of time) with the family to be able to balance the demands and cater to each in a timely and consistent manner; the results will be positive on each side.

It is very likely that you'll have many fires to fight at work that will require extra time and effort and hence life takes a back seat. In any case, the attempt should be to balance now and not to defer family or personal satisfaction to later. There's hardly any later in today's scenario; in most cases, later only brings in more work.

Why managers should encourage WLB

It may seem like managers should encourage employees to spend as much time at work, and put in as much effort as humanly possible, since more work done can only be good for the organization, but it isn't quite productive in the long run.

Even for a machine to be at its best, it requires some downtime and maintenance, so for a human to work at good capacity, caring and nurturing is required. The human machine also needs food and good working conditions, rest to recuperate, mental peace, and much more (refer to the chapter on Motivation) to perform at peak capacity.

The human machine is a really complex machine, and that's why managers are paid what they are paid to handle these complex systems. Creating conditions where employees can achieve their personal goals and ambitions and also their professional goals and ambitions is part of a manager's job. An inept manager will crank the machine and get the most out of it for a short period of time, but then end up with downtime later on and perhaps expensive replacements (attrition and hiring).

An individual's WLB is an employee's responsibility; managers only support it

Managers can't and should not be involved in managing WLB for employees. It's an individual's responsibility to manage his/her WLB. Managers are only expected to create conditions that help employees achieve WLB. Larger organization support is a must for a manager to succeed in creating good WLB conditions.

While creating WLB conditions, managers should never forget that WLB is not an end to itself. It's part of the larger working conditions that an organization provides. There are situations where an individual's WLB criterion does not go well with the organization requirements or culture. For example, someone just loves to work at night and consequently comes into the office only in the late afternoon. During the first half of the day, this employee spends time at some volunteer activity. This kind of schedule may not work with many organizations where a physical presence and close collaboration is required in work.

Common reasons of losing WLB

While each individual has his/her own priorities and ambitions, some common reasons for employees and managers to lose WLB are as follows:

- No real time management: Most of the employees never get an education in time management. Time management is just common sense till the employee reaches a point where things become tricky and some formal systems and techniques are required.

- I can do it all: Most employees think they can do everything that comes their way and then voluntarily sign up for more. Many never seek help to solve problems or let others who are better equipped handle those tasks.

- Flexible hours taken too far: Many MNCs offer flexible hours, and people end up spending too much time on work-related activities.

- Always ON: Given work from home, e-mails over mobile, chat over mobiles, and working with people in different time zones, people never really 'switch-off' from work. While this may be just fine for some, for many others, this may be a cause of constant stress.

Managing Indian Gen Y

Anyone born after the year 1982 is considered Gen Y. Gen Y is becoming increasingly important to the industry, as the number of people hired from campus, as well as people in their early career with 1-3 years' experience, is becoming a bigger percentage of the workforce.

I'm not sure how the term Gen Y came into usage, but it's often used and understood fairly well now.

Some characteristics of Gen Y

Every generation has some specific behavior pattern and thought processes, which are a result of their upbringing, that is, the way their parents treated them as they grew up, the economic and political environment around them, and their exposure to the world. Here are some things that shaped Gen Y.

Gen Y kids grew up in an environment where entertainment like TV, video games were always available, and later cell phones were all pervasive, hence the Gen Y person is very tech savvy and comfortable with technology.

Entertainment is just a remote click away, information is another Google search away, and friends are a phone call away. Pizza can be delivered within 30 minutes, and there are coffee shops everywhere. As a result, the Gen Y person is used to getting gratified very quickly. When they want something, it's within reach and can be achieved fairly effortlessly.

Gen Y parents are a liberated lot too, who gave a lot of time to their kids and had a more 'friendly' relationship with them, as opposed to just a generation back, when Indian parents were a law unto themselves. As a result, Gen Y's image of an authority figure is of a person who can help them, rather than an authoritarian.

Gen Y has also grown up while India was on an epic journey of economic liberalization, which has led to unprecedented economic growth and job creation. Hence Gen Y has a very positive view of the world and think the possibilities are endless. They usually don't want to settle with what they have and would rather take a risk than not in order to fulfill their ambitions.

Gen Y employee behavior

Shaped by the things mentioned above, Gen Y exhibits certain behaviors on the job; here are some key ones to look at.

Smart working

Gen Y believes in smart working, that is, getting things done. If that requires help or looking up references on the Internet or talking to someone else, they would do it rather than dwell through the process just by themselves. Gen Y uses all tools and resources at hand to get the job done and they believe that reinventing something is a waste to time; if it's out there, let's find it and use it.

Nothing is impossible

Gen Y has a very positive attitude about what can be accomplished. In general, everything is possible and it just requires to be worked at. As managers, feel free to give Gen Y some tough challenges and you'll be surprised at their ingenuity. Gen Y is open to taking challenges and failure isn't a driver; after all what is the worst that could happen?

Open and transparent

Gen Y is an open generation. There isn't much that they try to hide. In fact, everything is published. Where folks went over the weekend? What kind of food they ate, how frustrated they are, or the fact that they are ecstatic at some result. Facebook, Twitter, and Gmail statuses are ways to publish relevant and irrelevant details.

In general, the expectation is that everyone should be open, and secretive or bureaucratic processes put him or her off.

Secure – there's always another job

Gen Y feels secure because the belief is that there is always another job, and quite naturally, another job will also bring a small jump. This security allows Gen Y to go for their goals and take up challenges. Managers should look to leverage this and also foster this to create an environment of growth and job satisfaction.

Don't Alt-Tab

A Gen Y employee may not Alt-Tab out of a Facebook window when their manager walks-by. They don't necessarily think it is 'harmful' or incorrect to do so; after all, they are committed to work and will get the job done anyway. More importantly, they aren't exactly afraid of any reprimand from the manager for doing so. In their minds, the authority of a manager is over their work and not over them as a person.

Very social – diverse

Gen Y is a very social generation, although the means of being social have changed. A Gen Y employee is likely to be part of many different groups and keeps in touch with everyone, possibly through social media. Gen Y loves to connect and loves to contribute and leverage these social relationships, for fun, for work, and for learning.

Respect for the individual rather than the position

Gen Y respects the individuals for their achievements and contributions, but have little respect for just the position as such. If you try to push your authority as a 'manager', you are likely to see resistance, but if you earn your respect in Gen Y's eyes, by doing your job well as a manager and as a leader, you'll see unprecedented support and following.

By the same measure, Gen Y expects respect for them from everyone, including their first line manager and beyond.

Ownership, decision-making, and choices are important

Gen Y loves the fact that they own something and wish to be part of the decision-making process about the product or area that they work on. Participation in decision making and having choices is part of Gen Y DNA. After all, they grew up in an environment where parents gave them choices and they always had a significant amount of control over decisions in the household and choices for themselves.

Gen Y will respond well in situations where they are free to opine and participate in decisions that impact them.

Finally, there are a lot of contradictions and misunderstandings about Gen Y, and it is typical of a generation gap in a workplace. Most senior managers are from a different generation and are so engrossed in the work world that they fail to understand the reality of a new generation. Gen X managers have misconceptions such as the following:

- Gen Y is lazy and doesn't work as hard
- Gen Y is always looking for help
- Gen Y gets paid too much

Nothing can be further from the truth. The truth is that Gen Y is very capable and is way more productive than Gen X, not because Gen Y works harder, but more because they work smarter and leverage the tools available to get the job done. They get paid based on new economic conditions and the impact of globalization on India. Comparing their work and salaries to what Gen X managers had when they started their careers is an incorrect yardstick (just try asking your father or mother about their starting salaries and compare to yours when you started).

Overall, Gen Y is really taking on the challenge and will certainly take the Indian industry to newer heights of productivity, responsibility, and success.

Managing diversity

Every organization has a Workplace Equal Opportunities policy, and several pages of documentation to explain workplace equality and the organization's commitment to ensure that no one is treated unfairly on the basis of race, color, religion, sex, sexual orientation, age, mental or physical disability, gender, marital status, and many more criteria. This policy document, like many others, is likely to be not read by most of the employees. They know they have to respect diversity, but unlikely to spend half a day reading through the policy. Smart organizations know this and they create mandatory online trainings that are much easier to understand and drive home the point with real examples and interactive pop-quizzes. In any case, diversity is a really big deal.

Diversity is a big deal, because the world has a history of discrimination on the basis of personal traits of some kind. While the caste system was a dominant discrimination factor in India, it was color discrimination in the United States that haunted the workplace and life in general. In more recent years, several European countries have demonstrated a resistance to turbans and face covers (Hizaabs), leading to huge protests against such bans that target individual preferences.

Diversity is a big deal because it 'attacks' an individual. People feel they are being short-changed for no real reason, impacting individual performance leading to long-term impact on growth potential for the organization.

Diversity is a big deal because it suppresses individuals and denies the organization the best of the available talent. Talent and commitment from its employees is critical for any organization's success and awareness and respect for diversity is absolutely a must in today's global business environment. Just about every top business leader, like Vikram Pandit of Citibank, of Indian origin, or Hungarian born Andy Grove of Intel, would have never reached the top positions if they were discriminated against on the basis of their ethnicity or color or religion. Intel Corporation's stock value went up by 2400 percent under Andy Grove's leadership and Vikram Pandit led Citibank through the aftermath of the biggest financial meltdown.

Diversity is natural

No two people are alike anyway; even two brothers from the same parents, with almost the same upbringing have different viewpoints and styles of working and can even appear quite distinct from each other. Diversity is natural to the human race, and there are huge benefits in being diverse.

Shun stereotypes

Stereotyping is a direct result of not understanding diversity. Most people are so accustomed to hearing and experiencing stereotypes that they tend to believe it's ok to stereotype someone.

The start of diversity in the work place is to stop stereotyping, for anything whatsoever. Start with evaluating your own biases. Are there any that you hold? Once you know what to deal with, you can consciously attempt to shun those stereotypes. Encourage your team to do the same.

Early training

When people join your team, it is the best time to talk clearly and strongly about diversity and the value of it to the organization. New employees are in a state to absorb and mould their systems to fit into the new organization.

Diversity doesn't mean the 'same' treatment

You don't have to treat everyone the 'same' in order to be diverse; understanding each person's individual needs and acting accordingly is the correct way to deal with diversity.

For example, you may have an employee who has a physical disability and may not be able to speak clearly, while his communication over e-mail and in the written form may be immaculate. As an understanding manager, you can create more opportunities for him to do written work and publish various documents, rather than tedious conference calls that may be difficult for all concerned.

Similarly, if your work involves women working late nights, you may need to create systems that will ensure safety for women, such as additional security, GPS fitted cabs, and mandatory background checks for drivers and transport staff.

Creating and supporting a diverse environment may require extra effort from the manager. Be open to providing that support.

Celebrate the diversity

The best way to manage diversity is to embrace it with all your heart and celebrate the fact that there is diversity in the system. Invite the perspectives of different people from the team, and you'll be surprised that really good discussions happen and you get a better result.

Diversity brings in various perspectives, because each individual's opinions and thought processes are shaped differently. Hence multiple perspectives and ideas help shape a better product overall.

You can talk openly about differences in various cultures and discuss how things are done a certain way, but never let that conversation focus on an individual, from your team or otherwise. It is best to let the employee talk about their culture and systems, rather than anybody else. Everyone should be in an absorbing mode without evaluating what is being said, in his or her own scale of things.

As an individual, learn about different cultures

Just like you spend time in reading technical material and management books, spend some time to learn about different cultures—customs and cultures of people from different parts of the country and the world. It may help you better connect with them. In some cultures, making eye contact with a senior may not be a custom, while in others, it may be seen as a sign of evasiveness or not speaking the truth.

Be aware of various diversity programs run by the organization

Your larger organization is also likely to have many programs that encourage and celebrate diversity. Spare some time and get familiar with them. Encourage participation in such programs by all employees.

Enjoy the food

The most enjoyable way to celebrate diversity is to enjoy the food from different regions. Let the employees organize a lunch or a dinner at an ethnic place and let them explain the food specialties, if they wish to. Enjoy the food, and if someone wants to stick to a 'safe' dish, let him/her do so.

No jokes about a particular community

This is an often-repeated mistake, since jokes about communities are so easily heard and repeated in the society. However, the work place is not the place where employees should bring these jokes. I have even seen instances where people have sent really silly and offensive jokes about a community to an entire mailing list with hundreds of people.

As a golden rule, simply ban all such jokes from the work place and any gathering of the team, even in a team party or outing or even personal parties where team members are gathered together.

Be quick to stop a conversation that is bordering on discrimination, even in humor

Despite all efforts, there may be cases where insensitivity towards other cultures or plain simple discrimination shows up. Have a zero tolerance policy towards it, and stop such behavior when you observe it. When a manager ignores such behavior, other employees, including the victim of such behavior, will see it as acceptance.

Summary

We discussed some of the softer aspects of management in this chapter, which don't exactly relate to the delivery of work, but have a huge impact on the team and its long term sustenance.

Understanding the aspects like work life balance, diversity, Gen Y, and remote working not only enhances your work effectiveness, but also makes you a better human being and a more effective manager.

Another key aspect of being an effective manager is to plan effectively. In the next chapter, we'll explore the planning aspects of being a manager.

11
Effective Planning

I did my first – time-management course when I was about three years into work, and I must say it was very impressive. The theme of the program was very simple, that is, set some goals and then work towards them. We were given a folder to start managing better. The folder had sections for personal goals, to-do lists, and a daily timesheet where we allocated time based on to-do lists. The to-do lists were supposed to contain daily work items assigned to an individual, and every few weeks, one was supposed to create items in the to-do list that made you move towards your goals. It sounded pretty good, maybe a surefire way of achieving your goals.

I was very pumped up to change my life, become a more organized person, and achieve the goals on my list that was created during the program. One of the simpler goals was to save Rs. 10,000 in three months' time.

Six months later, the folder was part of my bottom drawer and the goals were almost forgotten. There weren't 10,000 rupees in my bank account.

Besides, every day the to-do list kept on getting longer and longer and every daily or weekly review only pointed to my failures in completing what I had "planned" for myself. After a month or so, I started to leave the folder in my desk drawer a little too often to avoid the guilt. By the end of the three months, not only did I fail in saving 10,000 rupees, but also considered that the planning model was a failure and not worth following.

That's the power of 'ineffective' planning.

Just adding items to to-do lists is not enough and relying on just a to-do list may make it harder than what it should be. Forcefully fitting items into the schedule will only add more pressure without adding any value. Perhaps, there should have been a rule to remove items from the to-do list.

When I look back now, I think the primary reason why the plan 15 years ago didn't work was because it wasn't created with execution in mind. It was created only with the end result in mind. I want to achieve 'X' and for that I need to perform A, B, and C actions and here's when I'll do those A, B, and C actions. HOW can those A, B, and C be done? WHAT capabilities I need for those actions? WHO else do I need help from? WHAT IF 'A' isn't done or delayed; where does that place me? These questions weren't considered then.

Effective planning starts with thinking about execution and all things related to execution. The players that will be part of the execution, the capabilities of each player, the environment in which the execution is to take place, and so many more aspects related to execution need to be thought through. In this chapter, we'll explore the aspects that impact planning and planning techniques to make our planning more effective.

Why plan?

Let's look at some compelling or non-compelling reasons for planning.

Making something happen

The primary reason to plan is to make something happen, such as delivering a software module or achieving a sales target.

Every step in a usual plan looks like something that we'd like to see happen. For example, milestones such as functional design, or code complete, or testing.

Stopping something from happening

The other primary objective of a plan is to make sure that an adverse result does not happen. There is a 100 percent chance that some things will go wrong and a plan may help avoid many such situations from happening, reduce the impact of others, and help handle them better to bring the projects back on track.

Educating and making people aware

Planning creates awareness about the project and its moving parts among the team responsible, other stakeholders, as well as the organization in general. A plan answers the question, 'Who is responsible for what task?'

Helping to prioritize

Every plan involves breaking down the task to smaller tasks and some actionable items. Looking at the smaller tasks forces people to think of all the different parts and prioritize one over another. Many projects face unnecessary delays because the sequence of dependencies and timing of deliveries, availability of resources, and so on, is not prioritized well.

The plan answers the question: What needs to happen first? Or what needs more attention?

Increasing commitment

Many managers develop the plan in consultation with other team members, especially seniors or key folks. Participation in planning creates a sense of ownership and helps in creating more commitment during the execution phase.

Commitment to the plan is a big deal and extremely important from key team members.

Showing the path – adds confidence, lowers anxiety

The plan shows the path moving forward to all concerned. Team members can understand their role and, to some extent, interdependence among different players and deliverables. Looking at a path to potential success increases the confidence in the team. Your management will also gain confidence in your ability to deliver by looking at a working plan.

Planning cycle

Planning is not a one-time activity; rather, planning and execution repeat themselves in a cycle:

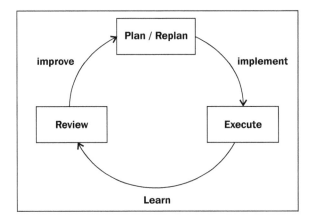

We need to view planning as a cycle, where the plan improves as more cycles of plan-execute-review happen. This also implies that planning is a continuous activity that is intertwined into the execution cycle.

Planning is a series of short cycles of plan-execute-review. After each short cycle, you may have to re-plan or adjust the plan for the next cycle. At the beginning of the project, the knowledge of the given work is at its lowest point; that is, every subsequent day from this day you will know more about this project than you do today. But ironically, you are supposed to predict how this project execution will progress over the next few months and with given resources.

You fall back on the experience of the past projects and your understanding of the technology to guide you, but no two tasks are alike in the knowledge industry. You are bound to make estimation errors and hence you want to be able to correct them as you go along.

Planning cycle does not mean you have unlimited scope to change a plan. Most commitments are made based on your early plan, and you want to make sure that you meet those commitments and hence fine-tune the plan for the next phase. Plans can be classified using many different criteria, such as:

- Domain: Financial plan, operational plan, administrative plan
- Time period: Five-year plan, long-term plan, short-term plan, weekly plan
- Purpose or intent: Strategic plan, execution plan

- Life of a plan: Standing plans such as procedure, rules, and so on, single-use plans like a budget that is valid for a specific one-time use only

We will focus on 'execution plans', largely around the 'project plan' and 'weekly/daily plan', since these are the plans that make the most impact on effectiveness and success of an early manager.

A good project manager

Here are some key traits and behaviors of a good project manager. Good project managers are:

- Flexible:
  - ° Flexibility is a core behavior of a good project manager. A flexible manager knows that things will change and is always mentally prepared to handle changes that will show up in due course of the project. He/she ensures technical design will accommodate changes. An effective project manager always looks out for changes in the project scope.
  - ° Open to critical feedback: A good project manager is open to any feedback, especially critical feedback. It does not imply that the project manager will act on all negative feedback that comes his/her way; rather, he/she will make an informed decision where this particular feedback may have an effect.

- Well connected:
  - ° A good project manager balances his/her time and energy to create connections and information channels. He/she reaches out to people in different areas who may be connected to the project. He/she uses these information channels to send and receive timely feedback and fine-tunes the execution as the external factors shift.
  - ° A good project manager is also well connected with his/her team. He/she knows the strengths and limitations of his/her team members and leverages accordingly to deliver on the objectives.

- Communicates well:
  - ° To the team: A good project manager keeps the team informed about anything that touches the team's work. He/she is connected with people and is available to listen to anyone who wishes to talk. This allows the project manager to be an informed manager. He/she knows how the team works and anticipates problems early and pro-actively resolves them.

- To stakeholders: A good project manager knows the requirements of different stakeholders. He/she knows that stakeholders feel better when they know about the progress of the project. A good project manager creates monitoring and reporting systems, so stakeholders can get relevant, honest, and timely information about the project.

- Seeks and creates clarity:
  - A good project manager strives to create clarity at all levels, within the team and outside the team. He/she understands where confusion can exist and actively finds information to remove and reduce confusion.

  - Define clear exit criteria per task – reviews, tests, and so on: A good project manager always ensures that each team member, especially the leads, understands the 'exit criteria' for the assigned tasks. This exit criteria is to be broken down into metrics that individual contributors can deliver. For example, customer requirements may be to deliver 99 percent error-free transactions. This will need to be broken down into metrics that can be applied per task. In this case, for a given sub module, this could be a set of pre-defined test cases with varying input types and performance.

  - Not afraid to ask questions: An effective project manager is never afraid to ask questions. Asking questions is the easiest and most effective way of getting to the right information and ensuring clarity.

- Understands priorities and focus:
  - A good project manager knows his/her priorities. He/she works with his/her management chain and different stakeholders to understand the priorities and plans accordingly. Prioritization helps the project manager to focus the energies where it matters most and also helps in cutting down work that is not a priority.

- Looks for wow factors:
  - Every project has something that you can make stand out. Something that management, or team members, or customers would cherish. A good project manager figures out ways and means of creating a wow factor around the deliverable.

What to consider when creating a plan

A plan obviously involves the breakdown of tasks, resource assignment, and scheduling, and any kind of plan will involve those. Planning aspects can be bucketed into four areas:

- Big picture understanding
- Work assignment and execution
- Monitoring
- Risk management

Let us now examine the considerations in each of the previous points.

The big picture

For a usual project to be delivered, a project manager can focus only at the deliverable at hand, but that will create all sorts of problems since a project does not exist in isolation. The big picture includes things that are beyond the immediate deliverable that may or may not impact the project deliverable.

Identifying the deliverable and greater purpose

The plan is obviously made for and should clearly state the deliverable for which the plan is created. For example, the purpose of the task may be to create a new utility for predicting the hard disk and memory needed as the number of users to the website increase.

It should also state the greater purpose of the task. In the last example, what kind of real life problem did this utility solve for the end user? How will this utility be used by its consumers? What are the other utilities that may be used along with this one?

Specifying the greater purpose and making it visible to the team helps individual contributors to focus on the finer points of the task. For example, if there is a financial implication of the calculation from this utility (like billing customers for usage), there should be a high emphasis on accuracy. If it's to be used as a guide for internal planning, even ballpark values will suffice.

Use project planning as an opportunity to align the project objectives with the organizational goals.

Know the larger 'program management' plan

Almost always the project deliverable is a small part of the larger plan that the organization is to execute on. The larger plan will typically be owned and maintained by a 'program management' function. This larger plan is typically the source of all work within multiple project teams and has many different elements like risk items identified, key contractual terms, customer concerns captured, and even some history on the deliverable. The larger plan is an important source of very relevant information that you would be able to leverage. Besides, you would be required to update and be in sync with the larger plan.

External environment and dependencies

No project is conceived and executed in isolation. Anything that impacts the larger organization will impact the project also. The impact on the project may be very severe; for example, an acquisition of a product may completely slow down or shut down your project due to a high overlap in feature set. Similarly, change in management may bring in new thinking and re-positioning of the project may be required.

As a manager, keeping an eye on the external factors is an important part of the plan execution. The plan itself will need to be adjusted to handle new threats from the environment and take advantage of the new opportunities.

Make provisions in the plan to spend time in keeping yourself connected to the external world. Attend other meetings in a related area, keep connected with different folks, demonstrate your product, share your progress, and seek ideas and participation. Make all of this part of the periodic milestones as well.

Governing rules and requirements

There may be some governing rules and requirements for a project, like the requirement to use a certain technology, or avoid a certain technology, or usage of specific versions of libraries, or testing automation and coverage, and so on. Also find out who is responsible for signing off on these requirements being met and make that part of the project plan.

Usually, such requirements generate more work. Consider the number of such requirements and the impact of these on the execution timelines. Consider if any new skills may be required for meeting these requirements.

Always spell out and highlight the requirements that are mandatory, as those can make or break the project. For example, third-party software usage is one such thing where all legal clearances and export compliances need to be sought before usage and release of the software.

Most government agencies mandate 'accessibility compliance', that is, the product must be usable by citizens with disabilities for any product that they buy. Governments in any country are usually the largest buyers in the market.

Know the stakeholders and their requirements

Every project will have many stakeholders in it, such as other project teams, sales organization, support organizations, program office, customer himself/herself, technical reviewers, security reviewers, and so on. Some of them will be very involved and others will be passive. As a project manager, you are expected to know all stakeholders and what each one expects from the project team. Some stakeholders will be very demanding and others will adjust to your needs.

Understand the level of tolerance for problems

Most of the work in the knowledge industry is very 'virtual', that is, there isn't much physical matter to look at in order to determine the quality of it; instead some other metrics are defined to judge the quality. For example, quality of a software module is often measured in the number of bugs and test cases being run in order to test the working of the system. The quality of a software module is very subjective and technically there is no end to how much time one can spend on quality. After a certain point in time, any more investment into quality will lead to negative returns.

As a manager, you'll need to manage the 'acceptable' level for problems in a certain area. In reality, we don't live in a problem-free world and this work will not be problem-free either. The nature of certain work is such that it has more problems than others.

Sometimes you may end with more than your fair share of problems in a certain area. Instead of trying to fix every problem that you see, first look at the acceptable level of tolerance and the kind of problems that can be tolerated. For example, in some areas, a slower system response may be acceptable, since it's a backend process and the user is not waiting for it to complete after a click on the screen. Instead of spending too much time fixing minor performance problems in this area, you may be better off fixing performance problems on a user interface.

Knowing tolerance levels helps to ignore stuff that you can live with and focus on what is really important.

Work assignment and execution

The core of project planning is the work assignment and execution of tasks by each team member. Here are the key things to know.

Start with a conservative and flexible plan

Effective planning starts with being realistic. However, there are so many unknown twists and turns in a project that there is usually more work than you thought you would have. When creating a project schedule, try to be a little conservative to start with. Remember, no one got shot for finishing early. A little buffer will give you a chance to manage the contingencies better. Perhaps a little extra time will allow you to do some more 'wow' factor work.

When scheduling, don't forget the standard holidays, expected vacations, and usual pace of work at that time of the year.

A plan must be designed to be flexible. Looking at the planning cycle, we know that a re-plan is part of planning. A re-plan doesn't mean a complete overhaul, but adjusting to changes and unexpected happenings with the objective of getting the planned result.

Leave room for 'mistakes', new work to be added, delay in tasks, and loss of resources. Ultimately, following the plan is a means to an end and not the end itself.

Players and their strengths

The outcome of best-laid plans is decided by the players in the team and in some cases, outside the team also. The success of the plan lies in the ability of each individual player and the ability of the team to work together.

A balanced team is better than just a highly-skilled one or a highly-experienced one. While planning, managers would be advised to create a team that has a mix of skill, experience, and youth.

Each individual should be assigned the tasks as per their strengths and interests. People's interests change all the time and more so in the knowledge industry. Very often the guy who really wanted to work on Java in the last project and did brilliantly may want to work in a different area.

Different interconnected tasks require different kinds of players. Each of them is necessary for the end result. Each works in their own way. You can't rush a guy who takes his time to think things through and implement.

In a way, every plan is a one-time plan since it has to consider the strengths of its current players and allocate accordingly. The moment a player leaves the project or a new one joins, the plan needs to be re-adjusted.

Choosing appropriate methods of execution

During the planning time itself, consider the method of execution to be used. There are many ways of doing the same thing and you will very likely have choices. For example, a software project can be delivered using a traditional waterfall model of development or you can apply a more iterative model of execution.

In most cases, the larger organization standards will influence the method of execution, but you may be able to tweak it to suit your purpose.

For example, if the deliverable is a routine deliverable, something that your team has done many times before, you may not need an iterative model since there is less chance of getting off the path.

The choice depends on many factors, including the availability of time, skills, resources, and requirements from the customer or peer teams.

What is a buffer?

We often hear the term 'buffer'; for example, "I added a buffer of about 10 percent to the overall schedule". This implies that you estimated some work to be completed in X number of hours or days, but you think it 'may' take up to 10 percent more time.

Buffer is the time for any unforeseen activity, like a customer escalation taking time away, or an unknown complexity that may surface, or a fire drill in the building that will make you lose half a day.

Many times, managers shy away from adding a buffer because they think it is the time that will be wasted. In some cases, it's true when people may work at a pace to meet the deadline just in time. In those cases, feel free to keep the tasks at your original estimate and add the buffer to the milestone date.

The more experience you have with a certain technology and nature of work, the less the buffer you will need to add. The more granular the task breakdown, the less buffers you need.

In reality, actual time taken by a task = time taken to complete the task in isolation + time spent on other tasks (buffer).

Execution plan

An execution plan includes:

- A list of tasks

- Time required to complete those tasks

- Start date, expected end date, actual end date

- Assignment of task to an individual

- Ordering of tasks

- Key milestones where multiple tasks must be completed to deliver something

This is the typical MS project © plan that some project managers paste outside their offices.

First of all, check with your manager and program management office about the company standard rules or customer-driven tracking requirements. Make sure you thoroughly understand the mandatory requirements. If you do not do this, you will end up with a deviation from the start, which will magnify as you move further ahead in the project.

Effort estimation is the backbone of any execution plan. While it's an inexact science, the goal is to get the estimation to be as close to reality as possible. There are many methods of estimation and we will not get into all the scientific methods of cost estimation for bidding for projects and so on. We will focus on a rather small (3-6 months in length) project execution estimation method since that is perhaps an ideal execution size to manage at a given time. Every large project can be broken down into smaller manageable projects to keep the execution efficient.

Step 1: Break down the tasks to a functional deliverable unit. For example, if you are planning a software module deliverable, break it down to 'UI Pages to be developed' or 'interest rate calculating routine' or 'bugs in area ABC to be fixed'.

Make sure that the deliverable unit is something that a team member can understand and execute as such. It should not be a fuzzy item like 'improve quality', which can be interpreted in many different ways.

Step 2: Allocate the task to a particular person.

Step 3: Estimate the time required for completing that task. Let's say this turns out to be five days. Use your experience in that area and capability of the resource allocated to estimate the time required.

If you know the area well and have done similar work earlier, your experience will be a good guide.

If the kind of work is new to you, spend some time to understand the details and look for an analogy in your earlier work—maybe you have done something similar. It is perfectly fine to seek help from other managers who may have done such a project earlier and check for their opinion on a typical time estimate.

Estimate the time required considering ONLY this task. Consider just the effort estimation, as if this task is being worked at in isolation.

Add some buffer time per task if the technology is new.

Add some buffer time per task if the processes are new.

Evaluate the completion criterion and look for additional tasks that may need to be performed in order to mark it complete. Add appropriate time for it if required.

It is ok to add additional time as a percentage of the initial time estimate. For example, if you evaluated that it would normally take three days to do something similar, you may add 10 percent for unfamiliarity with a process or additional closing criterion.

Add 5-10 percent for usual time spent on 'stuff that shows up'. These are unexpected tasks from your previous work or some urgent things that your manager will need you to look into. You can also add this as a buffer at each milestone level, but then the dates of individual tasks may be always off.

Round up the estimate to the nearest half a day. So if your estimate is 3.3 days, round up to 3.5 days.

Make notes against each task. These could be free form and may include relevant FYI kind of data, like 'very important for customer' or more significant ones, like 'this needs to be reviewed by the product management' or 'this is expected to change based on feedback from Mr. XYZ'.

Step 4: Continue steps 2 to 4 for the entire list of tasks.

Step 5: Apply the **two-day rule**, that is, no task should take more than two days of effort. For each task that takes more than two days (or you can make a three-day rule), break it down to smaller executable tasks. This rule is extremely useful in uncovering hidden work. It forces the project manager to dig deeper into the task and break it down into doable chunks.

Avoid listing tasks that take less than one day. Consider them as part of another task.

Step 6: Once the calendar dates are assigned to the tasks, start adjusting for lost time due to vacation, holidays, and other events. Insert those days as tasks in the plan itself. This will push down the other tasks by that many days.

Treating lost working days like a task makes the plan a single place to look at time utilization. It also makes it easy to adjust for lost days due to impromptu vacations taken.

Checkpoints

Create checkpoints in the plan. These typically mark the completion of a demonstrable feature. Multiple tasks may need to come together in order to complete a demonstrable feature, so in some ways, these are integration points also. Checkpoints are a great way to focus on 'completion' of objectives rather than trying to micro track each two-day task. You can live with any intermediate delay as long as checkpoints are met within acceptable limits.

Reviewing the plan

Share the plan with your key team leads and get their opinions. These are your leaders on the ground and will understand the execution issues much better that yourself. I have personally always found this to be an extremely useful activity and a buy-in from the leadership team and this automatically increases the chances of success.

Next, share the plan with your entire team in one large conference room and spend an hour or two going over the details. Let each team member understand the plan and their deliverables and opine about it. You may not address each concern on the spot, but note it down. Work with the lead in that area along with the team member to iron out the concern.

Finally, don't expect the estimation to be accurate and do not try to adjust the plan too frequently. Perhaps you can re-estimate and adjust the plan after you are 30 percent into plan execution. With the additional knowledge and comfort, you would be able to make better estimates.

Monitoring

Any planning will fail without proper monitoring. Even with the best of people in the team, monitoring will be required to ensure the plan is on track. Let's look at some monitoring considerations.

Completion criteria and success criteria

In the IT industry, completion isn't like crossing the finish line in a 400 meter race; instead everyone can have their own definition of completion. Code complete criteria can be code + test or it may be code+ test + automation + sign off.

Success criteria are even fuzzier. Everyone claims victory without exactly knowing where the finish line is and in what shape or time you were supposed to be there. For some, just completion is success; for others, completion is a bare minimum requirement.

It would be great if managers can figure out the different criterion that applies to the project. What is the bare minimum expectation? What would be a stretch goal? What would take it 'above and beyond' in terms of success?

The same applies to individual tasks as well, but it's not possible to detail multiple criteria at individual task level. In any case, many of those tasks are standard tasks with a standard expectation that will be understood by the team anyway.

For any task where a success criterion is special or more enhanced than usual, such as for additional testing and automation requirements, usually the expected criterion is 70 percent automation, but for this module, the requirement may be 85 percent due to the critical nature of the module. For example, additional sign offs required from key people, such as an architect sign off on a design document.

Not knowing the success criterion is a killer, as people work hard to get to a 'completion' point and then feel shortchanged when the finish line they were looking at turns out to be the half way mark.

Progress and visibility

Figure out what the progress indicators are, like demoing milestones and making sure you meet them or manage any delays in them. In many cases, managers and the team become so involved in their work that they forget to provide the progress updates to the rest of the organization.

In the absence of progress updates, confidence in higher management as well as other dependent organizations will get dented and soon the manager and the team will end up fighting a battle to protect the project from undue interventions.

Make progress and visibility part of the plan and allocate time for those activities as well.

Checkpoints and re-planning

Every project plan must have a set of checkpoints where you look at the real position versus the 'planned position'. Almost always there will be a gap between reality and plan. Checkpoints provide the opportunity to re-evaluate and re-plan the rest of the activities.

Review and re-plan are even more important activities than the creation of the initial plan. The review is of the actual happenings and tasks already completed, hence should reflect the reality accurately. With a view of the reality in place, you should be able to align the plan better. The re-planned 'plan' should ideally be more accurate than the original plan.

Advertising your plan and focus areas

Make sure everyone involved in the project knows the plan. It should be out there on the outside wall of your work area. It is not uncommon that many team members don't see the entire plan ever. Many times the plan is shared with the top management and looked at during the early phase of the project, then as the project progresses, there isn't enough time to update and discuss with the rest of the team.

This also goes on to say that you must make a plan that is maintainable throughout the life of the project.

Create a 'tag chart' that lists keywords related to your project. For example, zero customer bugs, 100 percent automation, sub second page response, and security. In some cases, target bug lists or the main focus area for the week can also be advertised on these tag charts.

Encouraging and expecting planning from your team

In order for the entire plan to succeed, everyone in the team may need to deliver on time with the expected criteria and within allowable flexible limits. While it's extremely difficult to force planning habits on people, it is important that everyone knows that planning is expected. Once the expectation is set and you show the appreciation for a plan, each individual will start to fall into place.

Weekly team meeting – last week, next week

This is a simple planning meeting that I used for several years as an early manager with direct delivery responsibility. The team size was under ten people, and this was a weekly status meeting. The routine was very simple; each person in the team had to talk about:

- Last week:
    - Tasks started
    - Tasks completed

- ° Any issues faced and possible explanation or analysis for the same
- ° Anything else worth talking about – good or bad

- Next week:

  - ° Tasks planned to complete next week
  - ° Tasks planned to start next week
  - ° Any help required from, or dependencies on other people for the next week

This was usually a one hour meeting and besides last week-next week updates, we discussed any other updates and key issues in detail. This one meeting forced people to plan their tasks so that they can report task completions and also forced people to plan out next week.

Since the manager records this, the data from the last meeting is readily available. In fact, pending items from 'last week' would usually become to-do items for 'next week'. Anytime a work item is getting pushed beyond two weeks, a closer look was required.

This meeting also helped create an environment of collaboration as everyone's status and issues were out there and suggestions to solve the problems were always welcome. An environment of openness and mutual trust was encouraged and it was easy for team members to come out with issues and discussions to find solutions. Plan changes were discussed in the same meeting, thereby generating more commitment to the plan going forward.

Daily stand up meetings – 15 minutes

Stand up meetings became part of the software development processes since the paradigm of 'extreme programming' or 'agile methodology' became widely popular. It's essentially an accelerated model of a status meeting, like the last week-next week model we discussed earlier.

I believe it's called a stand up meeting because people were encouraged to stand up in a circle and then go over the 'update' one member at a time. By standing up, there is a natural tendency to get going and hopefully that will set the tone for a short meeting.

The manager or any other leader moderates the meeting to the following rule:

- The meeting will be held at the same place and time every day
- Ideally, people should attend physically; however, it's quite common for remote members to be on the phone

- Ideal time for a meeting is 15 minutes, but half an hour is quite acceptable
- Each member must speak about his/her work for the last day
- Work done since yesterday (or last meeting)
- Issues faced or being faced
- Work planned for today (or till the next meeting)
- Each person should speak for about 2 minutes only
- Other members will be quiet when one speaks
- Others can respond to issues faced and solutions
- More than a short response needs to be discussed offline after mentioning it

Stand up meetings are great ways to be on the same page and collaborate across the team. Since these are short and sweet, attendance is found to be much higher. Participation from each team member creates a little bit of peer pressure to report progress, which implies some progress needs to be made.

Personal planning – 15 minutes a day model

Being organized and working according to a plan is a mindset. It's difficult, if not impossible, for someone to have a plan for everyone else but not for himself. A very simple trick that makes a huge difference in personal planning is a 15-minute a day routine. Every morning, allocate 15 minutes when you plan your day. Here's how it may work:

- Say 9.30 A.M. to 9.45 A.M. is your personal planning time.
- Between 9 A.M. to 9.30 A.M.: Check e-mail and list items on the to-do list or update the one liner on existing items.
- Do not entertain any interruptions as much as possible during this time. Knowing your schedule, pick a time slot where the least amount of interruptions is possible.
- Look at your calendar.
- Block time for tasks and move stuff from the to-do list onto your calendar.
- Remove things that may already be on your calendar and need not be done.

- Apply the urgent, important criteria to the tasks on the list:
    - ° Urgent: Stuff that cannot wait and needs to be done today
    - ° Important: Stuff that is important to do, but doesn't necessarily have to be done today

- If your day is full of urgent items, critically evaluate your planning and the criteria being applied.

Even though a manager's day is full of interruptions and a lot of action items show up over night, a daily planning routine will make a world of difference to the usual workday.

Managing changes and risks

The big challenge in any project is to manage changes in the planned work. There could be many types of changes, such as the following:

- Change in scope of the project
- Change of requirements
- Change in technical design
- Changes in dependencies that make you change too
- Change in timelines
- Change in availability of team members
- Change in the size of the team

Each of these changes will require some action from the project manager to keep the project on track. When these changes are within an acceptable or manageable range, it's business as usual. However, when these changes are beyond the acceptable range, these become a "risk". For example, losing one team member in three months to attrition is a manageable situation and business as usual, but losing three people in three months is a "risk" as it can adversely impact the project delivery.

What would you do to manage risk?

Looking at the basics of risk management, here are the obvious things to do:

- Completely avoid some risks:
    - ° If possible, take an alternative path that avoids the risk. For example, if certain technology skills are short supply and there's a risk that you may not be able to attract or retain the required talent, you may choose to use a different technology in your project.

- Assume cost of some risks:
  - Expect some risk and account for it beforehand. For example, if you feel there is a risk of losing people in between the project, you can hire one or two resources and add redundancy in the system. Also you can set the timelines in such a way that you can still deliver even if you lose a team member.

- Pro-actively prepare for risk:
  - For many of the risks, you can take early preventive measures. For example, if you know that some of the team members are low on certain technical skill that may be required later in the project, you can encourage them to get trained early on.

- Transfer risk:
  - Another strategy would be to transfer the risk to another team or person if that's possible. For example, many risks are routinely transferred to an insurance company in a contract. In most simple project plans, this may not be much of an option, however, you may have opportunities to transfer the risk to another team which may be better equipped to manage them. For example, a technical partner or another internal team which has the necessary skills or experience to make the delivery..

Preparing for risk

While the risk prospect turning into reality is not something you can control, the preparedness to handle risk is really up to you.

As part of planning, do a what-if scenario, thinking about various aspects of the project and especially around critical pieces. Look at hypothetical alternatives and lay some ground work, in case the contingency does arise.

For example, if your project has a high dependency on the skills of a specific programmer, plan to hire a similar skill set and help one or two people in the team enhance their skill set to handle things if the specific programmer is not available (could leave or be on vacation). It will take time to put this plan into action, but it will serve you well in any case.

Even if there isn't any immediate actionable task to be done to prepare for a contingency, just awareness will help prepare you mentally to face the scenario, in case it does happen. Also, at the back of your mind you may be able to find better solutions, set up key relationships, and find the required budget to handle a tough situation, if it indeed arrives.

A word of caution to be remembered when it comes to contingencies. Over preparation will lead to defensiveness in the approach and it's one of the worst things that can happen to a plan. A defensive attitude is easy to spot by team members and the management. It'll be interpreted as a sign of low confidence and weak leadership.

Being connected

Most of the risk can be spotted early on if the manager is well connected with the ecosystem. It may be very tempting to get involved with the day-to-day execution of the project and closely work with your team but project managers also need to spend time connecting with various people in the larger ecosystem. What's going on with the customer business? Maybe there's a risk of project scope change due to an acquisition that customer may have entered into. What's the feedback from various stakeholders after you published your weekly progress report? Which other project is using the same technologies and running into issues?

The idea is not to be specifically looking for a 'downside', but to be aware of what's happening in the world so you can spot any patterns of risk.

Planning gotcha: don't follow your plan too closely

Planning takes effort and a good detailed plan may take a very significant effort from the manager. However, even the best-laid plans will deviate from reality, since a plan is a projection (prediction) about the future and it's simply unnatural that all projections will be accurate.

At times, managers get too involved in the plan itself and ignore the reality. Good opportunities are lost because one may be following the plan too closely.

James moved to India and had a mandate of setting up a new team. There was a lot of work for him and he knew he felt really anxious about everything. However, he was a successful manager back in the US and had set up a team many times, although it was in a different environment. James laid out a plan that involved advertising for open positions, working with external recruitment agencies, and visiting key cities like Delhi, Mumbai, Chennai, and Hyderabad. He had the dates set and the team of people who were to travel to each location. He had set the expected number of candidates and was driving the recruitment agencies to get the candidates lined up for interviews. He could see the results showing up very soon.

Four months later, James was called up by his manager and was surprised to see that his manager was not very happy with the hiring so far and felt that this should have been much faster. Apparently, another team that started its hiring efforts much later than James was way more successful and was being talked about in the top management about their ultra short ramp up time.

James looked back and checked internally on how that team ramped up. Apparently, a couple of months back, a project got dismantled due to an acquisition and several members of that team were available for internal hiring. Since that bunch had worked together earlier, they were happy to move en-mass to the new team. The other team gained from quick hiring and more importantly, a pre-trained set of people who were already used to working together.

In his quest to hire the best, James ignored the internal organization, and while his plan would have been successful as such, he missed out on a huge opportunity. He also recalled that the news of that acquisition and the existence of overlapping work was not hidden from him, but he failed to make the connection. He was not attending many internal meetings due to his focus on traveling and working with the recruitment agencies to create a pipeline for the next hiring trip.

Nuances of planning in India

Planning and execution depends on the people, and the way people work depends on the work and social culture of that region. Clearly, India has its own set of nuances. Here are some that impact your plan.

Not saying NO

Indians always find it hard to say NO. I'm generalizing here, but it's true that we do have trouble saying 'no', especially to our managers. If you ask one of your team members to take on an additional task, very likely the answer would be 'Ok, I'll take care of that'.

While managers love the guys who are ready to take on more, there is a real chance that the guy may end up missing his deadlines. You may still love him for he took on the additional work; however, your plan may be off track.

Too much focus on work – desire to grow

Many professionals bite more than they can chew since they are eager to commit, mostly because they have an ambition to grow fast, really fast. My personal experience is that young professionals in the west are much more relaxed. They are looking to learn and live their lives.

In India, the start of work life is the start of pressure and slogging. The young crowd is constantly under pressure to prove themselves and 'get ahead'. In the eagerness to do more, people commit to more than they can handle; many a times they push their limits and make everything happen, but many other times they'll not be able to do so.

Performance can become inconsistent and planning for an inconsistent workforce is a nightmare.

'All is well' syndrome

Another manifestation of not saying 'No' is the 'All is well' syndrome. Many professionals have a hard time reporting a 'not good' status; instead they continue to report 'all is well', perhaps hoping that they will be able to somehow catch up and then report the good status. Even when a negative status is reported, people tend to sugar coat it so much that it seems like 'all is well' as something minor has gone wrong. Getting an inaccurate status is a plan killer. Project managers are unable to make any adjustments as nothing seems to be wrong anyway.

Too many young players – lack of experience

The Indian knowledge industry relies heavily on young talent. At times, the team may be 50 percent staffed with the campus graduates with less than a year of experience. With such raw talent, it's very hard to estimate the delivery capability. Invariably, the planning becomes conservative even when it may not need to be.

Regional and cultural issues

Each region in India has a very distinct character and local social, religious, and political issues. Location makes a difference to the execution, especially if there are many external touch points like local vendors to work with or travel required.

Each location has a slightly different set of holidays; for example, Rakshabhandan (the Indian festival that celebrates the brother-sister relationship) may be a holiday in Delhi but not in Bangalore. Try driving through Mumbai on Ganesha festival or through Delhi during 'Chhat Puja' (a revered festival celebrated in some northern states).

Planning becomes harder when you have to manage across multiple Indian locations.

Remote teams – out of the loop

A very significant number of teams in India are 'remote teams' that work closely with some team in the US or Europe. Most senior management and decision makers work out of US or Europe. The remote team in India is essentially out of the loop, and unless there are strong mechanisms to get the latest developments on a daily basis, information will tend to get lost.

Keeping a plan on track and responding to any changes becomes much harder when impacting decisions reach late and people have no control over them.

Summary

Planning continues to be a challenge despite all the efforts put into it. One big reason for this is that most of the work is highly people-dependent and the capacity and performance varies from person to person. Also, most of the work tends to be flexible, therefore increases/decreases in scope.

Always remember: planning is a cycle and not an event. By nature, it's cyclical and bound to change. To make a plan successful, the primary requirement is to make the plan flexible. It sounds a little counter intuitive, but that's what makes the plan succeed; that is, the planned goals are met in time with key objectives met with quality, and hopefully all this can be done in a great working atmosphere.

A well-executed plan is a wonderful feeling for a project manager. Repeated successes with planning will make you a super star in the organization. In the next chapter, we'll examine some more aspects of how to grow as a manager in the knowledge industry.

12
How to Grow As a Manager

Growth seems to be on everyone's agenda. A mid-size company wants to grow to a large sized one, a large size company wants to grow into a mega global enterprise, and even a startup wants to grow to become valuable enough for others to take it seriously.

So far, as a professional in the knowledge industry, you have grown as an individual contributor and then taken on some more responsibilities to take a lead position and perhaps a manager title. The first year of being a manager is very exciting and you enjoy the learning curve, the newfound authority, and figure your way out the various roles you have to play. The second year may be the year to take on some more responsibilities, some that you like and some that you would rather not take, but didn't have a choice in. In the third year, you start looking for your next promotion and wonder what it would take to get there. You may even ask your manager in a one-on-one, but he defers it to the next discussion and instead focuses on the deliverable for the next quarter. You are left wondering, am I doing something wrong? Am I missing something?

Vijay was doing well as a first line manager with five people reporting to him. In the last budget session, his larger organization got a larger budget to enhance the product for the next release. Vijay suddenly found himself with another six new positions to be filled. It took him another five months to fill those positions. Through these five months, he had to endure severe pressure from his manager on hiring fast. So much so that he could not concentrate on his deliverable. Once folks were on board, Vijay had no game plan for how to make them productive quickly. However, the new project work had to be started. Vijay went from a successful manager last year to a struggling manager this year, all because he wasn't prepared to grow and take additional responsibilities that the organization demanded.

Growth as a manager is a significant challenge, which is why there are many professionals who never grow beyond a certain level in the management chain. I know of many managers who may have had title changes, but their work content and responsibilities are exactly the same for the last five years.

For a fulfilling management career, growth is absolutely essential and individuals will have to work smartly, leveraging their skills and knowledge in the organizational ecosystem.

What does 'growth' mean to you?

Growth is not an absolute term. Different people see growth differently. When I look at various resumes of fairly senior managers, this is how they describe their latest 'enhanced' role:

- Managing a team of over a 100 people
- Managing a business worth USD 50 million or 100 million
- Managing a world-class product with over 1000 large customers
- Managing a distributed team of high performance developers and architects
- Managing a new line of business that is critical to the organization

Of course, each of them is an accomplsihed manager in their domain. Vijay is in the software services business for a large financial institution. Here the billing is based on work done, and the work done depends on the people on the project. Hence, the business success comes from a large number of people being managed for large customers. Today he manages a team of over 100 people and is a role model for growth in the organization.

On the other hand, Ram manages a small team of just eight people and delivers a product that is an important offering for the company he works for. The product is of high technology and well appreciated by customers. Ram feels proud to be leading a product like this, working with various stakeholders and top technical people to make it happen. He has certainly grown as a manager to handle this responsibility.

Figure out the direction of growth for you and plan your career accordingly. Is financial growth the final measure of growth for you? Or is it the position within the organization more important? Or is an opportunity to contribute at a higher level growth for you?

As a growing manager, spend some time introspecting to figure out what kind of growth you want. Perhaps you can evaluate the question five years from today:

- Is it important for you that you have more people in your organization? Even in a structure where your influence on their work content is limited.

- Would you rather have a small team (fewer than ten people) but technically challenging and critical-to-organization kind of work and have more influence over the work content?

- Is a title very important for you? Do you want to be called VP or AVP, even if the work content is the same as a development manager?

- Would you feel happier if you work with customers every day rather than engineers?

- Does it excite you to know that you have revenue responsibility of 10 million US dollars? Or does it put undue pressure on you?

- Is it more important to you that your team members love you as a manager versus your management loving you as a go-getter?

The previous questions are not mutually exclusive; however, you can't possibly have a role that allows you to do all of the previous points. If you do want all of the previous points, you perhaps need to start your own company. Here are some examples of senior manager positions:

- A project manager or senior project manager in a services organization: Somewhat larger organization with delivery focus. Work can be complex, risky, and can have a high impact on the customer. Likely to have many processes governing the work.

- A development manager in a large product development organization: Somewhat smaller team, say, 5-10 people. Smaller module level responsibility but more control over the content. Ability to shape the product in your area. Technical depth is valued more than sophisticated people-management skills.

- A senior support manager who handles the first line support for customers: May require high patience and ability to handle pressure. High on problem solving and strong communication.

Similarly, there are many more manager profiles that you can study and perhaps you may like one or more of them. Talk to those people and understand the requirements of the job and match that up with your talents.

Another way: find your way one step at a time

Another way to grow is to focus on doing what you enjoy doing. Most CEOs would have never thought about a game plan to become a CEO in the early stages of their career. What they focused on was just doing a great job, following their instincts, and adding value to the organization. Of course, these guys were very talented and had the required skills to survive and succeed in a very competitive space and would have put in an enormous amount of time. However, regardless of the career stage, these guys prepared themselves well and took a shot at growth, perhaps because they believed they will have even more fun in the next role.

So while you wish to grow, there isn't a set formula that will work for you. Instead, you can always look for improving and learning. Perhaps that's the reason why you are reading this chapter.

Pre-growth checks

Here are some things you can do before you shoot for growth.

Are you having fun?

Growing in any job is not going to be easy. It'll require a 100 percent effort almost 100 percent of the time. There is very little chance that you can give your 100 percent every day if you aren't really 'enjoying' the job. The choice of the word 'enjoying' is deliberate here. What do you enjoy? That is a question which only you can answer for yourself.

Take a good look at what your day is like and how you enjoy the different components of it. You need to be in a job that you really enjoy in order to have your best shot at growth.

Are you able to leverage your unique talents?

Think about what you are really good at. What kind of activities you really do better than everyone else you have seen. What gives you the satisfaction of a job well done at the end of the day?

Usually by the end of five to seven years of work life, it is possible to look back and list where you stand head and shoulders above most people. It may not be one thing but a valuable combination of skills; for example, you may have average technical skills but better than average communication and empathy skills for a technical person. This combination can be very valuable in many areas.

If you are working from your strength areas, you'll find growth much easier than otherwise. Do you get the opportunity to leverage your strengths in the current organization? Will your management allow you to take on more responsibilities in the areas you think will leverage your unique talents?

Do you fit culturally?

As you grow as a manager in an organization, it becomes increasingly important to embrace the organization culture. Do you find yourself at odds with the organization's culture?

For example, you may believe in consensus building with making key decisions while the organization may be very 'top-driven' and autocratic in nature. Your pace of decision making will not fit with the expectations of the rest of the management and increasingly you'll find yourself getting pushed into making a decision or your boss will make it for you.

Find yourself a job where you fit culturally.

Bare essentials for any growth

The basic requirements for any growth, not just managerial growth, are the following three aspects. What ever you do, don't mess these up.

Capability

Every new level of responsibility will require the skills and personal traits to deliver at that level. Just as an individual contributor, a manager also needs to continuously enhance the skills required for the job. Very often, these skills will be a combination of broad technology/domain, people, and communication skills.

Developing capability is entirely up to you.

Credibility

Credibility is your status in the eyes of other people. Are you seen as someone who can deliver, who can be relied upon, and a person of integrity?

In general, credibility takes a long time to build up and hence folks need to be around long enough to get a chance to build credibility. At no point in time should there be a case where credibility is in question.

While building credibility is up to you, it depends on other people too, especially your immediate manager.

Opportunity

Opportunity is elusive by nature and shows up unexpectedly. Suddenly one day, there is additional responsibility, a key project that the top boss wants to see started, or a customer comes in with a critical job requirement due to a government regulation change or even the usual fact that a key position opens up in the organization.

Opportunity is completely out of your hands.

The trick to be 'ready' when opportunity arrives and hopefully there is enough credibility built that you can be seen as a potential person for taking on a new position.

Also, in order to better your chances of getting the right opportunities, you must be present at the place where opportunities are available or getting frequently created. While opportunities are not in your hands, being in a place where opportunities are likely, certainly depends on your initiative.

Some dos to grow as a manager

Here are some ingredients that will be required for growth to happen.

Grow your people

Let's face it, the team always does the real work and the manager essentially plays all those roles we discussed back in *Chapter 1* to support the work being done. A manager's capacity is limited by the capacity of his team and by the same token it can be increased with the capacity of the team. For a manager to grow, the team members must grow in terms of numbers, skills, and responsibility.

Delegate

The model to follow is to delegate everything that can be delegated. Delegation does not mean that you need to be cut-off from the work being delegated. You can choose to be connected, contribute, and follow up as necessary, but it's someone else's responsibility to make progress on the ground. Become a resource for that person.

Empower your team to take decisions instead of coming back to you for everything. It is likely that some mistakes may be made and let them know that it's ok to make mistakes. Wherever mistakes are to be absolutely avoided, create a closer monitoring system, but still allow the decision making to be de-centralized.

Don't be afraid to let go of responsibility and authority. It is supposed to be given away and your team will appreciate it. Empower the team and develop leaders in the team. For any delegation to happen, it requires the team to be strong. A strong team requires investing in the team and building the required capability. This takes time and effort from the manager and the rest of the team and is one of the primary responsibilities of the manager.

Almost redundant

It's a little bit radical, but in my opinion, the test for a strong manager is that the business can function without him being there. The team and the leads in the team should be capable of running the business on their own at least for a short while. It's likely that the 'effectiveness' may be a little less and many different people may have to take on parts of the manager's role, but the operations must go on.

When you look at any of the top managers today, even to the level of a CEO of very large corporations, you'll find that the number of direct reports to the top boss can be counted on your fingers. The only reason the top boss can function is because he/she has very capable managers; almost each one of his/her top line managers is capable of being the top boss himself.

Once you have achieved that level of operational independence, you are ready to take on more. As you grow, the value added by the manager needs to be more than operations. For yourself, figure out what value you add beyond day-to-day operations.

Trust your team

Trust in your team and the team's trust in you is absolutely essential for a manager to succeed. Trust is like a catalyst for all activities. When people lack trust in each other, the guards are up and folks stop and evaluate when they hear something and are watchful when they act on something. Once trust is established, everything becomes simpler as people focus on work, and can be assured that they are getting the correct picture of something.

Trust is not provided by the position alone and managers will need to focus on creating an environment of trust.

Make decisions

Decision-making is the top skill for top managers. As you grow and take on more responsibility, it is expected that you make more decisions. These could be all kinds of decisions; whether to hire someone, or to approve a design, or to approve a business trip or expense.

You must feel confident in your abilities and make a decision. This is where the strength and trust of your team comes into play. Very often, the decisions you make will be based on the data being provided by your team. You can't possibly spend the time to get into the details of everything.

There is huge value in 'timely decisions' and a manager who is unable to take a timely decision will have huge problems at hand as execution will suffer.

Don't keep going back to your manager to validate your decisions. Have confidence in your own decisions. Even if some of the decisions don't turn out stellar, you'll realize that the sky still stays up. You just have to buckle up and do a course correction after you own up to the decision being wrong. If you have the ability to course correct, you become even more valuable to your managers.

Take risks

The formula of 'higher risk, higher rewards' still holds true and always will. The corollary to it is, 'lower risk, no rewards'; low risk is not rewarded anymore. There is no glory in doing a job that anybody can do. Taking on risks shows confidence and you'll be surprised how others will rally around you once you are committed to a tough challenge.

There are hundreds of competent and competitive people who are ready to take those risks today. While Indians were not risk takers in the previous century, the scenario has completely changed today. Hundreds of startups are dreamt up every day and people take up a challenge with confidence in their ability as the rest will be 'figured out'.

Nerves

Managers will get into tough situations all the time, some tougher than you would think. Imagine you have the responsibility to tell someone that he has lost his job, then that person breaks down and cries in front of you, telling you that he needs the job and he has put in his best effort, but his commitment to his family held him back, and thus he couldn't complete the task assigned to him. Unfortunately, you have no choice at this point in time as the deal is done.

A more common one would be when the software module you own has bombed big time in the production environment. Everyone is putting pressure on you without any meaningful help to get the problem resolved. You need to stay calm, focus on the issue, and get the right people involved, while managing the bad publicity being generated.

You need nerves of steel to manage through these situations. There's nothing that will prepare you to work through these situations, except the situations themselves. Every tough situation that you face will make you stronger.

Deliver consistently

The key word here is **consistently**. Erratic delivery is a career killer. No business has the luxury of sitting on its laurels. The expected delivery must happen, and happen every time. This is what builds credibility.

Get diverse experience – projects, people, location

Once you become a manager and deliver in a given business unit, it's very likely that the next project or the next 'work' will be along the same lines as the last project. It makes business sense, since it allows the business to take advantage of your specialization. It's important that we continue to leverage our skills for the organization and must do so for a significant amount of time. However, it is also important that you work in other areas and get a diverse experience.

In the long run, the attempt should be to get a rich diverse experience; this means working with different people, different countries or multiple locations, different kind of projects and different customers. The reason being that the world and the business are extremely diverse in reality, and the kind of problems, the way of working, and many other things, differ from one scenario to another. Exposure to a different situation is what makes you grow as a person and as a manager.

Make linkages and network

Networking is a key aspect of business. Despite all the technology and globalization, the trust required for business is established between two individuals only. As you work through various projects and deliverables, don't forget to make linkages with people that you come across. Don't discriminate when creating a linkage. That means don't be eager to make a linkage with someone who is important today and ignore the fresh grad in your team. That would be selfish and a meaningful relation will not be created with that mindset. Contribute to your relationship with the fresh grad as a mentor, with the team lead as an advisor and reviewer, and in as many ways as you can. Stay in touch with folks as and when the opportunity arises, and be open to an e-mail, a phone call, or a meeting with anyone. Today's business and social networking tools make it super easy to maintain and grow your network.

Spend the time – the eight-hour workday is history

Growing in career requires extra work that will eat into your family time and personal time. As you grow, the responsibilities grow and invariably the number of people you talk to increases exponentially. In the Indian knowledge industry, that means late night calls since the workforce or customers are all over the world.

There will always be more to do and quite honestly, if you can't spend the extra hours, you probably aren't cut out for the job that requires the extra hours. Work with your family and friends to set up an ecosystem that can support you to spend the extra hours. Leverage the flexible timings if you have the option to balance out the work and life.

The trick is to work hard and also play harder. Figure out how you can spend quality time with family or spend the time on personal development. Organizations support this in many ways, but the responsibility still lies with you.

Grow in stature

As a person in the business and society, grow your stature. Be humble and kind and establish a long-term reputation of honesty and integrity. Be a person who is known to be fair in his dealings, whatever the size or value of the deal. Treat others the same way as you would like to be treated.

Don't model yourself on people with poor personalities. Just because someone treated you badly, you don't have to treat someone else badly. Don't pass on the bad stuff. Communicate effectively with everyone and don't keep people guessing if they are hearing the truth from you.

In the end, it's the person that people will interact and work with, and personal credibility, the way things are done, make a world of difference.

Some don'ts to grow as a manager

Avoid the following as you take on more responsibility.

Don't compete with your own people

Every manager should remember that he/she is the leader of the team. A manager gets to contribute to everything that the team accomplishes and hence is always eligible to take credit for the same. So technically, a manager should never feel threatened by his team.

However, most times the people in the team will be more technically accomplished. As the manager spends less and less time on the technical stuff and more and more on all the other aspects, the knowledge level on technical things will certainly drop over time. Rather, the technical knowledge gets broad and less deep.

Managers don't need to compete with their own team members in any aspect. If someone is technically stronger, encourage him and let him represent the team wherever possible. If someone is coming up as a good people's leader, encourage them and create opportunities for them to contribute more. If someone is good with customer interactions, let them participate in customer-facing activities.

Don't get sucked into the 'busy' paradigm

As the workload grows, you get 'busy' and that is to be expected. However, there is always a real danger of getting sucked into the busy paradigm. The busy paradigm makes people believe they are always busy. Busy implies that you are actively engaged with something; most likely work and not leisure.

The busy paradigm makes you think you have no time for anything more than what you are doing and if you do take on more, that essentially means you'll be stretching yourself. With a busy mindset, you always think you are taking on more than you can or should handle, and there will be more on the plate to do than can be done. The pressure built up is a sure gateway to loads of stress. And we all know that this kind of stress can't be good.

Managers will need to actively plan and organize their own time and priorities, such that everything can be done without 'feeling busy'.

Don't get blind in defending your team

It is natural for good managers to be close to their team. However, it does not mean that team deliverables or decisions can't go wrong. When something does go wrong, the manager will hear about it either from the direct manager or from other stakeholders.

Instead of defending the team or decision, be open to an analysis and steer the discussion towards that. Defending everything that the team does or team member does is not required and will only point to group thinking.

Here's an example seen many times: Mahesh went for a US visit for two weeks, and with all the travel, stay, and food expenses, his credit card bill swelled up. Mahesh was not familiar with the process of filing for expenses from the US and quite frankly was very busy too. On returning from the US, he got over the jet lag, organized the bills, and filed the expenses. Unfortunately, by that time, the credit card company slapped on delayed payment charges. With the expenses in USD, the charges turned out to be more than 7,000 rupees. Promptly, the late payment charges were rejected by the company finance. Mahesh came to his manager, Ashok, and in no time, Ashok shot out an e-mail. Ashok argued that this was not Mahesh's fault as the procedures to file for expenses from the US were not clear.

If Ashok could step back and be objective, he would have seen the problem here. It is a traveling employee's responsibility to know the procedures, and if those are not clear, then get clarity. Ashok also escalated this to his manager to put pressure on finance. Ashok's manager, Bill, handled it well. He first wrote a mail to finance and accepted that a mistake may have happened and asked if there's a way around this issue. The finance department pointed Bill to a corporate card policy where a waiver can be requested once in a year if there isn't a history of late charges. Fortunately, Mahesh's credit was in good standing and the charges were waived.

Ashok could have done the same thing and saved Bill's time, if only he wasn't too quick to jump in defense.

Don't be self-righteous, be open to a compromise

In an organization full of smart people, every one is 'correct'. Then again, there are so many viewpoints on any subject and that's what smart people are supposed to bring to the table. Debate various viewpoints and find solutions that work well for the organization. There are times when this debate becomes never ending with people unable to make a call.

Through any such debate, don't try to take a moral high ground on issues that don't need to be debated at a moral level. Avoid projecting an image of self-righteousness. It puts people off and they'll find it hard to have a good debate on the issue. Self-righteousness is essentially seen as pretentious and arrogant behavior. Here's a simple example:

Gaurav (programmer): Our solution looks good and it'll solve the problem with the least impact on the existing system.

Mohan (manager): We don't apply such designs in our product. I'd rather live with the problem than use such a design approach.

It is very possible that the solution being suggested by Gaurav is acceptable if Mohan can come down from the moral high ground. Mohan may reject this solution in favor of another one which may be much more expensive for the organization. The issue is not whether the solution is correct or not, but Mohan's response to this situation that prevents him from looking at other functional solutions.

Another aspect is to be open to a compromising solution. Once again, the idea is not to be stuck in a decision jam and move ahead after a debate has taken place. The more you grow, the more you have interactions with senior folks in the organization. Many a times, it is important to accept another viewpoint, despite not fully in agreement. Compromises will have to be accepted in the interest of moving ahead.

Don't forget the real job skills

While a lot of your time goes on meetings, discussions, and administrative work, don't let your 'real' job skills get rusty. If you are in a software industry, don't forget to code. If you are in sales, don't forget to sell on the ground.

Several managers become so oriented towards people management that they forget what they are really managing. It's hard to do an estimation if you are far removed from the technical knowledge. It's hard to hire a good candidate if you can't do a good technical round. It's hard to do a performance evaluation if you don't understand what the employee accomplished. And finally, it's near impossible to get your team's respect if you can't understand what they are saying.

Summary

Being a manager is wonderful, but sustaining growth is a difficult thing to accomplish. One may become a manager just because he/she has the most experience in the team, but without the basics discussed in this chapter, real growth may not happen. Growth is not to be measured in just titles and money, but also in your effectiveness as a manager. As you grow, one day you will become a manager of managers and the functioning will dramatically change. The learning and pressures only keep increasing, and that's the way it's supposed to be.

At this point in your career, lay the foundations for a long career in management by doing things right and it'll pay off over and over again in the years to come. Make sure you are having fun along the way.

The journey is the real thing. Each destination in the managerial journey makes it imperative to move forward to the next milestone. We have also reached the milestone in the journey of this book, and in the next chapter, we will peek into some key learning from the journey so far.

13
Summing it Up

It's very likely that you have reached this chapter by skipping through a bunch in between. Maybe you skimmed through some, looking for anything that catches the eye. Technically, I should be offended that my writing is not interesting enough for you, but I won't be, because the truth is that most managers will do exactly that.

With so many issues to worry about, so many people to talk to, so many e-mails to reply to, and so many expectations to meet, time and attention is at a premium for most managers. As a result, most managers start to move into a model where they try to find the 'core' of the matter and grasp as much as possible in a few minutes.

Here's a quick recap of some key elements from various chapters.

Know what you manage

The first order of the task is to know what it is that you manage. Answer some basic question about the business you are in. What is important to the business and what is expected of you? How are you connected with others in the organization? What are the priorities of the larger organization and of your immediate organization?

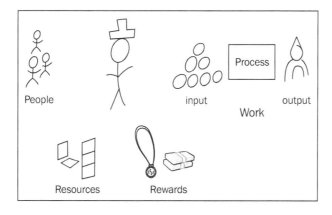

Along with knowing what you have to manage, you must also spend time to understand what the priority is among all the things that you manage. At a given point in time, taking care of people will be most important and at another time, you may have to ignore people in the team to take care of other issues.

Transition requires a mindset change

As you transition from an individual contributor to a manager, it requires a shift in the mindset, from that of an actor to a director.

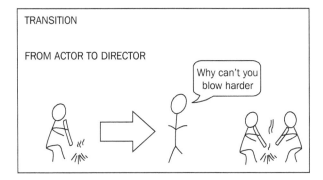

As an individual contributor, the inclination is to do everything by yourself, while as a manager, the inclination should be to help others do their job well. Remember the 'farmer mentality' to invest into people, hold your patience while they learn, and then reap the benefits of your investment, effort, and patience.

Help yourself, get help

Don't be afraid to seek help as you transition into a managerial role:

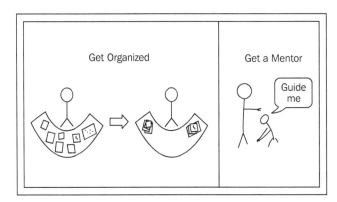

As you take on managerial responsibilities, be aware that many changes in your current style of working will be required. Be open to learning a new set of skills. It'll be of great help if you can find a mentor who you can go to when you need help.

Know your success measures

You can achieve success only if you can meet the organizational parameters of success:

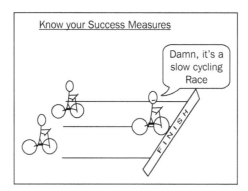

At any given point in time, you must know what is considered "success" and "failure" in your current organization. Every organization has its own measures of what it considers as real success. Always make sure your manager and you have the same definition of success.

Managers wear multiple hats

Being a manager is a fun, multi-faceted role:

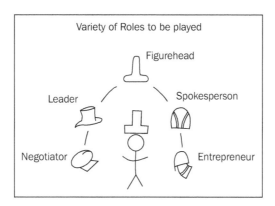

The nature of managerial work is to play different roles, and almost on a daily basis, many of these roles will need to be played. You may start the day checking your e-mail and monitoring the status of work, while planning the priorities for the day. You may allocate work to some team members and allocate required resources to others. By noon, you may talk to someone in product support to solve a customer issue, discuss extra space required for your team, or even meet the HR manager to help with some salary issues.

Managers are supposed to have the ability to switch context as and when required.

Manager as a conduit

Managers act as a conduit, that is, a connection between the team, the management, and the rest of the organization:

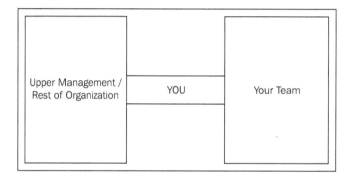

Managers are the interface between their team and higher management. A lot of the team 'image' depends on how a manager projects the image and manages himself in the other forums where he represents the team. A lot of what the team 'gets' is also through the manager's conduit:

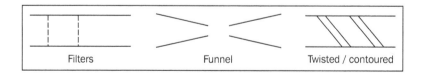

A manager can also enhance and shape some of these items, hopefully for the better of the team and the organization. Bottom line, a manager has the control and the responsibility to deliver the goods to-and-from the team.

Team building – define playing positions

Building a great team is essential for managers, now and for the future:

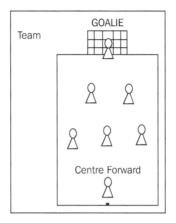

A team is not merely a collection of smart people; rather it is a group of people who can be very diverse from each other in experience, skill set, and many other aspects. Each person has a distinct role to play and that role may be as important as any other in the team.

Team building – winning as a team

There's a difference between individual success and team success. Team work is all about making the team successful at whatever it has taken up:

Help people understand the meaning of "team victory". Everyone will win when the team wins. This also implies that everyone will lose when the team loses. This sense of collective responsibility makes people of different skills, experience, and personalities come together and work towards a common goal.

Communicate in a timely manner – reduce layers, add clarity

Communication is the key to management in the distributed environment. Open, consistent, and in-time communication keeps everyone informed and reduces the risk of misinformation and guesswork. Work on reducing the layers between you and the ultimate recipient of the messages.

Motivation – Maslow's hierarchy of needs

Understand what motivates people in your team and what you can do to help them stay motivated:

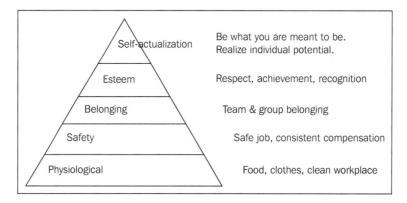

Motivation is a delicate and very fuzzy subject, but it's central to work and the quality of work. Motivational theories like Maslow's explain some of the very ingrained basics of motivation. They apply to any industry and are still very relevant.

Different people have different motivational factors. As the life-stage of an individual changes, the motivation factors also change. Understand the motivations that appeal to each individual and do the best you can. However, every individual is responsible for keeping himself/herself self-motivated.

Hiring

Hiring is among the top agenda for any manager in the knowledge industry. Always remember that hiring is part of the larger "team building" process and not isolated by itself. You are not just looking for the best guy out there, but the best "fit" for a specific position in the team. Let the team help in hiring and they'll automatically pick a candidate that may 'fit' best amongst them.

Also, if the team and the work are really good, you'll 'attract' excellent candidates without even 'seeking' them out from the market.

Attrition – expect it, manage it

Everyone who joins the team will leave the team as well. The question is: how do you manage when that happens?

Attrition is part of the team life cycle and a certainty. The challenge is in managing attrition by making sure that the business does not suffer when someone leaves. Strong managers create systems and structures that make the entire team strong enough to handle someone leaving.

Planning and execution

Execution is the basic 'purpose' of your existence and of the entire organization's existence. You and the rest of your team and everybody around you are paid to execute to the best of your ability. As a manager, always be on top of execution.

Planning is a great tool towards better quality execution. Remember, planning is a cycle of plan-execute-review-re-plan.

Decision-making

The art of decision-making is at the core of being a manager. All the aspects of understanding people, technology, core business, administrative functions, rules and regulations, external environment, hiring, performance management, and so on, are really surrounding the central theme of being a manager, that is, to make sound decisions, considering various aspects, and then own these decisions to handle the impact.

Manage – all aspects

Remember you have to manage everything that comes your way. Understand the management style that works best in your situation. Remember you must be able to manage a variety of aspects. Build a diverse team and respect the individual for his/ her talent, skill, and contributions without any prejudice towards any other factor. Strive to get the best from your young and old contributors, men or women.

In every problem, there is an opportunity. The more challenges you take on, the more you grow as a manager and as a person. Growing as a person is extremely important as well. It also applies to people in the team. Grow your people to become better contributors and better individuals.

 Manage your time, work, and personal life. Make sure you are having fun doing what you are doing.

Summary

Phew! Here we are now, at the summary of the summary chapter and perhaps there's just one thing that can always be repeated.

It's all about the people!

Index

Symbols

24x7 teams 71, 72
360 degree reviews 183

A

accessibility 52
admin costs 209
All is well syndrome 267
ambiguity 54
appraisal form 180
appraisal form, sections
  about 180
  competencies 180, 181
  development plan 182
  final rating 182
  goal setting, for coming year 182
  goals, from last year 181
  key dimensions 181
  open-ended questions 181
appraisal models
  360 degree reviews 183
  about 182
  employee - manager review 183
  external reviewers 183
  peer reviews 183
approachability 52
attrition
  about 200, 289
  benefits 213-215
  cost 209
  facts 200-202
  managing 217
  watch out 215-217

attrition, cost
  about 209
  direct 209, 210
  indirect 210-213
attrition, managing
  about 217
  attrition, expecting 217
  cross-area awareness, encouraging 219
  documentations, creating 220
  expectations, managing proactively 218, 219
  openness, promoting 220
  staying connected, with individual in team 218
  team capabilities, enhancing 219
  trainings, providing 220

B

background check process 210
bad news
  communicating, to individual 111
balanced team 254
basic requisites, for growth
  capability 273
  credibility 273
  opportunity 274
behavioral interviews
  about 159
  using 159, 160
bell curve
  about 185
  using, in performance evaluation 185
bell curve fitment 186
benefits, attrition 213-215

body language 55
bonus discussion 111
buffer 255

C

campus day 1 169
campus hiring
  about 168
  allocations 171
  boot camp 172
  campus day 1 169
  compensation rules 170
  elimination process, followed by selection
    process 170
  interviewing, at campus 171
  one job offer per candidate 170
  pre-join attrition 172
career growth 201
career planning 179
casual chat
  engaging in 108
checkpoints 258
Cisco TelePresence© 228
clarity 95
commitments 12, 33
committees 72
communicating 93
communication 288
communication channels
  shortening 105, 106
communication, in distributed team
  about 115
  accent 115
  acknowledgement response 116
  alignment, checking frequently 115
  different energy levels 116
  extra communication required 115
  mix methods, for communication 116
  questions 116
communication model
  setting, for team 103, 104
communication needs, of organization 102
communication needs, of roles 102
communication, scenarios
  bad news, communicating to individual
    111

communication, in distributed team 115
difficult discussions 113, 114
everyday communication 107-109
keeping mum 117
personal problems, sharing 110
unwelcome news, communicating to group
  112
communication skills 54, 93
compensation
  about 164
  at par with team member, with similar
    profile 165
  based, on market data 166
  by negotiation 166
  facts 166-168
  previous compensation + 20% 165
compensation discussion 104
compensation rules 170
competencies 49, 180, 181
completion criteria
  monitoring, for execution plan 258, 259
concise 97
conduit 23, 24
consumers 62
context 95, 96
copy cat attrition 213
core values, managers 53
corporate greed 54
courtesy
  rules 98
crack teams. *See* SWAT teams
cross-area contributions 219
cross organizational team 72
culture mismatch 205
customer orientation
  about 62
  expectations, from managers for 62, 63
Customer Orientation
  ratings example 191

D

daily stand up meetings 261, 262
decision-making
  about 59, 60, 290
  well informed decisions myth 60

decision-making roles
  about 17
  disturbance handler 18
  entrepreneur 17, 18
  resource allocator 19, 20
defensive approach
  about 35, 36
  overcoaching 36
demotivation
  about 134
  factors 134-138
demotivation, factors
  about 134
  disrespect 135, 136
  fear 135, 136
  lack of adequate, and timely compensation
    136
  lack of learning 138
  lack of opportunities, for showing potential
    137
  no social status 135
  poor working conditions 136, 137
  threats 135, 136
  uncertainty 134, 135
demotivators
  about 122
  versus motivators 122
desire 120
development manager 271
development plan 182
dimensions, social competence
  empathy 65
  social skills 65
direct costs, attrition
  about 209
  administrative costs 209
  hiring cost 209
  training costs 210
disconnected managers 188
disseminator 16
disturbance
  about 18
  examples 19
disturbance handler 18
diversity
  about 240

celebrating 241
early training 240
managing 240-242
natural, to human kind 240
no jokes, on particular community 242
stereotypes, stopping 240
dream job offer 170

E

effective interview
  conducting 154, 155
  hiring decision 162, 163
  interview plan 154, 155
  interview tips 155
  resume, analyzing 155
e-mail communication
  watching out 98
Emotional Intelligence 63, 64
empathy 51, 65
employee - manager review 183
enjoyment test 234
entrepreneur 17, 18
esteem needs, Maslow's hierarchy of needs
    theory 125
every problem is my problem to solve myth
    58
execution 290
execution plan
  about 256, 257
  checkpoints, creating 258
  reviewing 258
exit interviews 201
external reviewers 183
extroversion 51

F

facts, attrition 200-202
family 67
farmer mentality 52
fast moving managers myth 52
feedback 178, 184
feedback recording 160, 161
figurehead 13
final rating 182
flawless execution 61

frustrations, in new managerial role
  about 36
  information gaps 39
  no satisfaction 39, 40
  overwhelmed attitude 40
  slow world 38
  thought process 36-38

G

Gen Y
  about 236
  characteristics 236, 237
  employee behavior 237-239
Gen Y employee behavior
  about 237
  choices 239
  decision-making 239
  diverse 238
  nothing is impossible 237
  open and transparent 238
  ownership 239
  secure 238
  smart working 237
goal setting 184
good communication
  elements 94-100
good communication, elements
  clarity 95
  concise 97
  context 95, 96
  courtesy 98
  simple vocabulary 100
  timely 99
  two-way 97
gossip channel 106
grapevine 106
group
  unwelcome news, communicating to 112
Groupthink 90
growth
  about 269
  basic requisites 273
growth, for manager
  don'ts 278-281
  dos 274-278
  overview 270, 271

H

Halo effect 189
Herzberg's motivation 127, 128
hierarchy model 25-27
Hi exchange 108
high self-appraisal 193
hiring
  about 145
  for potential skills 146, 147
  optimal requisites 146
  risk process 147
hiring cost
  about 209
  background check process 210
  candidates, searching 209
  induction and on-boarding costs 210
  interviewing costs 210
  relocation cost, for new employee 210
hiring decision 162, 163
hiring process
  about 78, 289
  advertising 149, 150
  closing 168
  difficulties 79
  pre-interview 148, 149
  rules 78, 79
  sourcing 149, 150
  talking, about challenges upfront 148

I

indirect costs, attrition
  about 210
  copy cat attrition 213
  loss of productivity 211, 212
  opportunity cost 212
individual
  bad news, communicating to 111
individual contributor
  transition, to manager 284
industries
  characteristics 9
information
  about 33
  disseminating 16
information gaps 39

information processing roles
  about 15
  disseminator 16
  monitor 15
  spokesperson 16
information sharing 33, 34
interpersonal communication 101
interpersonal roles
  about 13
  figurehead 13
  leader 14
  liaison 14
interviewing, at campus 171
interviewing costs 210
interview plan 154, 155
interview tips
  about 155
  behavioral interviews, using 159, 160
  deep drill, on key areas 156, 157
  don't ask same questions to people, at
     different levels 156
  feedback recording 160, 161
  listen, to candidate 155
  look beyond technical skills 157, 158
  look for application, and not just theory 157
  past work 158
  warm-up questions 156

L

layoffs 179
leader 14
leadership deficit 89
leadership role 21
learned traits 48
liaison 14
life 233
listening skills 55
love needs, Maslow's hierarchy of needs
    theory 124
low motivation
  about 121
  signs 138-141
low motivations, signs
  absenteeism 139
  avoidable errors, making 140
  dragging feet 139

  lack of attention to detail 138, 139
  less social interaction 140, 141
  no contest 140

M

mai-baap manager 21, 22
management 9
manager
  about 8
  as conduit 286
  awareness, about communication 100
  core values 53
  custom orientation, expectations 62, 63
  decision-making roles 17
  expected competencies 50
  expected key skills 50
  expected traits 50
  FAQs 28, 29
  grip, on technical knowledge 61, 62
  information processing roles 15
  interpersonal roles 13
  job challenges 10
  job description 8
  multi-faceted role 285, 286
  patience, displaying 54
  re-planning 20
  role play, summarizing 21
  roles 13
  scenarios 11
  success measures, knowing 285
  tolerance, for ambiguity 54
managerial model
  about 22
  conduit 23, 24
  hierarchy 25-27
  orchestra conductor visual 27
  visualizing 22
managerial responsibilities 285
managerial role
  considerations 32
  frustrations 36
managerial role, considerations
  about 32
  commitment 33
  defensive approach 35, 36
  information sharing 33, 34

time 32, 33
tolerance 34
will, enforcing 35
managerial role, easing
about 40
getting organized 44
information needs 41, 42
NO approach 43
relaxing 41
sharing 45
signing up, for formal training and
education 45
success measures, knowing 42
Maslow's hierarchy of needs theory
about 123, 288
esteem needs 125
love and belonging needs 124
overview 126
physiological needs 123
safety needs 124
self-actualization 125
maximum output myth 57
McClelland's motivational needs theory
about 129
all three factors 130
need for achievement 129
need for affiliation 130
need for power 129
Minefield game 223
money factor, for motivation 141, 142
monitor 15
motivation
about 64, 119, 288, 289
factors 130-133
overview 120-122
theories 122
motivation, factors
challenge 132
hope, for better future 134
hope of individual's greatness 133
manager's, belief and confidence in
individual 133
power 132
success 131
team bonding 131

motivation theories
about 122
Herzberg's motivation 127, 128
Maslow's hierarchy of needs theory 123-
126
McClelland's motivational needs theory
129, 130
motivators
versus demotivators 122
multi-faceted role, manager 285, 286

N

National Geographic channel 67
negotiation 20
negotiator role 20
nice manager myth 51
NO approach 43

O

once-a-year appraisal process
steps 184
once-a-year appraisal process steps 184
one-on-one review meeting 184
open door policy 52
open-ended questions 181
opportunity cost 212
orchestra conductor visual 27
organization
communication needs 102
organizational improvements 180

P

peer reviews 183
people 10
performance
about 176
key aspects 177
scenarios 176
performance appraisal process, issues
about 186
difficulty, in remembering details 188
disconnected managers 188
Halo effect 189
high self-appraisal 193

hurriedness 187, 188
inconsistency in ratings, by different
    managers 192
managers, shying away from disagreements
    190, 191
non-ethical behavior 192
proximity effect 189
remote manager 193
subjective ratings, depending on
    interpretation 191
uncontinuous activity 187
performance evaluation, objectives
about 178
alignment 178
career planning 179
feedback 178
layoffs 179
looking ahead 178
personal development 179
positive side effects 179
reflecting 178
reviewing 178
reward calculations 179
performance evaluation process
about 180
appraisal form 180
appraisal models 182
bell curve, using in 185
objectives 178-180
once-a-year appraisal process steps 184
performance management
about 57
maximum output myth 57
performance ratings 180
perpetual teams 70
personal competencies 64
personal development
about 179
progress, tracking over years 179
personal planning 262
personal problems
sharing 110
phone screening 151, 152
**physiological needs, Maslow's hierarchy of
    needs theory 123**
plan
about 60

classifications 248
considerations 251
plan, considerations
about 251
advertising 260
big picture 251-253
buffer 255
changes, managing 263, 264
checkpoints 259
completion criteria, monitoring 258, 259
execution plan 256, 257
progress indicators, monitoring 259
proper monitoring 258
re-plan 259
risks, managing 263, 264
success criteria, monitoring 258, 259
tasks execution 254, 255
visibility, monitoring 259
work assignment 254, 255
planning
about 245, 290
encouraging, from team 260
expecting, from team 260
need for 246, 247
nuances, in India 266, 267
planning cycle
about 248
plan-execute-review 248
planning gotcha 265
pre-growth checks 272, 273
pre-interview
about 148, 149
phone screening 151, 152
screening process 150, 151
pre-join attrition 172
problem solving
about 57
every problem is my problem to solve myth
    58
program management function 252
project delivery teams 70
project execution 61
project management 60, 61
project managers
about 271
key behaviors 249, 250
key traits 249, 250

Q

quitters
  categories 202-208
quitters, categories
  about 202
  dissatisfied 203, 204
  fearful 208
  growth-oriented 203
  mismatched 204, 205
  purposeful 207
  still searching 206, 207
  whimsical 206

R

remote employee
  managing 224-227
  overview 225
remote management situation 223
remote manager 193
remoteness
  about 224
  managing 224
  strategies 227
remoteness, strategies
  about 227
  clear goals, setting 229
  communication, formulazing 228
  expectations, setting with remote employee
     for more communication 228
  frequent checkpoints 229
  getting, into details 229
  indulging, in chitchat 227
  making travel meaningful 231
  new technology, embracing 228
  no excessive reporting 230
  open sessions, conducting 229
  travel budgets 231
  two-way communication 228
remote team
  about 268
  managing 224-227
resource allocator 19, 20
result orientation 58
reward calculations 179

reward collaboration 83
risk management
  basics 263, 264
role mismatch 205

S

**safety needs, Maslow's hierarchy of needs
    theory 124**
sample interview plan 154, 155
sample phone screen
  about 152
  basic technical questions (10 minutes) 153
  closing (5-7 minutes) 154
  code writing capabilities (10 minutes) 153,
    154
  domain experience (5 minutes) 153
  recent significant projects (10 minutes) 152,
    153
  warm up (3-5) minutes 152
screening process
  about 150
  key criteria 150, 151
**self-actualization, Maslow's hierarchy of
    needs theory 125**
self awareness 64
self evaluation 184
self-motivation 122
self regulation 64
senior manager positions
  examples 271
senior project manager 271
senior support manager 271
Seven Habits programs 45
skills
  about 48
  developing 48
skill in accomplishing 49
skills mismatch 205
Skype© 228
S.M.A.R.T. goals
  about 182
  Achievable 182
  Measurable 182
  Relevant 182
  Specific 182
  Time-Bound 182

social competence
  about 65
  dimensions 65
social skills 65
spokesperson 16
stereotyping 240
subjective ratings 191
success criteria
  monitoring, for execution plan 258, 259
success dose 83
success measures
  knowing 285
SWAT teams 71

T

tactic knowledge 211
talent 48
talkative 55
team bonding 131
team bonding needs, Maslow's hierarchy of
    needs theory 124
team building
  about 56, 287
  difficulties 74
team capabilities
  enhancing 219
team composition
  about 74, 75
  difficulties 75-77
team goals and individual goals
  visible alignment, creating for 80-82
team member
  things, to remember 73, 74
teams
  about 56, 67
  building 73
  communication model, setting 103, 104
  need for 68, 69
  planning, encouraging from 260
  planning, expecting from 260
  reasons, for failure 88-90
  types 70-72
team spirit
  about 56, 84

brainstorms 84-88
  nurturing 56
teams, types
  24x7 71, 72
  committees 72
  cross organizational 72
  perpetual 70
  project delivery 70
  SWAT 71
technical knowledge 61, 62
timely communication 99
training costs 210
traits 48
two-way communication 97

U

umbrella dimensions 181
un-reward non-collaboration 83
unwanted communication
  controlling 104, 105
unwelcome news
  communicating, to group 112

V

video conferencing 228
visible alignment
  creating, between team goals and
      individual goals 80-82

W

web conferencing 228
weekly team meeting 260, 261
well informed decisions myth 60
work 233
work life balance (WLB)
  about 233
  achievement 234
  enjoyment test 234
  fulfillment 234
  need for 235
  overview 233, 234, 235
  reasons, for losing 236
Workplace Equal Opportunities policy 239

Thank you for buying
Management in India: Grow from an Accidental to a
Successful Manager in the IT & Knowledge Industry

About Packt Publishing

Packt, pronounced 'packed', published its first book "Mastering phpMyAdmin for Effective MySQL Management" in April 2004 and subsequently continued to specialize in publishing highly focused books on specific technologies and solutions.

Our books and publications share the experiences of your fellow IT professionals in adapting and customizing today's systems, applications, and frameworks. Our solution based books give you the knowledge and power to customize the software and technologies you're using to get the job done. Packt books are more specific and less general than the IT books you have seen in the past. Our unique business model allows us to bring you more focused information, giving you more of what you need to know, and less of what you don't.

Packt is a modern, yet unique publishing company, which focuses on producing quality, cutting-edge books for communities of developers, administrators, and newbies alike. For more information, please visit our website: www.packtpub.com.

About Packt Enterprise

In 2010, Packt launched two new brands, Packt Enterprise and Packt Open Source, in order to continue its focus on specialization. This book is part of the Packt Enterprise brand, home to books published on enterprise software – software created by major vendors, including (but not limited to) IBM, Microsoft and Oracle, often for use in other corporations. Its titles will offer information relevant to a range of users of this software, including administrators, developers, architects, and end users.

Writing for Packt

We welcome all inquiries from people who are interested in authoring. Book proposals should be sent to author@packtpub.com. If your book idea is still at an early stage and you would like to discuss it first before writing a formal book proposal, contact us; one of our commissioning editors will get in touch with you.

We're not just looking for published authors; if you have strong technical skills but no writing experience, our experienced editors can help you develop a writing career, or simply get some additional reward for your expertise.

Maximize Your Investment:
10 Key Strategies for
Effective Packaged Software
Implementations

ISBN: 978-1-849680-02-8   Paperback: 232 pages

Accelerate packaged (COTS) software implementations, increase returns on investment, and reduce implementation costs and customizations

1. Develop implementation approaches that maximize packaged software advantages and minimize packaged software challenges

2. Reduce implementation costs, increase knowledge generation, and reduce non-value-added implementation activities

3. Enable customers to lead during the implementation to maximize long term success

User Training for Busy
Programmers

ISBN: 978-1-904811-45-9   Paperback: 92 pages

Develop effective software training classes quickly and easily

1. A complete guide to creating software training courses and materials

2. Concise and practical step-by-step approach

3. Check-lists ensure that you are fully prepared

4. Based on proven educational techniques

Please check **www.PacktPub.com** for information on our titles

Google Plus First Look: a tip-packed, comprehensive look at Google+

ISBN: 978-1-84968-534-4   Paperback: 208 pages

Get up and running with Google+ fast

1. Written in plain but entertaining English by the author of over 100 books and a few zillion Internet posts

2. Leads you gently through understanding how Plus works and shows you tons of examples of how to make it work for you

Oracle Fusion Middleware Patterns

ISBN: 978-1-847198-32-7   Paperback: 224 pages

10 unique architecture enabled by Oracle Fusion Middleware

1. First-hand technical solutions utilizing the complete and integrated Oracle Fusion Middleware Suite in hardcopy and ebook formats

2. From-the-trenches experience of leading IT Professionals

3. Learn about application integration and how to combine the integrated tools of the Oracle Fusion Middleware Suite - and do away with thousands of lines of code

Please check **www.PacktPub.com** for information on our titles